Mama's Dark Secrets
Unmasking Evil

Please leave a
review on Amazon.
Thank you,
JoJo Maize

Mama's Dark Secrets
Unmasking Evil

By

JoJo Maize

Published by

AMAIZEing Press

I have tried to recreate events, locales, and conversations from my memories of them. To maintain their anonymity in some instances, I have changed the names of individuals and places; I may have changed some identifying characteristics and details such as physical properties, occupations, and places of residence.

This publication is not designed to provide authoritative information regarding the subject matter covered. The buyer should understand that the publisher is not engaged in rendering legal, accounting, or another professional service. If legal advice or other expert assistance is required, the services of a competent professional should be engaged.

ISBN: 13: 978-0-578-56269-8
Library of Congress Control Number:2019914784

Cover Art by
Ryno D. Bones

"silhouette: Freepik.com"
This cover has been designed using
a resource from Freepik.com

For my husband, who taught
me what it meant to be
confident in myself and
has been unfailing support
throughout the years.

For my daughter, who is the
joy of my life. She and I
share a twisted sense of
humor that I love.
I am so proud of
her strong, independent and
confident personality.

And for the daughter we lost
far too soon. You are missed
every single day.

My mother, age 14. 1949.

Preface

The title, Mama's Dark Secrets, refers to all the secrets I was sworn to keep while growing up. I called her Mama until I went No Contact. At that time, I began calling her Mother. No Contact is the term used by survivors of narcissistic abuse when they finally cut their abusers out of their lives once and for all. It doesn't feel good to call her Mama. Nevertheless, they were Mama's Dark Secrets.

I've also included my experiences in the U.S. Air Force. Because I was so damaged and had been groomed to accept inappropriate attention from people in positions of power, I was an easy target. Sexual assaults and sexual harassment in the military is so common, it's expected. I joined the Air Force in 1977, and it's still happening in 2019. Those narcissistic abusers don't see anything wrong with their behavior. It's time they are held accountable, not protected.

I spent years justifying the lack of values I saw in the people around me; their ability to cheat and lie without remorse. I was convinced these people would not deliberately treat me so shabbily. However, once I removed the blinders from my eyes, with extensive help in the form of therapy, I realized that's exactly what was happening, and there was no justification. I deserve to be treated with respect, as do we all.

By the end of my memoir, I intend to show how I overcame the need to please and finally see the narcissists for who they are — morally ambiguous and self-obsessed, which had nothing to do with me. My hope is my experiences will help others recognize the narcissists around them, thereby enabling them to see how people have systematically been destroying their self-esteem and breaking down their identity.

It is also my intent to encourage others to choose joy, rather than allow our abusers to continue an unhealthy hold on our psyche. Too many female veterans are committing suicide after having been assaulted and made to feel it was their fault.

I have carefully altered the identities of the people described in my story to protect confidentiality. I have re-created dialog from memory. However, the experiences described are quite real, as I remember them. *My perception is my reality*.

JoJo Maize
Yukon, OK
October 2019

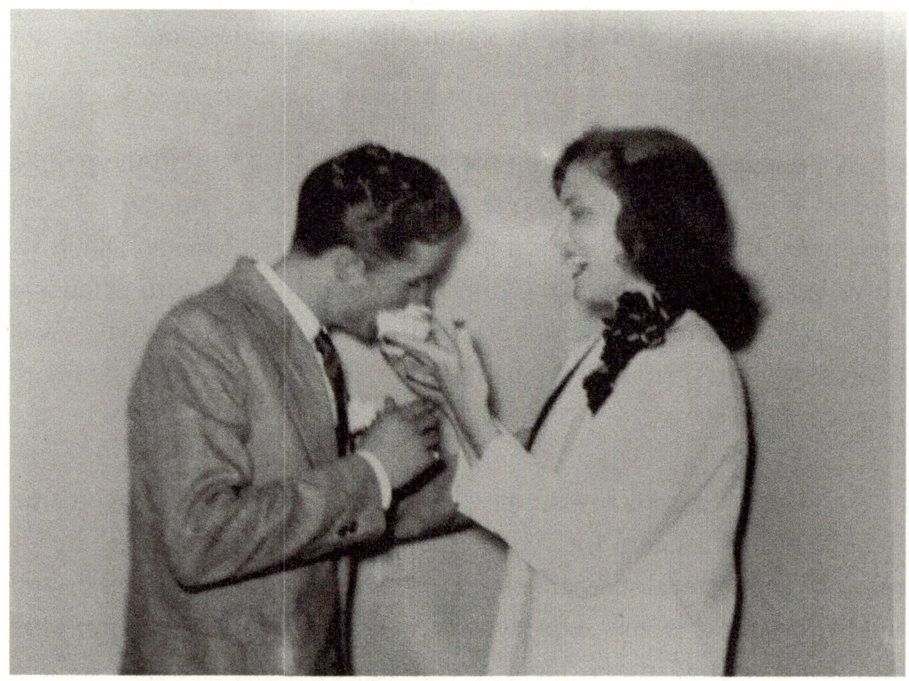

My parents on their wedding day, 1953

Acknowledgments

I would like to say, thank you. To Jeanette Truong and Sharon Webb, for encouraging me to put my story on paper. Without your confidence in my ability to do the work, I doubt this book would have ever come to fruition. And to my Write, Publish and Marketing teacher, Andrea Foster, thank you for leading me through the quagmire of information. I could not have done it without you. Demaris Brandt, you deserve a special thank you for putting me on track to help other veterans. You are a special friend.

Veterans!

Apply for the benefits you deserve!

www.ebenefits.va.gov

Mother, after she cut her hair. Age 15.

Table of Contents

Part 1

I'm not crazy; I'm just a little unwell.
Rob Thomas

Mother, age 17

Chapter 1

Dead Babies

*D*uring my birth, my mother had what she called a "near-death experience." She would relate her experience to anyone willing to listen.

Childbirth was difficult for my mother. She was diagnosed with Infantile Paralysis in 1937 at the age of two. Also known as Polio, the disease affected the lower left side of her body, from the waist down, causing her to suffer paresis, a partial paralysis, with diminished muscle tone. As an adult, Mother's left foot was three sizes smaller than the right. The muscles in her abdomen were affected as well. When she would bear down to give birth, the baby was pushed to the left by the stronger muscles on the right side. Rather than pushing the baby out, she was pushing the baby to one side. Today, Mother would have had a Cesarean, but in the mid-1950s, Cesarean births were considered major surgery. Doctors avoided Cesareans whenever possible. Only one out of twenty births was Cesarean, whereas today the number is one in three births.

When I was born, Mother died giving birth to me and was brought back to life by the medical team. However, before being resuscitated, she found herself in Hell, where the Devil met her. He gave her a tour of Hell, where she saw people writhing in pain and suffering every kind of horror.

The Devil, she told me, then turned to her and said, "This child you are bringing into the world will end up in Hell."

Now, I don't believe she met the Devil in person. But what a great story to tell an eight-year-old about her birth. *Fait Accompli.* I did, indeed, end up in a living Hell.

I never felt that my mother wanted children. She never appeared to like children; her own, or anyone else's. Mother told us she deliberately got pregnant with my sister because our father was threatening to leave her. She easily could have named my sister, Ulterior Motive.

Three years later, I was born. Mother never said why she got pregnant with me. She didn't say what motivated her. She didn't say if the pregnancy was deliberate or an accident, but there were seven other pregnancies she *deliberately* ended. Years later, my sister asked me if I ever thought Mother might have tried to abort me. I suppose we'll never know for sure, but evidence points to the likelihood she did, indeed, attempt to abort me. Coincidentally, I have a severe sensitivity to Sulfates. Which could mean I was, at some point, exposed to Quinine Sulfates, Mother's choice of *birth control*.

In 1968 Mother was playing on a *Ouija* board with a family member at my grandmother's house. Mother expressed doubt, calling the *Ouija* board a hoax. Her newly acquired stepsister suggested she ask a question to which only she knew the answer. Thinking this other woman knew only of my sister and me, she asked, "How many times have I been pregnant?" The planchette slowly moved across the board directly to the Nine. Mother threw the planchette across the room and said that proved the whole thing was bullshit. That evening, our mother told my sister and me that the *Ouija* board scared her because the nine pregnancies answer was true. At which point, she confided the story, making us swear never to repeat it to anyone else. Mother caused several miscarriages at home using Quinine Sulfate tablets. Historically, quinine has been used as an abortifacient.

Mother would take the whole bottle of Quinine tablets and wait around the house for the cramping to begin. Finally, when she felt the time had come, she would sit on the toilet until she voided the unwanted fetus. After flushing the toilet, she would make a trip to the emergency room for a D&C (dilation and curettage). Then she told us about the final abortion, which had occurred just a few months earlier. She said she had gotten curious and removed the amniotic sac from the toilet before flushing. She tore the sac open, removed the offending fetus, and said the baby was a boy with arms, legs, and definitive facial features; which describes a fetus of sixteen to seventeen weeks. At this point, he went into the toilet and was flushed away. Mother was very matter-of-fact, telling this story to her then ten and thirteen-year-old daughters; never showing any sign of regret, remorse or shame. Instead, she showed a kind of awe, like he was an eighth-grade science project.

On the other hand, she watched our faces for any reaction or judgment. I instinctively knew not to show any reaction on my face of the horror I was feeling inside, the deep sense of sadness. *What is she saying? Did she kill those babies? Was that baby boy alive when she flushed him down the toilet? Is she a monster?* She was a classic Malignant Narcissistic Psychopath.

Dr. Les Carter, Ph.D., has written several books, such as *When Pleasing You Is Killing Me, The Anger Trap,* and *Enough About You, Let's Talk About Me.* Dr. Carter talks about Narcissists and the People Pleasers they create. He has opened my eyes to the many ways I have sabotaged myself over the years. Growing up with a narcissist, I assumed the insanity was a normal way of life since constant turmoil was all I knew. *If something doesn't feel right, the fault must be mine. There's something wrong with me.*

I have learned, in my research, everyone has some narcissistic tendencies. I know I have a few of these traits myself. The difference is, *a true narcissist refuses to recognize these traits in themselves, denying any character flaws*. So, if you refuse to acknowledge any of the symptoms listed at the end of this chapter, you may have to consider the possibility you are a *true narcissist*.

But let's be clear. A narcissist doesn't describe my mother's ability to abort her babies in a manner some might call murder. Nor does Narcissistic Personality Disorder explain her desire or attempt to murder one of her husbands. Nor does NPD explain the death of the girl on a motorcycle, caused by my mother's insanity. These traits may well describe a psychopath. These things are what my mother did, and so much more. I will go into all of that in later chapters.

Mother controlled me in many unhealthy ways over the years. A few extreme instances led to my decision to get some counseling. For example, after several occasions when she told me my husband wasn't treating me right or wasn't good to me, Mother convinced me I needed to leave him and to leave my child with him.

I can look back, capable of seeing how crazy I must have seemed to my husband on the day I walked through the front door and said, "I'm leaving you, and I'm leaving our daughter with you." I cannot rationalize my thought process, only that my mother said leaving them was the best way to accomplish what she felt needed to be achieved. Like someone under a spell, *I had to do what she told me to do.*

Thankfully, my husband, being calm and rational, quietly said, "Okay. Well, how about you talk to someone. Someone who doesn't have a motive to lead you one way or the other. Maybe a professional counselor? Would you be willing to put a pin in this idea until then?"

I felt such relief. My husband had thrown me a lifeline. I was saved, for the moment, from having to do what she demanded. I hadn't wanted to leave him, and I certainly didn't want to leave my child. I was unable to tell my mother *No*. He had given me something to grasp onto until I could figure out a way to disobey her without the consequences. At least for the time being.

The first time I walked into a psychiatrist's office, I had a one-hour appointment scheduled. I told him my mother told me I should leave my husband. I told him my husband suggested I see the psychiatrist, to discuss the matter. Suddenly, before I knew what had happened, two hours had gone by, and the doctor was saying to me, "I don't think you have a problem with your husband. But I can assure you; you definitely have a problem with your mother."

After much counseling over the years, I've learned I am a Chronic People Pleaser. Pleasing others rather than oneself comes from years of being taught to do what was expected of me or suffer the consequences. *Submissiveness gets you less grief. Just go along and fly below the radar.* The result is, one never learns to trust oneself to make decisions based on their own needs, but always first to consider others' needs. If you don't take their needs into account first, then you are selfish. Sound familiar?

Negotiating a relationship with a narcissist is possible, as Dr. Carter advises, through behavioral and talk therapy, although, he agrees, negotiating said relationship is not always advisable. In my case, I felt safer removing myself from the situation. I wasn't just dealing with a narcissist; my mother was scary-crazy. I didn't reach that point in my relationship with my mother for several more years. Some people never reach the point where they feel ready to "cut the cord." However, when it became clear my children were at risk, the choice was made for me.

As I relate stories in my book, I talk a lot about situations that took place away from me. Mother would tell us what happened and what was said, but I have no way of knowing how truthful she was being. I only know the results. For example, the man who died after *he* suggested they trade cars; her Rambler for his Cadillac. Then she told us he had asked her to help him die. That was her story, but I have no idea what the actual circumstances may have been. As she told the story, she was a merciful angel helping him to end his life. *As she told the story.* I have personally witnessed a great many of her lies and distortions. She was always very convincing. *Classic Narcissist.* I will tell these stories, as she told them to me because they had an impact on my life. They became a part of my story.

My hope is my book will help others to recognize in themselves all the ways they were raised to deny their own needs and sacrifice their health to please the narcissists around them, and how they can break free of self-sabotaging ways. The chapter in which I discuss the miscarriage I suffered will sound extreme but is a classic example of denying my own needs and sacrificing my health not to be a burden to those around me, all due to the training I received at my mother's hands.

Today, I write from a new perspective, that of an adult who can, finally, see the dysfunction, and hopefully, make better choices. Healthier choices.

I am in no way an expert on Narcissistic Personality Disorder. I'm not an expert on anything. I enjoy cooking, but I'm not a great cook. I'm a pretty decent scrapbooker, but you won't see any of my pages in a magazine layout. I have tried my hand at crocheting and cross-stitch, eventually getting bored after a year or two. More recently, I've done some plaster stenciling of which I'm very proud. But an expert? If I could lay claim to being an expert at anything, I suppose slogging through life with my mother, and the many other narcissists I have dealt with makes me an expert on avoiding their vengeance. Recognizing the narcissist in other family members has helped me expertly negotiate those relationships. I survived to tell the tale, and that's an achievement in itself.

I realize, having a crazy mother doesn't make me unique. Everyone has someone in their life who is an irritation. I know every mother figure in my life was, to some degree, a narcissist. I decided to write my story because my mother was a special kind of narcissist.

I could have turned out like my mother. Thankfully, I had people in my life who influenced a desire in me to go a different route.

The Mayo Clinic gives the following overview and list of symptoms describing Narcissistic Personality Disorder.[1]

Overview

Narcissistic personality disorder — one of several types of personality disorders — is a mental condition in which people have an inflated sense of their importance, a deep need for excessive attention and admiration, troubled relationships, and a lack of empathy for others. But behind this mask of extreme confidence lies a fragile self-esteem that's vulnerable to the slightest criticism.

A narcissist causes problems in many areas of life, such as relationships, work, school, or financial affairs. People with a narcissistic personality disorder may be generally unhappy and disappointed when they're not given the special favors or, admiration, they believe they deserve. They may find their relationships unfulfilling, and others may not enjoy being around them.

Symptoms

Signs and symptoms of narcissistic personality disorder and the severity of symptoms vary. People with the disorder can:

- Have an exaggerated sense of self-importance

- Have a sense of entitlement and require constant, excessive admiration
- Expect to be recognized as superior even without achievements that warrant it
- Exaggerate achievements and talents
- Be preoccupied with fantasies about success, power, brilliance, beauty or the perfect mate
- Believe they are superior and can only associate with equally special people
- Monopolize conversations and belittle or look down on people they perceive as inferior
- Expect special favors and unquestioning compliance with their expectations
- Take advantage of others to get what they want
- Have an inability or unwillingness to recognize the needs and feelings of others
- Be envious of others and believe others envy them
- Behave arrogantly or haughtily, coming across as conceited, boastful and pretentious
- Insist on having the best of everything — for instance, the best car or office

According to the Society for the Study of Psychopathy, psychopathic traits include:

- Lack of guilt/remorse
- Lack of empathy
- Lack of deep emotional attachments
- Narcissism
- Superficial charm
- Dishonesty
- Manipulativeness
-

Chapter 2

Divorce and the Ignoring Mother

*M*other was a charmer. She was beautiful. When she walked into a room, people turned to stare at her gorgeous, thick, auburn hair, her bright blue eyes, her huge, dazzling smile.

Based on her interest in you, your first impression would cause you to assume Mother was going to be your friend, your confidant. Mother would encourage you to confide your deepest, darkest secrets to her. Once she had you in her web of deceit, Mother began to bring you down systematically. My mother would use the very mistakes you had confided in her as evidence of your shortcomings. Eventually, you would question your sanity. Behind your back, Mother was telling people horrible things about you, including embellished accounts of the very secrets you'd confided, all while she was screwing your husband. The woman could charm the pants off someone's husband while throat punching the unsuspecting wife. My mother refused to accept responsibility for her actions; she had an utter lack of remorse. The woman experienced no empathy. Which is not to say she didn't recognize your feelings; she used them against you, to undermine the foundation of your self-esteem. The ruse was all premeditated. Everything Mother said, or did, was goal-oriented.

Charm:

adjective

Delightful, pleasing, agreeable, likable, lovable, sweet, appealing, captivating, engaging, enchanting, fascinating, bewitching, beguiling, spellbinding, mesmerizing, seductive, desirable, irresistible.

Charm is not a personality trait. Charm is something worn like a cloak. While these adjectives may not be dangerous, *they often hide a dangerous, sociopathic, or narcissistic personality*. The person in question wants something, so he or she is particularly complimentary. When the charmer no longer wants something from you, he may be derogatory or cruel. He is skilled at projecting an attractive behavior to entice people to want to be around him. Watch for glimpses of what is behind the mask. Trust your instincts. Question your objectives. Why are you attracted to this person? What qualities do you see in this person making him a candidate for a deep emotional attachment? If you've ever described someone as charming, watch for the traits they are hiding. The charmer will catch you off-guard. Beware! Ted Bundy used charm to entice his victims, before the kidnapping, torturing and murdering of them.

Children's talent to endure stems from their ignorance of alternatives.

Maya Angelou

Before my parent's divorce, life seemed pretty normal for my sister and me. However, what was normal for us was distinctly abnormal for other children.

In the spring of 1964, my Uncle Jack, Dad's brother, died in a terrible car crash. He was racing a friend on a freeway near San Francisco.

His friend relayed the story saying Jack had just bought an old police unit at auction; they were racing late at night when the tie-rod broke on my uncle's car. The front wheels made a sudden, sharp right turn. The car went off the road, hitting a pole. The sheer velocity of the impact killed my uncle instantly.

Five months later, Dad filed for divorce from my mother. In 1964, a full year had to pass before divorce became final. My parent's divorce was final in September of 1965. In October of '65, one month later, Dad married his brother's widow.

When Dad filed for divorce, my mother, my sister and I went to live with my mother's parents. A short time later, Mother found a small house to rent in San Bernardino, near her parents. Mother claimed, while she was moving into the house, a neighbor lady came over. The neighbor told my mother the last woman who lived in that house had drowned her children in the bathtub.

Rather than move into the house, Mother agreed to move in with a man named Winfield. I suspect getting him to suggest she move in with him was the plan all along, but I can't know for certain.

I don't remember Mr. Winfield's first name. I remember he had a son with one arm, a prosthetic hook on the other. The son's name was Biff. Mother and Mr. Winfield drove down to Tijuana to get married. Her divorce wasn't final from my father, so this, her second marriage, wasn't legal.

While we lived with Winfield, Mother decided to make me wear toddler's plastic pants to bed, because I was a bedwetter. My sister, Lisa, and I had to share a room with Biff, so having to sleep in plastic pants was extremely embarrassing. Biff was a bully who insisted on tormenting me. He told all the kids who lived near us that I was a bedwetter who wore plastic pants to bed. But, more importantly, Mother wouldn't have to clean up after I wet the bed. My sister and I felt Mother seemed happiest when we were not a bother.

"Mama," I begged, "please don't make me wear plastic pants to bed." She made me promise, if she let me sleep without plastic pants, I would clean up after myself. I was six-years-old. I would get up in the middle of the night and get a dirty towel from the clothes hamper to cover the wet spot. In the morning, I would put the towel back in the hamper, leaving the bedclothes open to dry.

While we were living with Winfield, I got very sick with pneumonia. My grandmother told me later, she and my grandfather had come to our house. When they saw me on the couch in a makeshift bed, Grandmommy checked on me, telling my mother I appeared comatose. My grandmother insisted Mother take me to the hospital.

At the hospital, tests were done to determine the illness. The diagnosis was pneumonia. They admitted me to the hospital, where I stayed for a week. In the 1960s, people were still dying from minor cases of pneumonia. New types of medications were being developed, with limited knowledge of the side effects, in the hope of saving the patient's life. I was given Tetracycline before my permanent teeth had broken through the gum tissue, resulting in severe staining.

Mother would come to the hospital, paying little attention to me, only to the baby in the oxygen tent sharing my room. I assume the narcissist in her wanted other people, like the parents of the other child, to think she was this wonderful, caring woman who was brought nearly to tears for their little one. She would *charm* them. *Wasn't she just the kindest woman to care about their child?* When, at the age of six, I complained she wasn't paying enough attention to me, she called me selfish and spoiled. I have always held any criticism I've received close, not wanting to repeat the same mistake. First, to avoid Mother's disapproval, later to avoid anyone's disapproval.

At times, Mother was the classic Ignoring Mother. She was incapable of caring about anything or anyone but herself. If something didn't benefit her in some way, she managed to avoid the situation.

The Ignoring Mother will not teach her children about hygiene. My mother didn't teach me to use a hairbrush under the back of my long hair. As a child, I ran the brush down the sides of my head. Eventually, she discovered the matted, snarled hair at the nape of my neck. I distinctly remember her taking me to a salon to get someone else to take care of the problem. Initially, she took me to have my hair cut. Mother was told the tangles would need to come out before they could cut my hair properly. Two stylists were working on my hair at once, trying to detangle the mess. Mother just kept laughing, talking about how lazy I was. I remember the two ladies not laughing at all, just looking very stern. I internalized their scorn. I didn't know how to please my mother, as well as these women at the same time. The event was traumatizing. Now I think perhaps they saw the state of my hair as neglect on her part. Once they had the tangles out, they washed and cut my hair. She kept my hair in a Pixie style from then on.

When Mother's relationship with Winfield ended, she moved us to an apartment in San Bernardino, followed quickly with another move, closer to my father. A basement apartment in Redondo Beach. The divorce was getting close to being final. Perhaps that move was motivated by her desire to convince our father to come back to her.

My sister, Lisa, and I were nine and six-years-old when we moved to Redondo Beach. After my parents separated, we never had a babysitter unless we were with my grandmother. Once we left San Bernardino, Mother left us home alone to care for ourselves. In Redondo Beach, we wore swimsuits under our dresses to school. After school, Lisa and I would go directly to the beach where we would swim until Mother drove up, honking the horn; at which time we would collect our things to join Mother in the car. Mother would then take us home where we would shower off the sand, have dinner, and go to bed.

Lisa and I didn't mind this at all. We loved the beach, which was only two or three blocks from our house. There was a set of stairs going from the street down to the sand, followed by a short walk to the water's edge. We rode the waves on our bellies, dove under the waves, swam out as far as we could, again riding the waves back into shore. I don't remember there being a lifeguard on duty, but none of the adults on the beach seemed too concerned. We felt complete freedom, which we loved. As a parent myself, I now realize the neglect and danger we experienced.

While living near the beach, my parent's divorce became final. Dad remarried the following month, in October, so Mother remarried, too, that same month. Her third husband, Alex, was five years her junior. He just happened to be the man she was dating at the time of my father's second marriage. We moved in with Alex, the fourth school I would attend in the first grade. The following summer, we moved again, this time to Illinois.

By now, I was starting second grade. Having spent the first seven years of my life in Southern California, surrounded primarily by family, I had never met an African American. My first association with a person of color was in this small-town elementary school.

The year was 1965. With the Civil Rights Act of 1964, as well as more recently, the Voting Rights Act which had gone into effect in August of 1965, the news outlets were full of the changes our country was experiencing. These changes seemed to be taking place at a slower pace in the small community in which we were living. Halloween came around, the newspapers making it clear, October thirty-first was the night white children would go Trick-or-Treating. The *Negro* children would go the next night, November first. People weren't to leave their homes after dark unless it was their night for Trick-or-Treating. Lisa and I found it all very confusing. *Why do we have to go on different nights?*

Mother's husband, Alex, said, "Little white girls do not need to be mixing with n*****s. They have their place, and we have ours." Lisa and I looked to our mother for clarification, but she didn't say anything. Alex had boldly made the statement, and Mother let the word sit there like the proverbial elephant in the room.

Before this time, she had made clear to us; there was no difference between the races. She taught us not to use the N-word. Now, when the opportunity came for her to set the example, she didn't object to Alex's racist remarks. Naturally, we couldn't question either Mother or Alex. This was a very confusing time for us.

I remember, in the 1990s, Oprah Winfrey said something on her television show which resonated with me. She said, "If you don't speak up against racism, you are just as guilty." Oprah went on to say,

"Even if it's a racist joke. If you laugh at it or don't speak up against it, you're just as guilty." Powerful, powerful words.

During one of my father's visits in the '90s, I had some of his cousins over to my house for the evening. My Dad's cousin began a joke that included a "n****r." A plethora of thoughts went through my head in the split second after he had used the offensive word, including the time my mother didn't speak up against Alex using the word, yet, not a full second went by. I said, "Excuse me, I'm going to have to stop you there. We don't use *that* word in this house, and I don't want my children to think I'm okay with the use of the word." I almost threw up, so terrified of speaking up to an adult, even though I was an adult myself. Making the statement was a pivotal and defining moment in my life, standing up for my integrity, and my values.

The next day, my cousin called me and said, "Thank you for calling me out on that. It's a word I grew up with while living in the South. I hadn't given it any thought or considered what an offensive word it is. But I promise you; I will never use it again." I have never felt so validated.

As a child, I was an impulsive wanderer. If I got an idea in my head to walk down the street, I walked down the street. If I got invited into a house by one of the kids in the neighborhood, I went in. While not a good or safe practice, it was what I had always done. Mother just said, "Be home before dark."

One evening, I was playing in a little girl's bedroom when her mother stuck her head in the door, asking my name. She said there was a woman outside yelling for me. The sun had gone down, but I hadn't noticed. I jumped up, ran downstairs, out the front door, like my butt was on fire. Mother was mad as any mother would be, but in my mother's case, she wasn't scared for me. I felt my mother was mad because she had to come looking for me. When we got home, Alex wanted to spank me. He had a paddle he had made himself, with holes drilled in the wood. His children lived in California with their mother. I had watched him make the paddle. The paddle was intended for my sister and me. Mother let him use his weapon on me, yet she had never spanked me. I thought, *why is she letting him do this*?

Mother was never physically abusive with us. Lisa and I felt her contempt for us; we were beneath her consideration. She told us, daily, what she could be doing if she hadn't had us. If we expressed dislike for something, a piece of clothing or a certain type of food, she would begin screaming at us about how ungrateful we were. We learned not to be honest with her. Because she claimed to have had a terrible childhood, we were never allowed to express joy. We were made to feel guilty for being happy. We couldn't express disappointment; she would blame everything wrong in our lives on our father for abandoning us, for choosing a different family. Every emotion we felt, we learned to keep to ourselves.

On the other hand, if she did something for us, we were expected to show exaggerated gratitude, even though the deed was for the Glory of Mother. Photographs of us opening her gifts at birthdays or holidays always show an exaggerated joy on our faces. She taught us to overemphasize our joy at the gifts we received from her. With Alex, there were many instances he showed his hostility toward me. He made sure I understood, my being friends with a black boy at school was not appropriate. Then there was the time I asked Alex why he added vinegar to his spinach. He handed me the bottle and said, "Try some for yourself." I accidentally splashed too much on my spinach, and he made me eat the spinach anyway. Reminding me, I had done it myself.

Lisa and I never lived in a happy, accepting, and fulfilling home. We were never made to feel encouraged or supported. There was always tension.

Before Alex moved us to Illinois, we lived in a duplex with a shared closet between two bedrooms. I thought running between the two rooms was great fun. Every night, I would run into their room to kiss my mother goodnight. One night, when I ran into their room, Mother wasn't there. Instead, I found Alex standing nude in front of the dresser mirror, arms over his head running a brush through his hair. His penis was hard, standing out in front of him like a flagpole. He made eye contact with me, never adjusting his posture in any way. I turned to flee back to my bedroom. That may have been an innocent mistake on both our parts, but let us not forget, he knew I would be coming in through the closet.

One evening, a policeman knocked at the door of our home in Illinois. He told my mother her father had died. She said, "You mean, my mother."

"No, Ma'am," the officer said, looking puzzled. "The message said your father has died." We didn't have a home phone, so a family member in San Bernardino had called the local police department, asking them to make notification. Mother went to her mother-in-law's house to call her parent's home in California. Indeed, her father had passed away that afternoon.

My mother's father was a big, strong, John Wayne-type of man; he had hoboed around the country as a young man, hitching rides on boxcars, and he had been a short-order cook in cafes. My grandfather was best known as a rodeo bronc buster. He had gained the nickname, Booger Red, based on a famous bronc buster from the 1920's of the same name. Family members still call him Uncle Booger when they speak of him to this day. They all describe him as a great man with a great sense of humor. He was 6'2" with red hair, which played into the name as well. He was never sick a day in his life.

On the morning of his 54th birthday, he awoke not feeling well. By November 22, 1965, he was a Body and Fender man at an automobile shop located across the street from Goodwill, where his wife, my grandmother, was a seamstress. My grandparents always drove to and from work together. That afternoon, Grandpa walked across the street to tell Grandmommy he wasn't feeling well; they needed to go home. Upon arriving home, Grandpa told her he felt like he was going to throw up. Grandmommy told him to lie down on the couch, and she would bring him the trash can.

My mother's father, "Booger Red" in 1933.

My grandmother walked into the kitchen to get the trash can. When she returned to the living room, she found him dead. He'd had a massive heart attack.

My grandmother, Ruth, was a tiny little thing. Standing just five feet tall, weighing less than one hundred pounds when they married, she couldn't get pregnant right away. The young couple had been married for three years before they discovered they were expecting.

My grandmother was born in Hugo, Oklahoma, in 1913. Her father, at the age of eighteen, had married a twenty-eight-year-old widow with three children. Together, they had five more children, four boys, with my grandmother, the only girl, in the middle.

Ruth was eleven years old when her mother died. Her half-siblings were gone. Ruth, being the only girl still living at home, she became the lady of the house. She cooked, cleaned, hand-washed the clothes, tended the vegetable garden, for her father and brothers, until the boys all left home. The youngest brother, Reggie, had polio and was severely handicapped. Reggie died at eighteen from pneumonia, shortly after recognizing symptoms of polio in my then two-year-old mother.

My grandmother, her father, and brothers, all had a hard life. The struggle was all they knew. No different than other families around them in their small community of Hugo, Oklahoma.

Mother was born in her father's lap. When the birthing process became too much for my grandmother; her sister-in-law told my grandfather to get behind his wife, hold her legs up to relieve some of the exhaustion. My grandfather held his exhausted little wife like that until finally, the baby girl came into the world. The new father swore his wife would never go through childbirth again. She never did. After my mother was born, my grandparents took whatever precautions were necessary to prevent getting pregnant.

After giving birth to my mother, Grandmommy put on weight, becoming this jolly-little-round woman whom everyone loved. A benevolent, generous, happy little lady was the only way I ever knew her. My grandfather adored her. They were very much in love.

My mother's mother, in 1934.

However; my grandfather spoiled his daughter, which meant his wife had to be the disciplinarian. My mother told my sister and me she hated her mother. As unreasonable as Mother's hatred may have been, Mother never forgave Grandmommy for ever having said *No* to her, or for any spanking she had received as a child.

Mother was two years old, playing on the floor while her mother was working in the kitchen. My grandmother's disabled brother, gravely handicapped by polio throughout the entire right side of his body, noticed something about the two-year-old which was concerning to the teen. He realized the baby wasn't walking at all. Reggie told his sister, "Doris can't walk. When she tries to walk, she's dragging her left foot. I'm afraid she has polio." In 1937, polio was a real concern throughout the country. Cases were showing up more frequently.

When my grandfather came home from work, the young family went to the local doctor for his opinion on why the baby had stopped walking. The doctor diagnosed the child with Infantile Paralysis, also known as polio.

The most common result of the Polio (Poliomyelitis) Virus is "drop foot" when the Tibialis Anterior muscle is paralyzed. The Achilles Tendon is weakened and contracts, causing the toes to "drop" toward the ground. In my mother's case, it was just the opposite. However, in all of my research, I have been unable to find any reference to what must have been an extremely rare result of the poliovirus. The Achilles Tendon on her left foot was long, while the muscle in the front of the ankle was short, causing her toes to pull back toward her leg.

When Mother was in elementary school, her parents took her to a specialist. He recommended releasing the muscle on the front of her foot, allowing it to relax. She was happy her parents chose not to go this route. Mother had heard horror stories of patients spending the rest of their lives in a wheelchair after similar procedures.

Mother never lost the ability to walk. She couldn't run, but for the most part, she didn't allow her disability to limit her. However, as she became menopausal, she gained weight. Obesity took a toll on her ability to walk and caused her to develop issues with her spine. Shortly before she passed at the age of sixty-two, Mother was looking into getting a scooter to help her get around.

For the most part, people didn't notice her disability. About the time Mother bought a little beer bar in San Bernardino, at the age of forty, her limp was beginning to be more pronounced. The regulars at the bar sometimes asked questions like, "Hey, Doris, why are you limping? Did you hurt your foot?"

Mother told me she had discovered if she told people she had had polio; they would become uncomfortable and apologize for having asked. So, when anyone asked about the limp, she told them she had a horseback riding accident as a child. People seemed to accept this explanation without feeling uncomfortable for having inquired about the limp.

As a child, my mother began to realize she was different than other children. She noticed the things her handicap prevented her from doing. As her friends and cousins began to outrun her, she began to feel left out. She told me about being left behind when her cousins would play games outside that she was unable to play. As time went on, Mother became bitter. She began to *look* for instances where she perceived people deliberately leaving her out.

As an adolescent, Mother's disability began to show up in her everyday life. She became resentful, and angry, getting in fights with the other children. Mother told my sister and me of the fights she had with her cousins. She said her mother would "beat" her for fighting. She told us of being held down by her cousin, while his brother put a dead grasshopper in her mouth, and how it made her feel helpless. When they let her up, she caught one of them and began brawling with him. Recently, the older of the two brothers told me she and his younger brother were both beaten for fighting.

As a teenager, Mother had grown into a lovely young woman, although self-conscious of her disability. Mother's father always made sure she had a car to drive. When she wrecked the car, he would provide her with another car. Then he would repair the damage to the wrecked car and sell it.

The boys were attracted to her, and the girls were envious. Consequently, the girls in school began to bully and demean our mother. She told us of the time, while in choir, two girls behind her were pretending to spit on her beautiful, long auburn hair. Mother went home, grabbed her mother's scissors, and headed for the bathroom. When she came out of the bathroom, she had cut her hair off. She came out with a bob just below her ears. Mother told us the bob was a popular style at the time. She had been begging her mother to let her cut her hair, but my grandmother had refused.

The incident was one of many times my mother would disobey her parents. Each time, she claimed, her mother would beat her. Then her father would buy her a gift.

In her thirties, Mother applied for a job as a telephone operator. She was told, "We don't hire the handicapped." At a time before the Americans with Disabilities Act of 1990, prohibiting discrimination based on disability.

Mother learned to be bitter and resentful at an early age. She became overly suspicious of motives. When a new policy at work went into effect, she assumed the policy was intended to cause her a hardship. Many years later, when Mother arrived at a Family Reunion, she saw a sign at the entrance to the facility that read, No Smoking. By the time I arrived with my family, Mother had left. A family member told me my mother had seen the sign and felt it was a direct assault on her. She left the reunion, driving the three-hours back home, never to return.

Mother flew, along with my sister and me, to California for her father's funeral. My grandfather dying was my first experience with death. I remember thinking, *I'm supposed to cry. If I don't cry, will I look like I didn't care? Mama will want me to cry.* I shouldn't have worried. As soon as I saw my grandfather in the coffin, I began to cry. He was a sweet man who loved us very much. His loss left a huge hole in our lives.

Once we returned to Illinois, things went back to normal. Alex didn't like me. I didn't like Alex. I asked my mother if I could go live with my father. In her mind, I suppose, *one less kid*. We went to a neighbor's house, where Mother called my father, *Collect*. When he agreed to accept the charges, she handed the phone to me. "Ask him," she said. Dad immediately said I could come live with him, his new wife and her two children, my cousins.

Chapter 3

A Strong, Independent, Capable Woman

*M*other was many things. At times she could be the Child, sometimes the Prostitute, on occasion she presented herself as the Victim. Often, she was the Saboteur.

The woman could be whatever character she felt was required to accomplish her goal at any given time.

At times, my mother would treat me as her surrogate parent. When she wanted me to take care of her needs, acting like the Child was how she achieved her goal. I didn't always recognize what she was doing. She had used this ruse so often over my life; I just did what was expected of me. Until the day she threatened to kill herself. I made it clear I was done being the mother figure in our relationship.

While narcissists have been known to commit suicide, they don't typically harm themselves. Instead, choosing to harm others. Having said this, those on the spectrum of The Dark Triad: a combination of narcissism, sociopathy, and psychopathy (Machiavellianism); depending on other factors, such as substance abuse, the likelihood of suicide increases. In this case, it was the one, and only time she had threatened suicide and never had she attempted it. I was convinced it was an idle threat.

"The vulgar crowd always is taken by appearances, and the world consists chiefly of the vulgar."

Niccolo Machiavelli

Mother was often the Prostitute, taking in men, women, and children; making promises about how she would reciprocate favors, with no apparent intention of following through, unless it benefitted her.

The woman could get her house painted or cleaned. Her car washed, her laundry done, her tire changed, you name it. She was an expert at convincing people to do favors for her, with no payment or favor returned.

As the Victim, she would use her handicap, exaggerating her limp to appear more delicate and or helpless. Mother referred to this as "acting."

My mother was a strong, independent, extremely capable woman. She was physically and intellectually capable of accomplishing anything she set her mind to achieve. However, if she could convince anyone else to do the "heavy lifting," she chose to go that route.

Mother made numerous court appearances over the years, never being convicted of any crime. Her "go-to" character in these situations was always the Victim. She would exaggerate the limp, roll her shoulders to make her 5'8" frame appear smaller. Then her acting chops would kick in; the free-flowing tears, the hiccups, and loss of breath. She could appear intimidated by the judge, the courtroom, and the lawyers. I'm not certain anything or anyone had ever intimidated her. My mother was a master manipulator. If you didn't know her on a personal level, it would be very easy to fall for her act. She was good.

The woman had used this character in court on two occasions concerning child support.

Which brings me to the Saboteur. I remember the time she took our father to court in 1968. My father had flown his brother down with him. Mother, Lisa, and I made the one-hour drive to Los Angeles for the showdown in court.

Mother pointed out to Lisa and me that our father flew his

brother down with him but wasn't willing to give her more money to raise his children. This was Mother's way of sabotaging our relationship with our father. "He doesn't love you. He doesn't want to support you. He's trying to get out of paying any child support. He wants Lois and her children to be his family, not us."

Mother began the brainwashing, convincing us that she was the only person who loved us and was the only adult we could always depend on for our personal care. Which, of course, was her last priority. She made sure we got fed. Not necessarily by her, but that was the only thing she made sure of concerning personal care.

Any relationship we had, that didn't keep her as our top priority, she would sabotage. She poisoned our feelings towards our father, his parents, and his siblings. She had us convinced that our grandparents, aunt, and uncles didn't care about us. She tried to sabotage our marriages. She even fed us poisonous fruit about her own mother, convincing us that Grandmommy did for us out of guilt for a past transgression.

She claimed, when Lisa was a baby, our grandmother reached to take Lisa out of her crib. Lisa swatted her chubby little hand and hit Grandmommy's glasses, knocking them askew and hurting Grandmommy's nose. Mother said Grandmommy had slapped Lisa.

There were no witnesses to verify the truth of this account. I had never seen my grandmother lose her temper. Never, not once.

Mother always ended the story with one of her patented, "make the story better" lines. She said she had told her mother, "If you ever strike my child again, I'm going to take you outside and stomp a mudhole in you." Verbatim. Every time. And she told that story to us often, emphasizing her role as Hero in the story.

Early on, I believed the story, thinking the only reason Grandmommy wasn't abusive to us was out of fear of our mother, our protector. Over the years, I realized Mother liked to embellish and make-up scenarios. She liked to repeat them until I think she, herself, believed them. When it all became so clear to me, I began to take everything she said with a grain of salt. Eventually, I got to the point

I just assumed everything she said was a lie. Literally, I just ignored anything she said about anyone else.

Unfortunately, I took everything she said about me to heart. It was all in the training I received. I was worthless, and I was a bad mother, I wasn't smart or pretty. The only thing she ever said that wasn't negative about me was truly the most negative. She told me that I was a good dancer. She never encouraged me to attend a school of dance. Oh no. The only thing she said was, "You should move to Las Vegas and become a topless dancer." She wasn't joking. She repeated the advice to become a topless dancer every time she reiterated, "You have no other skills. What else will you do to support yourself?"

December 1965

I was very happy living with my father and his new family. I knew them all, they were already family, so fitting in was easy.

Dad and Lois were living in a two-bedroom house, so my now stepsister/cousin, Calley, and I shared the secondary bedroom, and Greg, my stepbrother/cousin, slept on the couch.

Calley was five, Greg six, and I was seven years old. We went to school together, and we walked home together. We played together, fought like siblings, and fell into a routine I happily enjoyed. It wasn't a fairy tale existence, but it was safe. I was still careful not to make an adult mad, but generally, I was happy.

Calley and I were best friends. She followed me around like the proverbial puppy dog. She went wherever I went and tried to do whatever I did. I enjoyed the experience.

One evening as we were preparing for bed, I was in the bathroom brushing my teeth. Calley followed me in the bathroom, carrying her pillow. She put the pillow on the edge of the bathtub and sat down to talk to me. Almost immediately, she fell over backward into the tub, hitting her head on the backside of the bathtub. She hit it hard. Once Lois got her calmed down, we went to bed.

Calley threw up all over the bed, a couple of times during the night. The next morning, Lois called the doctor's office to get Calley checked out, worried she might have a concussion. I can't remember what the doctor said about Calley, but when he was done with my "little sister," Lois asked if he could determine why, at seven years old, I was still wetting the bed. I clearly remember getting up on the examination table, but I don't remember the exam. Then he told her, "She has a lazy bladder and is probably a deep sleeper. She'll outgrow it." I remember what he said like it was yesterday. I've thought of it often over the years. Lois was telling my father a distorted version of the truth.

The doctor's comment had stuck with me because, when my father got home from work that evening, Lois told him the doctor said I was too lazy to get up and go to the bathroom during the night. Even at seven, I knew it was a lie. The doctor's explanation of the "lazy bladder" was relatively clear to me, but I certainly wasn't going to correct Lois. I had learned, grown-ups don't like to be corrected.

I wet the bed the following night. The next morning, Dad called me into his bedroom and closed the door. He asked if I had wet the bed the previous night. I said I had. He asked if I was just being lazy about getting up to use the bathroom. I mumbled something like, "I don't know."

As the child of a narcissist, you learn early on. The wrong answer can bring down the Wrath of God, or the wrath of an adult. Answering certain questions is like walking through a field of landmines. One wrong step and Boom!

When I told my father, I didn't know if I was just lazy, I was really saying, *I don't know how to answer your question. Do I tell you what I heard the doctor say, and call Lois a liar? Do I say, yes, I was lazy?* Rock, hard place meet JoJo. I got my one and only spanking from my father. Dad didn't act like he wanted to do it, but I guess he felt it was his responsibility. I didn't stop wetting the bed until I was fourteen years old, but I never got another spanking for it, either.

The Dysfunctional "Lazy" Bladder Syndrome in Children[2]

> The cystometrographic studies using a Stadham transducer and a polygraph were of particular interest because of their characteristic abnormal pattern. A normal cystometrogram was characterized by occasional small contractions and by a gradual elevation of intravesical pressure which initiated involuntary bladder contractions on reaching approximately 15 to 20 cm. of water pressure. If the patient did not respond to the urge to void, the contractions disappeared, and the intravesical pressure decreased temporarily to rise again gradually to the previous level at which involuntary contractions appeared. By contrast, in the dysfunctional "lazy" bladder syndrome, the cystometrogram showed a gradual elevation of the intravesical pressure beyond the physiological limits, which normally initiate involuntary bladder contractions.

In addition to Dysfunctional Bladder Syndrome, I also suffer from Urethral Stricture, with no known cause. It's a struggle. For a child, it is involuntary. As the doctor told my stepmother, the child will outgrow the bedwetting, as they learn how to contend with the issues.

I had a chance to be around my father's extended family, even my stepmother's family. However, my stepmother's sisters didn't seem to know what to do with me. If I spoke to them, they mumbled and seemed to be tongue-tied. Consequently, they ignored me and avoided me. I wasn't sure what I had done wrong, so I would spend the next forty-plus years trying to make them, and other people, like me, confirming the People Pleaser Syndrome.

Dr. Carter goes into detail about the People

Pleaser Syndrome in his book, *When Pleasing You Is Killing Me.*[3] He lists the requirements of people-pleasing.

1. Being Responsible for What Is Not Yours.
2. Enabling Others to Be Unhealthy.
3. Denying What is Healthy.
4. Showing Disrespect Toward Yourself.

He goes on to say, "Most people pleasers have lived so long with controlling, imposing people that they automatically acquiesce to certain do's and don'ts such that this pattern of behavior has become unquestioned. Despite consistent attempts to appease them, the controllers remain judgmental, causing the pleaser to become wary about being authentic and voicing any residual discomfort or doubt. Over time, perhaps subconsciously, the pleaser succumbs to unspoken rules of engagement that perpetuate an inner strain in order to keep an outer semblance of peace." These are self-imposed requirements.

At the end of the school year, we all moved. It was another two-bedroom house, but this time the secondary bedroom was large enough, Calley and I shared one bed, with Greg using a twin bed in the same room.

I have some fond memories of that house. Dad and Lois always had someone over to play games, and our company usually brought their children to play with Greg, Calley, and me.

My Dad's brother, Charlie, and his wife, Nancy, would come over with their two boys, Kevin and Scott, who were Greg and Calley's ages. The house was next to an elementary school, so we had plenty of room to play outside.

I remember a time when the adults were sitting around the table playing dominoes, and suddenly both women began screaming.

We kids' ran in to see what was happening. There was a mouse! The women were on top of the kitchen counter screaming, and the men were trying to catch the mouse or kill the mouse and yelling at the women to be quiet. Calley and I jumped up on chairs. Greg, Kevin, and Scott were trying to get in the middle of the "mousetrap." It was complete chaos. The men finally killed the poor mouse. That evening proved to be an evening of grand excitement.

One day, Uncle Charlie and Aunt Nancy rode over on a new motorcycle. Charlie let my Dad take Lois for a ride, but they were gone a long time, and I was beginning to worry. Residual feelings of abandonment. I remember sitting on the curb, waiting for them. Charlie came out and sat by me. He said they were probably having fun and would be home soon. When Dad and Lois finally came home, they were in the back of a taxi. A teenage girl had pulled her car out in front of them, and they had crashed into her car. Dad had a cast on his right arm; Lois had a cast on her left arm.

Not long after, the phone rang. My mother was calling. She told my father she had left Alex and was living with her mother in San Bernardino. Mother wanted me to come back and live with her. I could hear their conversation. "She's happy here, and we like having her," my father told my mother.

"Put her on the phone," Mother told him.

Dad handed me the phone. She told me to tell him I wanted to live with her.

This was a woman who had trained me to do as I was told, no questions asked. I told him I wanted to go live with my mother. I *didn't* want to go live with her, but I didn't feel like I had a choice, so off I went to live with my mother, the woman who treated me like an inconvenience. She told me I should feel lucky if I got a C on a test in school. The same woman who mocked everything I said or did. Lisa was the pretty one, the smart one. Lisa could take care of herself, and she wasn't any trouble. As Lisa got older, she became responsible for me. I had no value to my mother, except to hurt my father. I was happy living with my father, and that didn't sit well with her at all. I went back to San Bernardino to live with my mother.

Grandmommy and me, 1965

Chapter 4

I'm a Girl, in Hollywood

*W*hen I moved back with my mother, in the summer of 1966, we were living with her mother, in the house where my grandfather had died. I soon discovered my mother was in contact with Alex, her last husband, the very man who caused me to go live with my father in the first place.

Mother and Alex were writing letters back and forth to each other; filthy letters, pornographic letters Lisa and I should never have seen, but Lisa found them, and we looked at the pictures together. Alex was an incredible artist. He used his talent to sketch incredibly graphic pictures at the bottom of his letters to our mother. I didn't want to see any more, so I stopped looking at them after I saw some of the illustrations he had added. I'm not sure if Lisa read the letters or not.

At the same time, Mother was seeing a fantastic man whom Lisa and I loved. Barry was a handsome, intelligent man with a career and a good income.

Barry gave me a Teddy Bear that his mother had given him on his 2nd birthday. Barry was two years older than my mother, so I knew Teddy was the same age as my mother. My Teddy was born in 1935. That's how I always knew how old my Teddy was. And my Teddy was my best friend over the next ten or eleven years. No matter where we lived, or what school I was attending, Teddy was always there, waiting for me in my bedroom to come to him when I needed comfort.

When my mother went off on me, in one of her rages, I could

only stand there while she ranted. Afraid to move, afraid to speak, afraid to even breath. Always afraid to make the rage worse. *If I don't move, speak or breathe too loudly, maybe she will let me leave the room sooner.* I loved my Teddy. I knew I could hold him close and tell him all my fears, pour out my anger and frustration. I could tell Teddy things that I couldn't tell anyone else. In the past, when I'd tried to tell my friends what kind of mother I had, they never believed me. They always said something to the effect, *your mother is great. I wish she was my mother.* My friends loved her because they only saw what she wanted them to see.

Lisa and I thought Barry was perfect; so, of course, Mother dumped Barry and remarried Alex. Her fourth wedding, to her third and fourth husband.

Mother and Alex in Hollywood, 1965.

I had started the third grade in San Bernardino, but Mother and Alex moved us to a one-bedroom bungalow in Hollywood. The little bungalow was part of a courtyard, similar to that in *Swing Shift*, the Goldie Hawn and Kurt Russell movie depicting life in the 1940s. Several little bungalows along a central sidewalk. Lisa and I shared the bedroom while Mother and Alex slept on a bed in the living room.

Mother had chosen Alex over a man who could have provided us with a nice home and plenty to eat. Instead, she remarried a man whose general lack of income caused her to steal milk from the stoop of the next-door neighbor. This was back in the day when a milkman would deliver milk to the door in glass bottles. The neighbors had moved but hadn't canceled their milk order.

The day we moved into this little bungalow; I was standing on the running board of the trailer filled with our furniture. A boy walked by and kept staring at me. I just stared back at him. Pretty soon, he came back by and asked if I was a boy or a girl. I just said, "I'm a girl." When I told my mother about the boy wanting to know if I was a boy or a girl, she thought it was funny, and for years she retold the story, with her embellishment.

She always told people I had said, "I'm a girl" and punched him in the nose. I don't know why she felt the need to say it, but she was always making stories "more entertaining."

The little boy lived two houses down from us. He asked me where I was going to school, and who was my teacher. When I told him, he said, "I went there last year, and she was my teacher." He was a year older than I but had stopped attending public school. His name was Vincent. He would always be sitting on my front stoop when I got home from school. He and I would play until dinner time and then go our separate ways. One day, after dinner, I knocked on his door. His father answered the door, and I asked, "Can Vincent come out to play?"

Vincent's father said, "He goes to school in the evening." My mother guessed he was an actor on the studio lot, and they conducted his classes in the evening. I just know, one day we might be playing cowboys and Indians, hanging my doll from the clothesline, and the next day playing secret agents and jumping from roof-top to roof-top. The houses were very close together, with cinder block walls between them. Vincent and I would jump from one roof, to the wall, and on to the next roof. Most of the time, we were riding our bicycles all over the city of Hollywood. He and I did some seriously dangerous things in traffic, but as long as I was home by dinner time, my mother didn't worry.

One day, Vincent and I were out riding our bikes, when we saw a limousine pull up in front of a music studio on Sunset Blvd. We stopped to see who was inside the limousine. Out of the back stepped two people we recognized instantly. Sonny and Cher. They smiled and waved at us, then walked into the building. We were so excited!

It wasn't unusual for us to see actors from the current batch of sitcoms. We saw Adam West and Victor Buono from *Batman*, on separate occasions. We used to see Erin Murphy, from *Bewitched*, grocery shopping with her mother at the Market Basket on Ventura Blvd. I once saw Butch Patrick, from *The Munsters*, at the bowling alley with his friends. My sister went to school with Sheldon Collins from *The Andy Griffith Show*. Those were exciting times for a couple of kids who didn't know better. Lisa and I didn't know we were poor.

From the little bungalow, Lisa and I were moved to North Hollywood, the third school I would attend in third grade. Our little "family" rented the one-bedroom servant's quarters of a mansion on Orange Grove Avenue. We lived two houses off of Hollywood Boulevard, above a five-car garage.

I never saw Vincent again. We thought we saw him at the end of a movie, *Wild in the Streets*, 1968. But he wasn't in the credits.

A flamboyant party planner and caterer, Lionel D. lived in the Greek Revival style house. A white two-story, with a huge Grecian fountain in front, and six two-story columns. The columns stood at ground level, appearing to hold-up the roof. Alex had met him through the company he worked for, doing maintenance on restaurant-style kitchen equipment. Lionel D. offered up this garage apartment to Alex and his family at a reasonable price, so we moved into the apartment above his five-car garage.

The apartment was dark and unadorned. There was a set of stairs along the far-left side of the garage. At the top of the stairs was the beginning of a long, sinister hallway; without windows, it ran the length of the garage below. There were four doors along the right side of the hallway; first was the kitchen, next was the bathroom, followed by the one and only bedroom and finally, the living room. I spent very little time indoors. I tried to stay outside as much as possible, away from Alex and my mother.

I had great freedom while living there. When I wasn't in school, I would get on my bicycle and just go. I rode my bike all over North Hollywood, in and out of traffic at break-neck speeds, through underground garages and across parking lots, down streets filled with shops like *Frederick's of Hollywood*, costume stores, porn theaters, and head shops. I rode like the wind.

Hollywood was filled with quirky characters who came out at night. We were so poor; for entertainment, we would park in the heart of Hollywood and just "people watch." My favorite people to watch were the transvestites. They were always so colorful, vibrant, and sparkling. Alex said they acted that way to attract clients. He said they were hookers. I didn't fully understand what "hooker" meant, nor did I care. They were glittery and pretty.

Mother seemed to be happy, as long as Lisa and I stayed out of her way. She would go and visit the owner in his "big, fancy" house. Mother said they were having coffee and talking. I was never allowed in the big house. This was all right with me; I was too busy exploring the city, and enjoying the wonderful neighborhood in which we lived, filled with mansions and "beautiful people."

Lisa and I would go for walks across Hollywood Boulevard and up into the Hollywood Hills. At that time the houses were smaller and more like cottages than you see today. The people we saw living in the hills were more eclectic. Mama Cass Elliot, of *The Mamas and the Papas* singing group, lived up there. We saw them all, one day, sitting around an outdoor table. They were laughing and talking on a covered patio in front of one of these little cottages. Now, when you go driving through the Hollywood Hills, all the little cottages have been razed, and mansions have been built in their place.

Mother had some friends, the Valentinas. Harry and Dorothy gave her a loan, in the summer of 1967, to get a *Winchell's Donut* franchise in Hawthorne. The four of us moved to a two-bedroom house in the suburbs of Hawthorne, and I began the fourth grade.

Grandmommy moved in with us to help with the donut shop. She had a twin bed in the laundry room off the kitchen. My grandmother could come in through the backdoor, right into her makeshift bedroom.

On Sunday mornings, after working all night making fresh donuts for the day, my mother would bring home "day old" donuts for me to sell at a stand in front of our house. Similar to a lemonade stand, but I sold "Day Old Donuts," cheap. The ladies on the block loved it. They would come, in housecoats with curlers in their hair, and buy donuts from me so they wouldn't have to cook breakfast before getting the family ready for church.

One evening, Lisa and a friend from school took me with them to a traveling carnival in town. Mother and Alex dropped us off with enough money for ride tickets and snacks. I remember the three of us on The Octopus, a carnival ride that would whip you around and around. I was not enjoying it, so Lisa's friend kept trying to get me to laugh, saying silly things. Finally, at one point, Lisa said, "I think I'm going to vomit!" I began to laugh at that, but by the time we got off the ride, Lisa was really sick to her stomach. She and her friend decided to ride the Ferris Wheel, hoping it would settle Lisa's stomach. I had decided to stay off the ride and just watch.

Lisa was sitting with her head resting on the side of the seat. She had very long hair, and suddenly she began to scream. Her hair had gotten tangled around the rim where the seat attaches to the rotating wheel. Lisa's hair was tightening the further around the wheel turned. Suddenly all the people around the girls began to scream as well. When the attendant realized what was happening, he quickly stopped the ride, but eventually, they had to get it around to where the seat could be removed from the wheel. I'm not sure when my mother arrived. She and Alex were there as Lisa was being removed from the ride. Lisa had a hunk of hair pulled out at the scalp, along with a portion of her scalp. She was never taken to a hospital or even a doctor. She was given aspirin and then put to bed.

Eventually, Mother and Alex began having problems. He didn't want to live with her mother or her children, and she didn't want his kids coming to visit. The final straw was when he came home one day driving a Corvair, without first discussing the purchase with her. One night, they got in a knock-down, drag-out argument with pushing and shoving. In the end, she threw an alarm clock at him as he stormed out. Alex got in his little Corvair and left the house.

Mother said to my sister and me, "Watch this." She dialed the phone and called the police. She was smiling gleefully with anticipation. When the police answered, her whole demeanor changed. She used to brag about her acting abilities.

The tears began to flow, "My husband is threatening to kill me. He just left but said he would be back later to finish the job. I'm here alone with my two little girls," she cried. Tears were running down her face. When she got off the phone, she wiped her face and told us they would be keeping an eye on the house all night.

Sometime during the night, Alex drove his car into the driveway and was detained before he got to the front door.

Mother got another divorce after moving the three of us to a one-bedroom apartment across the street from the donut shop. Grandmommy found herself a little one-bedroom efficiency apartment nearby.

One day Grandmommy told us she had gone on a date with a gentleman who frequented the shop. He had offered to take her to dinner, and she had accepted his invitation. Telling us about the date, Grandmommy was hopping mad. She said that he had insisted on giving her a kiss goodnight. She told us, "He put his nasty tongue in my mouth." We all laughed so hard at her facial expression telling us about his "nasty tongue"; we couldn't help laughing. Grandmommy was not amused.

Mother was the main baker at the shop. She would walk across the street at midnight and begin making the donuts for the morning rush. By the time she unlocked the doors at 6 am, the front display would be full of freshly made donuts; glazed and iced raised donuts, glazed and iced cake donuts. Maple bars, twists, and cinnamon rolls were generously displayed. There were powdered donuts and jelly-filled donuts; chocolate bars filled with freshly whipped cream, and tons of fresh coffee. You could never have enough coffee on hand.

The first people through the doors every morning were police officers. There's a reason police are associated with donut shops. The shops are always right downtown, where the homeless live, and people who are too poor to own cars have access to public transportation. Downtown also attracts seedier individuals. As long as police are offered free donuts and coffee, they are always nearby.

A donut maker is observed with the same interest people will watch a pizza maker throwing the dough in the air. Mother had her cutting table set-up next to a big, wall-sized window on the side of the building near the street, where people walking by would stop to watch the day shift baker making donuts.

Mother had decided it was time to train someone else to take over the midnight shift at the donut shop. She hired a young lady and began training her. After a couple of months, Mother had this woman go in at midnight by herself, to see if she could handle it. The first night, Mother was heading over to check on her at about 3 am.

Mother told the story many times over the years about the incident. According to Mother, she had walked through the courtyard of the apartment building and out to the street. Late at night, the windows from the inside of the shop are like mirrors. It's dark outside, so the light is reflected back to you on the inside. Mother could see someone standing outside the window watching this young lady make the donuts. When Mother was half-way across the four-lane street, with no traffic in the middle of the night, she realized it was a naked man, jerking off while watching this girl.

Mother quietly turned around and headed back to the apartment where she called the police. Before she could get outside and in front of the apartment building, the first police car was arriving. Within minutes, the building was surrounded by police cars. Officer chased the man down the alley behind the shop. They didn't catch him, and the girl was so spooked by the experience, she refused to return.

Grandmommy worked the display case at the donut shop, helping customers. My friendly and lovely little grandmother did well at this job, and all the customers liked this chubby-little lady with a quick smile. Her first name was Ruth, and they all called her Ruthie as if long-time friends. Grandmommy made everyone feel welcome. When my grandmother saw me coming with my little boyfriend, she would pull his favorite from the display case, a chocolate bar, and add more whipped cream, just for him.

One evening, when my grandmother was over at our apartment for dinner, she began to laugh while telling us about one of her customers who had asked about Mother.

"He asked me where my sister was," she told my mother. "He meant you!" In 1967 my grandmother was fifty-four years old.

"Well, we're just gonna have to start calling you Granny!" my thirty-three-year-old mother said.

Grandmommy looked horrified, "Nobody is going to call me Granny until I'm eighty," she grumbled.

Naturally, from then on, she would forever and always be Granny to us. Even my mother called her Granny. And Granny loved it.

I believe I've said before; my mother was completely self-serving. We had to give up the donut shop and move back to San

Bernardino, because Mother began having an affair with Mr. and Mrs. Valentina's son, Mitch. The very people who gave her the loan for the shop.

During the day, while Lisa and I were at school, Mitch would come over and spend the day in bed with my mother. His parents discovered what was happening when the school called them about his truancy. *He was a high school student and a minor*.

They threatened to sue her, have her thrown in jail, anything to get her out of his life. I don't know the details of the agreement, but we left the shop and moved back to San Bernardino. Mother openly explained to my sister and me what had happened. I was not yet ten years old.

Chapter 5

The Malignant Narcissistic Engulfing Mother

*A*s a child, I was often mistaken for a boy. My "dishwater blonde" hair was kept in a short Pixie style, and I was always in shorts and t-shirts. Mother loved to point at me and tell people, "This one is always getting mistaken for a boy." One of the things she told me about myself was, I wasn't very smart, but I shouldn't be ashamed. I was average. I got C's in school, which was average and perfectly fine. She said I wasn't ugly; I was average-looking, so that was okay, too. Not everyone could be like my sister. Lisa was gifted with beauty and intelligence, often envied; according to my mother. Occasionally, Mother would say to me, "You're just like your father," or, "You are just another Donald Ray Maize." I knew my father had had a limited education, but she never gave him any credit for all he had accomplished to improve himself, nor did I get any credit for any self-improvement. Of course, my self-improvement came after I left home for good.

I often wondered if Donald Ray Maize was my biological father. Mother often talked about my father's best friend, a man with blond hair whom everyone called Whitey. She told us many times; Whitey had propositioned her, "You know, Don cheats on you. You should sleep with me to get even."

Lisa and I talked about Mother's need to sleep with every man she ever met. Lisa said, "Why shouldn't we assume she slept with Whitey?" And, because I had blond hair as a child, Lisa wondered, "Don't you think there is a possibility Whitey is your real father?"

In 2017, I did an Ancestry DNA test, which linked me to all of my relatives who were on Ancestry. The connection wasn't random; my results were connected to the Maize side of my family. There was no doubt. Donald Ray Maize was my biological father. However, I still wonder, did my mother suspect he was not my biological father? She certainly treated me differently than she treated my sister, who looked like our father.

Upon returning to San Bernardino in 1968, Granny gave us the use of a house she still owned. The property she had bought with my grandfather before he died; a house with three-bedrooms, one bathroom at the corner of C & 10th Streets in San Bernardino. Granny moved into the small, one-bedroom garage conversion at the back of the property. A stand-alone building, steps from our back door.

Mother, Lisa, and I had to clean out a roach infestation before we could move into the house. Mother set roach bombs in every room, and we would go back the next day with brooms to sweep up the dead roaches. After the third round of bombs, the house was ready for paint.

As she was choosing paint, I was told my favorite color was blue, because she had chosen blue for my bedroom. Many years passed before I realized my favorite color was green. Similarly, for my thirteenth birthday, she made me an angel food cake with a watered-down strawberry glaze she said was my favorite cake. I don't think I'd ever had that particular kind of cake before. Nor did she ever make that cake again. Mother just made proclamations.

I turned ten in 1968, the year I started fifth grade. The school was within walking distance, and I was making friends. This was the year she became an engulfing mother, with no boundaries between herself and her children, she confided in us as though we were her contemporaries. Or, an extension of herself.

Dad came to visit Lisa and me, rather than us going to visit him, on one occasion in the summer of 1968. My father slept on the couch. I don't know why Mother didn't just give him my room, which was inside the closed-in porch on the back of the house. I could easily have slept with her in her double bed. Or Lisa's room, which was right next to the bathroom. But she did not do either of these things, instead, having him sleep on the couch.

However, after Dad went back home to Lois and her kids, Mother told us that Dad had been sleeping with her. Coming to her room after we went to bed and moving back to the couch before we woke in the morning. She told us they were having sex, and that Dad told her having sex with Lois was "like sticking it out an open window." Lisa and I were ten and thirteen years old. Not to mention, they were our parents. We didn't want to hear any of that. How is it possible that my mother saw me as a contemporary? A friend to confide in. And if it were true, our father obviously didn't want us to know. He was barely on the plane before she told us the gory details. A prime example of a malignant narcissistic engulfing mother.

The fifth-grade class was learning to square dance for physical education, the same way we had learned to play four-square, or dodgeball. This time, the teachers decided to invite the parents to come to watch our last "performance." Mother had never come to any of my school projects. This time she decided she would make me a Square Dance dress, kerchief for my head, and all. I begged her not to. I was a total tomboy, and the last thing I wanted to wear was a flouncy dress. I told her *nobody else would be wearing anything other than their usual street clothes.*

She replied, "Then you will be the only one dressed appropriately"; in her opinion, and who's opinion mattered more than hers?

When the dance routine was over, Mother received several compliments on the dress. "Oh, I made it myself," she bragged. Her need for attention had been fed. She ate up the *narcissistic supply* with a spoon.

Narcissistic supply[4] is a concept introduced into psychoanalytic theory by Otto Fenichel in 1938, to describe a type of admiration, interpersonal support or sustenance drawn by an individual from his or her environment and essential to their own self-esteem.

The term is typically used in a negative sense, describing a pathological or excessive need for attention or admiration from codependents, that does not take into account the feelings, opinions, or preferences of other people.

Upon her return to San Bernardino, Granny had resumed attending church; the same church she and my grandfather had attended before his death. Granny met a couple who told her about the lady's brother. They thought he and Granny needed to meet. I never heard about how they met, when they met, or if they dated. I just know, one day we were attending their wedding. His name was Walter.

Granny decided she and Walter would move into one side of a duplex she owned across town. She had been having problems with the renters, so the time was right to get them out. We all went with her to notify them they had four weeks to move out. When we got there, the woman had the water hose in the living room hosing off the hardwood floors. There was a waterfall of muddy water flowing out of the front door. Catching her in the act of destroying the hardwood floors gave Granny the impetus to evict. She didn't give them any notice; she just told them to be out by the end of the week, or the police would be returning with her.

As soon as they were out, we all went over to see what needed to be done to make the house livable. That's when we discovered the children had punched a child-sized hole in the wall between the two bedrooms. The whole interior of the house had been destroyed. In order to make the place livable, we all had to pitch in.

We repaired the drywall and the floors. We replaced the toilet and all the fixtures in the bathroom and kitchen. The walls were painted, and doors replaced. Once the house was fit for human habitation, Granny and Walter moved in.

Mother began dating Don A. He was a very nice gentleman, not her type at all, but Lisa and I liked him very much. So, of course, she broke up with him and married Jose Cordova on Valentine's Day 1969, just eight months after her second divorce from Alex. This time, she *really* brought a monster into our home. With her two, innocent little girls.

Before they could get their marriage license, Jose had to tell Mother his real name was Alva Baca. He had changed his name and fled Colorado. He was a Golden Glove boxer who had nearly beat a man to death in a street fight. Because he was a professional boxer, he was to be charged with attempted murder. His hands were considered "deadly weapons." This was his account of why he had changed his name. In all of my research, I have never been able to confirm his story.

Walter, Granny, Mother, and Jose, February 14, 1969

Right away, he became controlling and jealous in the extreme. As soon as they were married, he began tearing up pictures of men in photo albums, even family members. He destroyed her address book because there were too many men listed. Mother told us he would even follow her to the bathroom, to be sure she wasn't pleasuring herself. He was *that* jealous.

After two weeks she left his things on the front porch with a note telling him he needed to find someplace else to live. He began calling and dropping by every day. He had already threatened her, so she was legitimately afraid of him. We kept the doors and windows locked at all times, something we had never felt the need to do before.

One day, after school, my grandmother's car was parked at the school exit waiting for me. My mother was in the front passenger seat, Lisa in the back. Mother's face looked like the loser of an MMA fight. She was a bloody mess. Her entire face was swollen and misshapen, the right eye closed. Speaking was difficult with her lips busted and swollen.

Mother had been vacuuming when he snuck up behind her and pounced. He whaled on her, using his fists and feet to punch her in the face, head, and body. She said she kept telling him she loved him, trying to get him to stop. She tried to cover her head and protect her teeth. Her forehead had the imprint of his boot heel. She took a great deal of pride in the fact he had never knocked her unconscious. Misplaced pride? Or self-promotion?

When he finally stopped beating her, he had picked her up to lay her on the bed. He put a cold, wet washcloth on her face and told her he would go get his things and return.

She waited until she heard him drive away, then ran next door to the neighbor's house to call for help. The police came and took her to the hospital where she was cared for, and they took her statement.

The officer was taking her statement and showing legitimate

concern for her welfare when she asked him, "How can I legally kill this man?"

She said the officer didn't bat an eye, and he simply said, "You have to make sure he falls inside the house to claim self-defense."

The details of the beating and the advice Mother got from the police officer are not things of which I have first-hand knowledge; I only have her word that the events happened as Mother described them. The only part I can state as a fact is, she had been beaten.

Mother began planning a murder.

Granny's husband, Walter, was still considered a legal resident of Arizona. He said he could buy a gun in Arizona without the mandatory two-week waiting period. One day Mother and Walter drove to Arizona, where she bought a silver, pearl-handled .22 automatic, and came home the same day.

Mother called Jose and told him she wanted to speak with him. He said he would come right over.

Granny's house was set-up so you could sit at the head of the dining room table and see the front porch through a window. The visitor could be seen in profile when he reached out to knock on the door, which was located off to one side. Mother sat there; watching and waiting, with the front door open, only the screen door closed. The plan was, when he came up to the door, she would call out for him to come in. As soon as he stepped inside the house, she would shoot him and make sure his body landed inside the door. Mother explained to her children in great detail her plan to kill a man.

He never showed up. Perhaps he had an inkling of her plan. We never saw him again, but for many years we would get calls from him, just letting us know he knew where we were. No matter what state we were living in, we got calls.

Mother chose to stay in San Bernardino until the end of the school year. She allowed my sister and me to walk to school, with this threat hanging over us. I have to guess she was hoping he would call her bluff. He never did.

In the summer of 1970, Granny, Walter, Mother, Lisa and I all moved to Hobbs, Arizona.

The saving grace in my life was my grandmother. As much as my mother led me toward smoking, drinking, and promiscuity as a teen; Granny always set the example of a good Christian.

Although she never had extra money, she always made extra at meals, which she would then deliver to someone in need; usually, an elderly person living alone whose family didn't have time to care for their needs. She always found one person on the block she could help. Wherever she lived, her goal was to be a blessing to someone.

In the 70s, the fashion was to buy new jeans and boil the heck out of them to make them shrink. We wanted our jeans to be skin-tight. And for a while, jeans had to have a permanent crease down the front. I would take my new jeans to Granny. She boiled them for me; then she would iron the jeans to get a perfect crease down the front, and finally, she would make the crease permanent by sewing it on her pedal-powered sewing machine.

My favorite thing to do with Granny was to go to Goodwill to shop for quirky and unique clothes and shoes. When I found something I liked, she would tailor it to fit. I can vividly remember sitting on her bed talking while she sewed. Later, she taught me to sew for myself. I remember one conversation we had about her wedding night with Walter. She didn't go into detail, as Mother would have, but she let me know they had consummated their marriage. She saw my face and began to laugh, "You're old enough to hear that stuff now." I was probably eighteen by then. The look on my face wasn't caused by shock. It was probably more like, "Not my Granny!"

After the move to Hobbs, Granny and I were home alone one

morning. I was in the living room watching TV, and Granny had gone into the bathroom to take a bath in her cast-iron clawfoot tub. She hollered from the bathroom for me to come in there. When I came in, she was sitting in the bathtub giggling. Granny was always reserved and discreet. She would never be naked in front of us, but here she was, sitting naked in the bathtub, laughing. After pulling a towel over her front side, she wanted to show me what had happened when she pulled the drain plug in front of her but hadn't gotten out right away. The tub was empty, in front of her, but still filled behind her. Her butt filled the space from side to side. The water behind her hadn't been able to escape.

Chapter 6

The Bedwetters Club

*D*uring the summer of '69, we had all settled in Hobbs. A small town in the mountains of Arizona.

Granny and Walter bought a motel on the highway, which runs through Hobbs. The main house, which also served as the office, sat at the bottom of a flight of stairs coming down from a sidewalk along the side of the highway. All of the buildings on that block were below street level, including the post office and the one and only store in town. At the back of the house was a large add-on with an extra bedroom and bathroom. Mother, Lisa, and I lived there. Behind the motel was a trailer park that belonged to Granny and Walter as well. I say, "trailer park," because it was specifically for people traveling with a travel trailer to park overnight that included utility hook-ups, although there were two or three travel trailers that had been installed permanently for a monthly fee. Mother got a job at a local chicken ranch, candling eggs.

I loved my time in Hobbs. I rode my bike all through the hilly and curving streets of Hobbs. I hiked with friends in the hills around Hobbs and along dry creek beds looking for Indian arrowheads. We investigated caves and had some close calls, once with a mountain lion and a few times with snakes. As long as I was home before dark, I had complete freedom.

In the middle of the trailer park, and adjacent the motel rooms was a cabana. It was a large screened-in room with a roof to keep out the weather. There were picnic tables inside and bookcases filled with board games. The guests were encouraged to use the cabana. Late one evening, as the sun was going down, Mother and I were in the cabana with some of her friends. We weren't playing games or being loud in any way. We hadn't even turned on any lights yet. The atmosphere was subdued. And then suddenly, someone noticed a mountain lion walking by. I could not be more serious when I say this. The lion walked right past the cabana, continued on through the courtyard between the office and the motel rooms, up the stairs to the highway and looked around. She then turned around, came back down the stairs, back between the buildings, and walked right by us again. None of us made a sound. We were shocked and thrilled to be so close to that beautiful creature. We spent the rest of the evening talking about the experience and trying to figure out how she got so far into town. Behind the trailer park were paved streets and blocks of dwellings, at least a half a mile, or more, before leaving the populated area. We called the only law enforcement in town, a Deputy Sheriff, and let him know what had happened, so he could patrol the area and, hopefully, keep the lion from injuring anyone.

Then, there was the time I went walking along a dry creek bed with my friend. We were scouring the ground for arrowheads when we heard a very distinctive growl. There was a cougar, or mountain lion, somewhere close by. She could see us, but we hadn't spotted her yet. She warned us away with a growl. We didn't panic.

Instead, we turned around and walked away, rather than run, back the way we had come. Because it was so common in those hills to run across wildlife, we'd learned what to do in case we ever encountered a mountain lion. When I told Walter about it, he said we were very lucky she didn't attack us.

Shortly after moving to Hobbs, Mother met Tommy. Tommy was seven years younger than Mother. He'd been married before and had a young son, Little Tommy. He began trying to get her to marry him, but, to her credit, she told him she wouldn't marry him unless he quit drinking. He was a mean drunk, always starting fights with the biggest guy in the room. Tommy said he would quit drinking for her, and true to his word, he quit Cold Turkey. They married on the twenty-third of December 1969, ten months after her marriage and annulment from Jose.

We all dressed in whatever we owned that might pass for western wear. Mother, Tommy, Granny and Walter, Lisa and I, all went to the Justice of the Peace right there in Hobbs, and he performed the ceremony, in his office right next to the jail cell. We were in and out in less than thirty minutes.

Mother and Tommy rented a house that was across the highway from Granny's motel, on a hill above the little fire station.

Tommy was a very handsome man. At twenty-eight, he was as cute as a button. All the little girls with whom I went to school had a crush on him. He and I got along famously.

Granny and Walter loved him, too. The two couples would get together and play cards. Mother was at her best while she was married to Tommy. They were happy.

Tommy took me with him prospecting for gold and silver. He once took me with him to the Silver Mine where he worked. We found the perfect Christmas tree, so Tommy jumped on a dozer and knocked that tree out of the ground. He cut the roots off, and we took it home. Tommy took me deer hunting with him once, and because I had such a need for him to like me, I agreed to shoot my first deer. Thankfully, we didn't see any deer that day.

One Christmas, Granny gave Tommy a full-face stocking cap for him to wear to work during the cold winter months in the mine. Only the mouth and eyes showed through the knitted mask. It was the perfect gift for those cold winter days in the mine, but Tommy, being a great prankster, had an idea.

Mother, Tommy, Lisa and I had spent Christmas day at Granny's house. That evening, after we left to go home, Tommy parked the car just around the corner, and we all walked back to Granny's house. The back side of the house had a huge, screened-in window that looked out over her vegetable garden. Granny was standing at the kitchen sink washing dishes when Tommy put that mask on and stood right up against that window, scratching his fingernails on the screen. Granny turned to look and got the scare of her life. She stood there squealing like a stuck pig, "Oooh! Oooh! Oooh!".

Tommy could tell he'd really scared her, so he real quick pulled the mask off and started yelling, "It's me! It's just me!" Immediately, Granny began to laugh uncontrollably. She stood there laughing, with her legs crossed, while peeing down her legs. Granny always peed herself when she got overly tickled. We loved that about her. Her great big belly laugh shook her from head to toe. She had the best laugh.

I attended a local two-room school. It had first grade through fourth grade in one room and fifth grade through eighth grade in the other. With an average of four students per grade, there was only one teacher per room. The high school kids had to ride a bus down the mountain to Demming High School, twenty-five miles to the south.

At some point, I think Tommy must have decided he didn't like Lisa.

Lisa liked to read. She could shut herself up in her room and read for hours, which is what she did. She never helped out around the house. She seemed, to Tommy, like she was always there, just hanging around. This seemed to gripe the shit out of Tommy. He said she was lazy and spoiled.

Tommy and Mother liked to go to the local bars to socialize and have a few beers. Beer was not Tommy's kryptonite. Hard liquor was his problem. He could drink a couple of beers and be happy as a lark. Most times, they would take us with them. There were two taverns in town that served only beer and one bar that served hard liquor. Since it was such a small town, everyone knew everyone, very casual and relaxed. Lisa learned to shoot pool and became obsessed with it. After school, she would stop in at one of the bars and shoot some pool. If nobody was using the tables, the owners let her play for free. She stopped spending so much time sitting around eating and reading and began losing weight and turning into quite an attractive young lady. By the time she was eighteen, she had a room full of trophies. By the time she was twenty-one, she could have been a professional pocket billiards player and made quite a bit of cash off men who refused to believe a "girl" could beat them.

I had one good friend while I lived in Hobbs. Daisy moved to town when her grandmother, who had been raising her, passed away. Without a guardian, she was foisted off on her aunt and uncle, who'd never had children of their own. She started school in the same grade as me. Poor little Daisy, she was going through a really difficult time, something I was not sympathetic to, I'm ashamed to say. I hadn't been taught sympathy, or empathy, for others. My grandmother was such a huge part of my life, I talked about her all the time, but every time I mentioned my Granny, Daisy would begin to cry. At first, I felt bad, but after a while, I told her, "You can't start crying every time I mention my grandmother." I realize now I was cruel. You can't put a time limit on grief, but Daisy bucked up, and we became very close.

I began hanging out with Daisy. She was fun and always ready to get into mischief with me. We spent all our time riding bikes and exploring the hills around town.

Daisy's aunt and uncle lived in a very small travel trailer they had installed permanently in the mobile home park of my Granny's motel. It had a little cubbyhole where Daisy slept. Daisy, like me, was a bedwetter. Her life was as dysfunctional as my own, perhaps more so. I don't know why her mother didn't raise her, or why her grandmother had been her guardian, but now she was living with her Uncle Bob and her Aunt Linda, a middle-aged couple she'd never met before, and who never wanted children. When Daisy wet the bed, her aunt made her hang the yellowed sheets on the clothesline for all to see. I remember this vividly. In 1976, a movie called *The Loneliest Runner* came out about a boy who ran home from school every day to retrieve the yellowed sheet his mother had hung from his bedroom window, trying to get there before any of his friends passed by to see it. I remember, I felt lucky that my mother never did that to me. I didn't see how she shamed me in so many other ways. I was just lucky she didn't hang my sheets out on the line.

There was a street with a downward slope from the highway. It went down and around a curve, around the block, ascending back up to the highway next to the post office. My girlfriends and I loved to take our bicycles and ride as fast as we could down the slope and around the curve. Then, we'd finish our ride around the block and come back around to race down the hill again.

We noticed on one occasion, a mobile home had been installed parallel to and beside the street. There was a large living room window at the end, facing the highway at the top of the street. We'd made our run down the hill and around the block a couple of times when one of the girls noticed the man in the mobile home was standing naked in front of the window with a newspaper held up in front of his face. Of course, we had to ride around the block again to see if it was true. Sure enough, we headed down the hill, and there he was, dick hanging out for us to see. Then, as we started around the curve, he would run to the kitchen window and look out at us. We were curious twelve-year-old girls, so we did this several times before we began to get creeped out. Perhaps we all felt a little bit of guilt because we had kept going back to look. I just know I never told my mother, and nobody else's parents came around to question me about the incident.

One day, we had a new girl at school. She was our age, and in our grade, so Daisy and I made her feel welcome at school. She said she was an only child who had been living with her mother until her father could get them settled, and then she and her mother moved to Hobbs to join him. After her first day of school, she asked if we would come and meet her parents so that they would let her play with us. Her parents liked to know her friends, so, of course, we agreed. She took us to that mobile home. Daisy and I gave each other panicked looks, but we couldn't get out of the situation, so we went in with her, and she introduced us to her parents. She didn't return to school the next day. They left town. I wish now that I had told my mother. We might have saved that child's life. Regrets.

"Every man is guilty of all the good he didn't do."

Voltaire

When we left San Bernardino, Mother was driving a beige 1962 AMC Rambler Classic. She would laugh because she could speed on the freeway, right past police cars, and they would go after sportier-looking cars, never giving her a second glance.

Not long after we arrived in Hobbs, a gentleman who lived in Granny's trailer park made an offer; my mother said she couldn't refuse. This was the story she told us.

He was old and didn't need the big car he was driving. He really wanted her Rambler. He offered to make her a trade, across the board, his Turquoise 1962 Cadillac Sedan Deville for her '62 Rambler. They traded pink slips, and it was a done deal.

Then, she told us the old guy had come to her for a favor. He said he was dying and in a great deal of pain. He asked her to help him kill himself. Mother said she gave him a cocktail of prescription pills that would "ease his pain." She left the pills with him, and the next day Walter found him dead in his trailer.

She said, "He chose to take those pills. Nobody forced them down his throat." She seemed satisfied with that story, almost exhilarated. As though she had come up with the perfect scenario.

In my heart, I believe Mother murdered that man. I believe she wanted the car. When Mother wanted something, she went to any length to get it. Mother fell in love with that Cadillac the first time she saw it. She talked about it constantly. Then, suddenly, for no apparent reason, this old guy offers to give it to her. And within days, he's dead.

I suspect she flirted, possibly began a relationship with him and convinced him to trade cars with her. Wanting her to continue whatever they were doing, he agreed. Once she had the pink slip, she wanted nothing more to do with him. Knowing my mother as I do, this is what makes the most sense to me. Why else would he just trade cars with her? On the other hand, who can say for sure? Maybe it all went down exactly as she said.

An old friend of Tommy's came up to Hobbs for a visit and to meet my mother. He insisted they all go down to the one and only bar in town that served his preference of whiskey. And then he began pressuring Tommy to have a drink with him. A *real drink*. Eventually, Tommy gave in and had a drink. He never stopped drinking. Mother left him in the summer of 1971.

At about the same time, Granny had a heart attack. She was taken down the hill to Demming to a hospital. We were told that because of her high blood pressure, she couldn't return to the mountain. Returning to that elevation would kill her. A small apartment was rented in Demming. Mother left Tommy, and she and Lisa moved in with Granny.

I stayed with Walter and helped take care of the motel. There were four motel rooms. I would clean the bathrooms, replace the linens, and vacuum each room. I collected the dirty linens and washed them in the wringer washer Granny had on the back porch. I would then hang the sheets and towels over clotheslines that had been hung over her vegetable garden. At the end of the day, I would fold the linens and put them away. I had just turned thirteen that June of 1971. Walter gave me $5 a day. I had nowhere to spend it, so I felt rich.

The motel sold, and we all moved to Chico, California, a town in Northern California where my father had moved his family in 1969. My mother thought she would have better luck getting him to pay child support if we lived closer to him. I suspect she had other motives.

Chapter 7

The Five-Minute Mile Through Anxiety

*D*ad had his own drywall contracting business in Chico. He was well on his way to becoming a successful businessman. My father and his new family lived in a house that was well known in town. The house was in a long, wide curve in the road and sat up above, on a hill, looking down on Choat Road.

My father had learned the craft of drywall finishing when my parents had moved from Oklahoma to California. Lisa was just a baby when they moved in hopes of finding work. Moving to California was the best decision he had ever made. Dad not only learned how to do drywall taping and finish work, but he also shared his knowledge and craftsmanship with friends and family. He was very generous with his knowledge, and he was good at what he did.

Upon arriving in Chico, we rented a small house with an attic conversion. The attic had two bedrooms, so Lisa and I would have our own spaces. I know she was grateful, as I was still wetting the bed.

Mother got a job as a bartender at The Grotto. It was a local bar, frequented by my father and many of his friends and co-workers. She discovered that he had been telling people that Greg and Calley were his kids, and when Lisa or I would visit, we were his dead brother's children. Wasn't he a great man to take on his dead brother's children for summer vacations? Did she make this up to further gaslight our relationship with our father, or was it true?

I remember him saying to me, "Nobody needs to know our business. Let them think what they want. It doesn't matter."

I started the eighth grade in Chico. Greg was in seventh grade at the same school, but he avoided me like the plague. Calley was in sixth grade at the elementary school.

Calley and I spent as much time together as possible. If I wasn't spending the night with her, she was spending the night with me, but I think Lois preferred we stay at their house. No telling what my mother might do or say. I can't blame her there.

I made some friends, some not so nice. I began smoking and hanging out with some trashy kids who didn't set a good example. But, again, if I was home before dark, Mother didn't care.

About six weeks before the end of the school year, Mother told me to get my school records from the office. We were leaving Chico. Tommy had convinced Mother that he was sober and wanted us back. They agreed that the best thing would be to get him out of Hobbs, so they decided to move to southern California where Mother's cousin, John, would teach Tommy the business of drywall finishing. My Dad had taught John, so John was happy to pass along his knowledge.

The night before we left Chico, Mother took Lisa to The Grotto with her for a going away party. We had some friends, a couple of bikers. One of them, Steve, was known by the nickname, Blood. I'd had this extra-long, bright orange stocking cap with a large pom-pom at the end. He always wore a navy, skull fitting, knit cap. He insisted he loved my hat, to the point where he traded with me. He gave me lots of attention, and I adored him.

The last night we were in town, Granny and Walter had already left for San Bernardino. I was home alone, asleep in the attic. Suddenly, I woke up with Blood sitting on the side of my bed. He scared me. He said he had asked my mother about me at the party. She had told him I was home alone. He left the bar and came over to the house. He said he had found my mother's unlocked bedroom window, came through and snuck up the stairs. He said he wanted to tell me goodbye. He said when he saw my sister at the party and not me, he didn't think that was fair to me. He hugged me, said goodbye and left. As a mother myself, I realize how wrong it was of her to tell him I was home alone. If he hadn't been a nice guy, that could have gone badly.

Granny and Walter moved back to the duplex in San Bernardino where they had been living before the move to Hobbs. Mother, Lisa, and I rented an apartment in Cushing. Lisa enrolled at the high school in Niles with our cousin, Andy. I was enrolled at the local junior high school. This was a whole new experience for me, not the small-town atmosphere to which I was accustomed. I had a locker with a combination that I have nightmares of forgetting to this day. I had six classes I had to juggle and all the books that go along with that. I also had a gym class that required me to wear actual gym clothes. The eighth-grade boys had beards and smoked on campus. The girls teased their hair, wore make-up, and cursed. I was like a fish out of water.

The first day I was there, I was told that we had a substitute math teacher because the regular teacher was in the hospital. Some of his male students had beaten him so badly; he never returned to school.

Within that first week, I was chased home from school by three girls. Fortunately, I was always the fastest girl in school wherever I went. That day, I ran through the door of our apartment and had just enough time to tell my mother and sister what was happening.

When the girls knocked on the door, Lisa answered it. Lisa was nearing 5'10", so when she opened the door, they took a step back.

They said, "Send her out. We're going to kick her ass."

"She doesn't like to fight, but I'll take you on," Lisa said.

"We don't have a problem with you, but she *chose me out*," came the reply. I had never heard the term before, *chose me out.* I have no idea why they picked me as their target, but Lisa convinced them to leave.

The rest of the year, I ran home every day, a full mile, on the off chance someone might be after me. It was the worst six weeks of my life, up to that point. I distinctly remember that time being when sleep deprivation became the new norm for me. I would lie awake, thinking up ways to avoid a beating, or what route I would run home, or having imaginary conversations in my head, what I would say if so-and-so said this or that. This anxiety has never stopped; the anxiety of not being prepared for a confrontation stays with me to this day.

Mother's cousin, John, and his family lived just a few miles away in Niles. Lisa and I spent as much of our free time with our cousin Andy as possible. He was right between us in age. Andy was in 10th grade, and Lisa was in the 11th grade.

A girl that had a crush on him saw the three of us running around together and got jealous, not knowing we were family. She found out my sister went to school with her and Andy. She decided to target Lisa. One day, Lisa was walking between classes when suddenly this chick that Lisa didn't know, jumped her and started punching. Lisa's reaction was to hold off this girl and ask why she was hitting her. Lisa would push her away and say, "Why are you doing this?" She never got a verbal reply, just got attacked again.

At one point, the girl took off her belt and wrapped it around her hand, swinging the buckle at my sister. Lisa took the belt away, tossed it aside, and put the girl in a headlock, with her head at Lisa's side. At that point, Lisa looked around and realized they were surrounded by other students. Teachers arrived to break up the fight and took the girls to the office.

My mother got a call at home from the principal of the high school. He told her that Lisa wasn't in any trouble, but for her to come home was probably a good idea. He told my mother that witnesses said she only protected herself and never threw a punch.

When Lisa got home and changed out of her dress, she and Mother realized the side of her dress had blood on it. Apparently, while she held this girl in a headlock, this chick bit a chunk out of her side.

We later found out that this little hoodlum was living in a half-way house for troubled teens. She had stabbed a girl in a movie theater because she refused to share a joint.

That summer, I took a Greyhound bus to Hobbs to spend a couple of weeks with my best friend, Daisy. I had missed her terribly, but we had been writing letters since I'd left Hobbs the year before.

One afternoon, Daisy and I were walking along the highway when we saw Tommy's car driving down the road. I waved him over and asked why he was in Hobbs.

I asked him, "Did you and Mama have a fight?"

"Yes," he said, ducking his head in shame. I didn't know the circumstances, yet, but he said he didn't think he would be returning to California.

"I love you," I told him and kissed him goodbye.

When I got home, I heard the whole story. Tommy hadn't been going to work. John had called my mother to ask about him. When Tommy got home that afternoon, he and Mother began to argue. He had picked up a coffee mug and slammed it down on the counter, cutting a pretty bad gash in his hand. The next afternoon, he came home drunk. Granny and Lisa were there when he got home, so they verified the story of what happened.

Tommy came in and headed for the kitchen to make himself one of his favorite sandwiches, mayonnaise, and Tabasco on white bread. Mother began to argue with him, so the sandwich sat there getting soggy. At some point, he made some derogatory comments about Lisa, and she rolled her eyes. Her look pissed him off so, he picked up the sandwich and threw it across the room at her. It landed square in her chest and made a loud, squelching noise, and that set Mother off. She dove into him with all her might.

Mother's arms and shoulders were big and muscular due to her having polio, compensating for the lack of muscle tone in the lower half of her body. She and Tommy were pushing and shoving each other when Granny shoved an ottoman behind Tommy to catch him off balance. When he took a step back, he lost his balance and grabbed for Mother, in an attempt to right himself, grabbing the front of her blouse instead. She shoved him, and he fell over, taking her blouse, and bra, with him. During the ruckus, the cut on his hand had opened up, and there was blood everywhere. Mother pinned him down and told Lisa to call the police. When the police car pulled up, Granny told

Mother they were there, so Mother let Tommy up. She pulled the pieces of her blouse over her breasts and waited for them at the door. What they saw was this woman covered in blood and trying to cover herself with the pieces of her blouse. Tommy stood there, not saying a word. They cuffed him and walked him out the door. Mother never saw him again.

The next day, I saw him in Hobbs for the last time.

Before the next school year began, I called my father and asked if I could come and live with him. He said I could. I was ready to start high school, and I sure didn't want to do it in Cushing.

Dad didn't discuss with Lois whether I would be welcome in their home. He just bought me a ticket on a Greyhound bus and told me to come.

Dr. Les Carter has a series of YouTube videos called *Surviving Narcissism*. One such video concerns the covert narcissist.

> *Covert Narcissism: Control with a Sly Twist*[5]
>
> Dr. Les Carter's YouTube video concerning the covert narcissist is eye-opening. "Not being a trained professional, you may feel something isn't right with them, but you can't put your finger on it. Your initial impression may be that they seem modest, reasonable, mild-mannered even.
>
> "The covert narcissist gives a false sense of humility or approachability. They aren't argumentative, never outright disagreeing with you. But then again, neither will they fully engage. You may work hard to engage with them, but you always walk away, feeling frustrated with the outcome. You may think, 'What did I do to offend that person?'
>
> "The covert narcissist isn't going to ask you about yourself. Nor will they ask your opinion. They are

dismissive."

Dealing with Lois, you quickly realized her aloofness was more smugness than anything else. Rather than engage in a disagreement, she would withdraw. You got the feeling a discussion based on differing opinions would have been a waste of her time. You were never going to change her mind, and she didn't care about persuading you to see things her way. Unlike the overt narcissist, Lois didn't care about persuading you to her way of thinking. The overt narcissist will wear you down until you agree with their opinion. The covert narcissist simply doesn't care enough about you to make an effort.

A great example would be when Lois found out I am an Agnostic. Lois made no effort to learn about Agnosticism or my reasoning for converting from Christianity. She simply said, "I'll pray for you." Make no mistake; Lois was not benevolent. She was not attempting to gain goodwill or keep any sort of positive relationship with me. Her comment was intended to provoke. In a passive/aggressive way, she was attempting to gain control with the least amount of vulnerability. Covertly saying, "I will pray that God doesn't strike you dead for denying him. You stupid child."

Dad always knew when Lois wasn't happy with him because she would walk away. Lois had passive/aggressive behavior down to a science. She always managed to make him wait on her when she was mad at him. He would pace the floor waiting on her. I remember a time all three of us kids were sitting scrunched together, sweltering in the back seat of the car, while Dad sat in the driver's seat. He finally said to us, "Tell her I went on ahead." He got in his truck and left us sitting there waiting on her.

Lois was also covertly rude and ungrateful. The last time I gave Lois a gift was Mother's Day, 2009. I was visiting them when I noticed their toaster only heated one slot. So, while we were at Walmart that day, I bought a very nice toaster for them. One with four slots that could toast bagels as well as bread. She saw the gift bag in my basket, that was hiding the toaster, and asked if I had bought Greg a housewarming gift for his new home. I just said that I had because I wanted to surprise her. After we got back to their apartment, I put the toaster in the gift bag and proudly brought it out to her. She was obviously confused, but I explained that I had lied because I wanted to surprise her. When she opened it, she said, "We don't eat bagels."

There is a disconnect between heart and mind. They may say they know there are things they need to do to keep a relationship, but in the end, a relationship is just not important enough to put forth any effort.

Lois never exhibited love or respect for my father, *that I saw*. She appeared to tolerate him. I've heard her described as being *reserved*. Describing someone as *reserved* is a socially acceptable way of describing someone who is *cold* and *unemotional*. I'm pretty sure Lois loved her children and grandchildren, but I never saw her openly show it. The covert narcissist doesn't show joy and rarely shows gratitude. They certainly will never show joy for someone else.

If a covert narcissist is asked to help on a project, they might agree to help, never coming right out and stating that they don't want to help. But the help you received probably wouldn't be the help you asked for.

Lois had a way of influencing people around her, sending non-verbal messages that would make them feel "off-balance or insecure." I know I experienced her confusing messages.

I know her family has seen that side of her but may have never allowed themselves to acknowledge those negative traits. Calley talks about her mother as the benevolent one, someone who never had an unkind word to say about anybody. I believe she knows better but doesn't want to admit that her mother might not have been a saint.

I remember noticing that every time Lois had company, as soon as they left her house, Lois found something to criticize about them. As an adult, Calley fell right in with her mother. They could tear someone apart, feeding off each other's negativity. In 2009, I was visiting the family. As I was leaving, it hit me like the proverbial ton of bricks. *Oh, it's my turn. Let the feeding frenzy begin.*

I've spoken to many extended members of the family who have told me, "I never felt like Lois liked me," or, "She never seemed to warm up to me," or, "She treated me like an interloper." Maybe if it was just one person, I could doubt the validity, but several of my father's family members told me these things. And I heard for myself the way she talked behind their backs. I have to assume she did the same to me when I left her home.

When I was a kid, living with Lois and my Dad, she was constantly complaining about having to wash my hair. Lois complained and continued to bring it up until the day she died that I was so tender-headed, I made it difficult for her to wash my hair. As though I had a choice. As though I pretended it hurt, just to aggravate her.

When I lived with them in the ninth grade, she complained; about how I had collected the eggs, how I did the dishes, how I wore my hair and my table manners. Not that I'd ever been given a chance to learn "Table Manners According to Lois." When she took us shopping for clothes, she always bought me clothes that were at least two sizes too big, even though she continually pointed out my stick-like figure. When Dad had a CB radio, she gave me the handle, Tumbleweed. She said it suited me because I was all spindly limbs. It was true, but why buy me clothes that I couldn't wear?

She had bought me a t-shirt and shorts set when I was fourteen that I wore until I was twenty. The swimsuit she bought me that year had a halter top that tied around my neck and zipped up the back. It gave full coverage of my torso, which she deemed too skinny and needed to be covered. I had to roll the neck down to hand stitch it in place, just to make it fit. I had to wear shorts under the top because the bottoms were too big. I held on to that swimsuit, for years, in case it ever fit properly. The last time I wore it, I was twenty-six and pregnant.

Clearly, she didn't want to be responsible for me. Dad had handed over all the responsibility to her as soon as they were married.

Rather than tell him he needed to step up and be a father to his own children, she became passive/aggressive about the responsibility.

It was her job to buy and mail birthday cards/gifts and Christmas presents to Lisa and me. And later, our children. I'm sure she must have resented having to do that. But rather than telling Dad, so that he could make sure we were remembered, she just "forgot" or sent as little as possible. She wasn't hurting Dad with this passive/aggressive behavior; she was hurting innocent children. How cruel.

When I was in third grade, I asked my father for an Easy-Bake Oven for Christmas. I got a transistor radio that year. The following summer, right after my birthday, Lisa and I went to visit them. Calley had gotten an Easy-Bake Oven for Christmas.

One year, when my two girls were about six and eleven-years-old, Lois sent them each a blow-up chair, the kind intended for a toddler child. Each chair had a name printed across the back. Names I didn't recognize. I naturally assumed she got the packages mixed up, possibly sending Mellie and Karly's gifts to these two children. I called to let her know about the mix-up. She said, "No. Those are the gifts I intended to send to your girls." No explanation. No apology. Just another throw-away gift. Why send anything at all?

When I was pregnant with Karly, I received a package from Lois. It was a hand-made crib set; bumper and quilt, white eyelet pattern with tiny red strawberries. I was so thrilled that she had done this for me. I immediately called to thank her.

She said, "Your Dad made me do it because I make them for all of my nieces when they have babies.". In her flat, monotone voice. Why not just slap me in the face while you're at it. I put it in a black garbage bag and stored it in the attic. Twenty years later, when the bag disintegrated, I threw the whole thing in the garbage.

Chapter 8

Jump!

I rode a Greyhound bus to Chico, where my father and stepmother picked me up at the bus station.

The school year began with Calley in the seventh, Greg in the eighth and me in the ninth grades. There was a glass-enclosed porch on the side of the house where the laundry room was located. We could see the bus from there when it was still half a mile away, giving us plenty of time to walk down the long, gravel drive to catch the bus.

Because we lived on a rural route, where there are fewer children, all grades rode the same bus. Our bus, when it finished picking up kids, would stop first at the elementary school where Calley would get off, then at the junior high, where Greg would get off, and finally at the high school.

At the end of the day, the bus would start by picking up kids at the elementary school and make its way around to the high school, arriving about forty-five minutes after I got out of school. Rather than hanging around the school, I would walk home with my friend, Beverly, who lived five minutes from the school. We would watch *The Vin Scully Show,* and I would walk back over to the school and get on the bus.

Lois made sure we all did our homework while she made dinner. Dad would come home, and we would all sit around the table, having a family meal. It was as close to Ozzie and Harriet as I had ever come.

The kids all had chores and took turns doing the dishes. One of my regular chores was collecting eggs. Lois didn't have an enclosed chicken hutch, so they laid their eggs all over the place. She showed me their usual spots, and I would walk around hunting eggs.

One day, a batch of new chicks showed up. Lois accused me of not doing my job, to which I said I was sorry. I was always apologizing to people, rather than make excuses. Mother taught me never to make excuses; that would just get me into more trouble, but honestly, those eggs could have been anywhere. Lois's chickens were free-range before Free-Range was a thing.

The house sat on forty acres, but Dad had the use of the forty acres next door, as well. They had horses, in addition to the chickens. I was not a fan of riding horses. I liked them, like pets, but they scared me. Dad griped that I wouldn't ride a horse. He would say, "Even Calley rides. She's not scared." My fear may have been unreasonable to him, but it was *my fear*. A couple of times, Calley offered to let me ride while she walked the horse around the yard, thinking it might help with my fear, but all I could think was, *A horse can sense your fear.* How many times had I heard that?

Dad would often have friends or family come over to go for a ride in the hills behind the house. They would take the dogs with them and be gone for hours. I remember a time when he put me on with him, behind his saddle. I was okay with that. I had full confidence in my father's riding skills. We were walking along when the horse stepped in a hole and went down to his belly. Dad put his feet out on either side of the horse and pushed up. That horse stood right back up and on we went, never missing a beat.

There were half a dozen horses on that little ride, along with a few dogs. Dad told me, "Those dogs will take off when they get wind of a rabbit. I'll grab your arm and yell, 'Jump!' That's when I'll help you jump off the horse. You just wait there until we get back." I agreed, and off we went.

Suddenly, all hell broke loose. The dogs took off barking, people on horses took off after the dogs, and Dad grabbed my arm throwing me to the ground, where I landed on my fanny and heard him yell, "Jump!" He took off, and there I sat. It was the funniest thing that had ever happened to me. When he came back, he was laughing, but he apologized. I told him I thought it was great!

While living with them, I was taken to a dentist for the first time since I was five years old. I asked the dentist if there was anything he could do about the discoloration of my teeth. When he used a tool to sand the surface of my front four teeth, he accomplished two things. First, he discovered the staining went through the tooth and was not coming off. Secondly, he removed all the enamel from my front four teeth. From that moment on, I could not drink from a water fountain, because the cold water hurt. I had to keep my mouth closed in a cold wind. I could not bite into ice cream. I had no protection at all. In my twenties, I met a dentist who said my insurance would pay to get my teeth capped. That was life-changing, not only because I could bite into ice cream again, but my confidence grew exponentially.

Life with Dad and Lois took on a rhythm. We had a morning routine that included clean clothes and a hot breakfast. Calley fed the dogs, Greg fed the horses, and I collected eggs. Our homework was always done, and we were always ready when the bus came. It was such a change from what I was used to. I was flourishing. That year, I stopped wetting the bed and stopped biting my fingernails. I no longer had the anxiety that went along with living in an environment of instability. I felt safe and secure, until Mother called.

Lisa was a senior that year, going to school with Andy in Niles. She had been a straight-A student all her life. Dad had told her that if she went to college in Chico, near him, he would pay for it. She just needed to help by getting good grades and applying for scholarships. She had a goal.

The last time Lisa had visited our father, she was about fourteen-years-old. Her favorite show on TV at the time was *Dark Shadows*, with Johnathan Frid. Lois had specifically asked her not to watch that in front of her children, who were eight and nine years old at the time.

Lisa never included herself in anything we did as a family. She pretty much made it clear; she did not want to be there. Greg, Calley, and I played outside as much as possible. One afternoon, while Lois was doing some gardening or some such thing, the kids and I went into the house for a cold drink. Lisa had been alone in the house before that, so she was watching her show. Greg, Calley, and I sat down in the living room for a minute, just long enough for Lois to come in and see what was on the TV. She threw a fit, screaming at Lisa that she had specifically asked her not to watch that show in front of her children. We all, including Lisa, tried to tell her that they weren't actually watching the show and were in fact just getting ready to go back outside, but Lois was fit to be tied. She wouldn't hear a word of it. Lisa and I were put on a bus back home the next day.

Lisa never went back. Ever. She never went to Chico again. If my father ever saw her, it was when he drove from California to Oklahoma. When he called her house to talk to her, Lisa's husband answered the phone and took a message. Lisa never returned his calls. He made sure to tell me.

When Lisa's son was about ten years old, he returned a gift to them with a note, "If you can't treat my half-brother as your grandson, too, then I don't want your gifts." Lois never got over that. She brought it up to me all the time. She always said that he was ungrateful. She and Dad hadn't been able to afford to send my sister's stepson a gift that year. Obviously, that was a load of crap. She cunningly caused a rift and put the blame on a ten-year-old boy.

I was halfway through my freshman year in high school, and we were on our Christmas break. Lisa was halfway through her senior year when Mother called to tell me that Dad had told Lisa he wouldn't be able to pay for her to go to college. Lisa was so heartbroken and angry; she quit school on the spot. Mother wanted me to come back to live with her, to punish Dad, I suppose, but this time he stood up to her and refused to let me go. I'm disappointed in him for not following through with his promise to Lisa, but I'm grateful he kept me with him as long as he did. I just wish he had insisted I stay with them until I finished high school.

Instead, the following summer, I went back to Mother and Lisa. They had moved to San Bernardino, into the other side of the duplex Granny was living in with Walter. I had just turned fifteen-years-old that summer of 1973.

Winter of 1995

For many years, I heard Lois say that "Greg just can't catch a break." When I talked to her, or Dad or even Calley, they were always telling me that Greg had either started a new job or had quit a job. And according to Lois, the employers at the job *weren't treating him right.*

I knew Greg had a wife and three little boys, so I suggested he move out to Oklahoma. I told him, "Come on out and stay with us until you get settled in a job and get a place to live. Then you can send for your family to join you." He gave it some thought, then called to tell me that he was going to take me up on my offer.

He called me a couple of weeks later and said, "We have all of our belongings loaded in a rental truck, and my pick-up is loaded too. We're leaving in the morning and should be at your house in a few days."

I was stunned. "All of you? You're not going to wait to bring the family out until you get a place to live?"

"No," he said. "I'm not leaving my family out here without me."

Well, they were all packed and moved out of their apartment. I felt forced to allow the whole family to move in with us. He didn't leave me any choice. Now I'm aggravated, and feeling manipulated, not a good way to start off this new relationship. That was our first clue as to the kind of man we allowed into our home.

I knew that he had just gotten each of the boys a kitten. And I had two dogs living in my house at the time.

"You can't bring those kittens. It will drive my dogs crazy.

You're going to have to find homes for them," I told him adamantly.

He suggested they stay in a container outside. In the middle of winter, on my front porch. "No. I don't want them here. Period."

He agreed and said he would find a home for them.

When they arrived; Greg, with his wife, Lindy, and the three boys, were driving a rental truck. Greg's pick-up truck was on the back of a flatbed truck. Apparently, Greg had put *water* in the radiator, in New Mexico in the middle of winter. Naturally, the radiator cracked. A man overheard Greg talking about the fix he was in with his family and offered to haul the truck directly to my house for one hundred dollars, and Greg agreed.

While the man unloaded Greg's truck, Greg brought his family in the house. Then he went back out to pay the man and *thank him for his help*. When Greg came back into the house, he proudly told us that he gave the man twenty dollars. The guy said, "We agreed on a hundred."

Greg told him, "Take it or leave it."

That was the second clue of the kind of man we were dealing with. Within minutes we discovered something else. He had brought one of the kittens.

The next couple of months was a nightmare. The first night they were in town, I had made dinner. I knew they had had a tough few days, so when Lindy, Greg's wife, went in to start doing the dishes, I told her not to do them. I said, "I'll do the dishes. You've got to be exhausted."

The next night, after dinner, I said something to the effect, "Okay, I'll let you do the dishes tonight."

Lindy didn't get a chance to say a word, Greg came out with, "*You jumped down her throat last night and told her not to do the dishes. Make-up your mind.*" Lindy looked as surprised, or embarrassed, by the outburst as was I. The only person who had ever spoken to me in such a demeaning way was my mother. But I was so stunned, and I don't remember if I said anything at all. Lindy just said she was okay with doing the dishes.

It was a constant fight with him. I let them use my car to go job hunting. So, that left me without a car. My husband, Dan, took turns doing dishes and vacuuming.

One day Dan said something to Greg about helping out with the housework, and Greg said, "I don't do woman's work."

To which Dan said, "If I can help clean up after your kids and mine, you by God can too!" Greg didn't argue with Dan. Dan is hard to piss off, but when he gets mad, there is no mistaking it.

A friend of Greg's came through on his way to Missouri. He brought some cash for them that the church in Chico had collected for Greg and Lindy. To help with the expense of getting their vehicle repaired and get them into their own place. They used the money to drive to Missouri to visit their friends. A mini vacation. That pissed us off, but the only thing I said to them was, "Take the kitten with you. Find it a home."

After they got their truck back, and they were both working, I was scheduled to have some foot surgery. I told them, "You need to find someone to watch the little guy. The other two will be fine with me when they get back from school. Little Guy is too much for me to take care of with a bum foot."

Greg got irate, and he said, "Your surgery isn't going to be that bad. You can take care of him."

I looked at him and said, "I don't want to. Find someone to babysit for a few days. The lady next door babysits a few kids during the day, ask her." He just grumbled.

On the day of the surgery, they were getting ready to leave the house and leave the three-year-old with me. I said, "Hey! You can't leave him here."

Greg said, "We don't have anyone else to watch him. You'll be fine."

Dan, who was taking me for my surgery and would have to babysit, said, "No. That is not going to happen. I don't babysit anybody's kids, and I have to go to bed as soon as we get back because I have to work tonight."

Greg and Lindy went out to the den, where their beds were, had a short discussion, and Lindy came out in tears. She went next door and asked my neighbor to babysit.

Greg cut his nose off to spite his face. Instead of telling Lindy just to ask her to watch the three-year-old, he told Lindy to pay her to watch the two older boys when they got off the bus, as well.

The other thing we noticed was that Greg never stayed in a job for more than two or three weeks. There was always some excuse for him to quit. Usually, *his employers didn't treat him right.* That sounded familiar. His mother had said the same thing.

One day my Dad called to see how things were going. I didn't want to tell him it was a freaking nightmare. I kept that to myself. Dad asked me, "Is Greg still doing his three weeks in a job and quitting?"

I couldn't believe it. "Yes! How did you know?"

"He's always done that. He never stays for more than three weeks. But you can't say anything to Lois about it. She gets really mad if you say anything against Greg."

Dad knew who Greg was. Dad had set the example of a hard-working man, but Lois wouldn't allow him to speak to Greg about his habit of using people and feeling like the world owed him something. I remember a specific conversation I had with Dad when he told me he had loaned Greg one of his trucks. After about six months, Dad asked Greg when he was going to give him back his truck. Greg's response was, "You don't use it."

I don't know where that attitude comes from. *Give me! Give me! Give me! Oh wait, you don't give me enough!* To a user, it's never enough. The world and everyone around them will always owe them something. They never actually want to have to work for it.

> Self-entitlement[6] is when an individual perceives themselves as deserving of unearned privileges. These are the people who believe life owes them something; a

> reward, a measure of success, a particular standard of living. The self-entitled often appears totally oblivious to the inconvenience they have caused you.
>
> Additionally, their relationships tend to be one-sided, and they can be incredibly lazy. Socially expected norms are not performed, such as not helping to wash the dishes after a meal that has been cooked for them, or taking their turn making coffee in the office. The development of the idea of sharing has not taken place. With all the focus and determination of a two-year-old, no shame or guilt curbs their demands.

As tensions got worse, they finally found a place of their own. That's when I suggested they let the two older boys stay with us during the week, so they didn't have to change schools, again. They agreed. Greg and Lindy would pick-up their boys on Friday evening and return them on Sunday evening.

My daughter, Karly, and Greg's two older boys have always gotten along well. They are still good friends. None of us got to know the little guy very well. Their family all left Oklahoma after about a year, so we didn't get a chance to bond with him.

Throughout the years, my girls may have received four or five birthday cards, each, from Dad and Lois. In the case of Karly, whose birthday was on the fourth of the month, Lois would say, "I didn't turn the calendar page in time to get a card off to Karly. I'll just save it for next year." In the case of Mellie, whose birthday was in the middle of the month, and two days after Lois's own birthday, she didn't even bother to make an excuse.

In 1995, while Greg's two oldest boys were staying with us to finish out the school year, April rolled around, as did Karly's tenth birthday. Double digits. It should have been a memorable birthday. And it was, for all the wrong reasons. Karly received a birthday card, signed *Grandpa and Lois*. That's all that was written inside. Greg's oldest boy, whose birthday was three weeks later, asked Karly, "What did you get?"

"A card," Karly told him.

"How much money did you get," he asked her.

"Just a card," she replied.

"Huh, we always get money from Grandma in our cards," he told her.

Karly told me about the conversation. I told her that Grandpa and Lois were probably having some money difficulties. But at least she got a card, which was unusual in itself. I always made excuses for them. Always, no matter how they hurt my children, I made excuses. I wanted so desperately to have loving grandparents in my children's lives and to have loving parents in my life. I always made excuses.

Three weeks later, Greg's son received a card for his ninth birthday, mailed to our house. In it, he had five dollars, which he couldn't wait to show Karly. I told her not to be mad at him; he didn't know better. But it was that moment that Karly figured out where she stood with Lois. And by association, her grandfather.

April 19, 1995.

Dan was working the Day Shift. His district included our house in far west Oklahoma City. He had stopped by the house that morning to use the bathroom. As he walked into the living room, he stopped to tell me goodbye. Just then, the windows and blinds throughout the house began to rattle and shake. Dan reached out and grabbed me, both of us thinking in an instant, Earthquake! A moment later we heard a muffled, Boom! Almost instantly, we heard officers on Dan's handheld radio begin shouting about an explosion in downtown Oklahoma City. They weren't making any sense.

Dan looked at me and said, "I'd better get down there." He didn't hesitate as he headed out the door.

It was 9:02 am. I ran over and turned on the television. It took a minute or two before the news media broke into regular programming. There had been an explosion downtown, but they didn't know anything else.

The news station stayed *live*, giving updates as the information came in. The station I was watching had sent a reporter in a helicopter to see what they could find out by flying over the city. As the station went *live* to the reporter in the helicopter, they were flying over the south side of the building and around toward the east. The smoke was thick. The wind was blowing the smoke to the north, so the camera was showing the back of the Alfred P. Murrah Federal Building on the south side, which didn't look too bad. Just a lot of black smoke billowing out of the top.

As the helicopter made its way around to the east side of the building, the reporter and pilot saw for the first time the devastation. The north side of the building was gone. The reporter went silent. She was speechless. It looked exactly like pictures we saw of buildings that had been bombed in other countries. Like nothing we had seen here in the U.S., let alone in middle America, Oklahoma.

I never turned off the television all day. I watched non-stop. At some point, thinking to myself, "Thank God Dan was standing here in front of me when it happened. I wouldn't know what to do if he hadn't been."

We didn't have cell phones in 1995. There would have been no way to contact him. But I was one of the lucky ones. My husband was standing in front of me when it happened.

And then everyone around the smoking building on the television began to run away from the building. I didn't know what to think. The news anchor said that another bomb had been found in the rubble. Oh My God! Where was Dan?

I don't know how long I sat there before they announced it was determined to be a three-foot-long TOW missile used in the training of federal agents. It was unarmed and harmless.

When Karly and the boys got home from school, they told me they felt the explosion in their school. To this day, my nephews tell me that it is one of their most vivid memories of living in Oklahoma.

That night, Dan worked late. When he came home, he told me

what he was comfortable telling me. But he didn't tell me everything. Over several weeks he slowly began to tell me a little bit more.

When Dan arrived downtown, he said he had to park his car a block or so away from the building. He ran the rest of the way. He came in on the south side of the building, running along the back to where he saw other officers working.

He said it wasn't until the end of the day, walking back to his car that he figured out why he kept falling while running to help. The sidewalk had been lifted and slammed back down from the impact of the bomb. The sidewalk was broken and uneven. He kept tripping and falling, but his mind hadn't acknowledged the damage to the sidewalk.

When he arrived at the corner of the building, he said he began helping to extract small children and babies from the daycare. He has never told me what he saw there. He says he has talked about it with other officers who were there. That was their therapy. Only the people who were there; who saw, smelled, and felt what the others saw, smelled and felt could relate to the trauma. Dan said it was not something that can be explained; it had to be witnessed.

That is Dan's to tell. I've never heard him tell anyone anything he hasn't already told me.

Chapter 9

Passive Aggressive Behavior or The Pouting Toddler

*I*n 2003, Dad and Lois came for a visit. They stayed in our guest room. Karly still had a couple of weeks of school in her senior year, so she was getting up early to get ready for school. The first morning Dad and Lois were there; they got up and took over the hall bathroom before Karly was ready for school. All of her things were in the hall bathroom, but she had to make do with what was in my bathroom. I told Karly I would ask the folks to wait until she got ready for school before taking their showers, which I did.

The next morning, Dad and Lois didn't come out until after Karly had left for school. I said, "Y'all slept late. Did you sleep well?"

Lois said, "We stayed in bed until Karly left. We didn't want to get in her way," with that simpering voice people use when they're pouting.

Instead of saying, "Grow the hell up!" I said, "I'll have her move her things to my bathroom so you can use the hall bath." Sometimes, I get really mad at myself for not having the balls to stand up to people.

During a visit to Chico in 2009, Calley and I were sitting with Dad and Lois in their living room. Lois said to me, about my then twenty-four-year-old, married, grown-ass daughter, "Tell Karly, if she would send us birthday cards, we'd send her birthday cards." Right out of left field. Nothing led up to her comment; she just blurted it out. Even as I sit here writing this, I'm gobsmacked. I can't imagine what the expression on my face may have been.

Calley quickly tried to defuse the situation by saying, "They just miss hearing from her."

I stood up and said, "I should probably get my things packed and ready to head home tomorrow." Luckily, I was leaving the next day.

I was sleeping on an air mattress in their spare room; I lay awake, all night fuming. I seriously contemplated calling a cab to take me to the bus station to get a ride to the airport in Sacramento.

I couldn't complain to my father. I didn't want to put him in a position to have to choose between his wife and me. I knew I would lose that one, so why make that inevitability a reality? Just like I didn't tell him what my sister and I had a falling-out over. I didn't want him to feel he had to choose between us. I told him, "She's your daughter, too. I don't want to bad-mouth her to you." A few years later, when he told me to stop being stubborn and call my sister, I felt hurt that he had assumed the fault for us not speaking was mine. I told him what Lisa had done, making it clear that I was not *stubborn.* I was standing up for my convictions.

I became resentful; I began making excuses not to visit. I rarely called anymore and honestly had no desire to see any of my Maize family. I realize now; I was passive/aggressive.

Calley is just as critical of me as her mother. Calley has taken subtle jabs by giving backward compliments. Calley once told me, "You have nice legs... when you carry some extra weight." I feel Calley really does care about Karly and me. She was just taught some hurtful behavior by her mother, much like I received from my mother. The difference? Calley either isn't aware or doesn't care.

Karly flew with me to California when Lois died in October of 2015. We went to support my dad and Calley through this difficult time. Our great-aunt volunteered to play the piano before and during the service, out of respect for Lois.

After arriving at the church, I looked for my father. Greg hadn't yet arrived with Dad. I greeted people I knew and introduced myself to others, many of whom remembered me after some prompting. Karly stayed with Greg's sons, her cousins.

Calley was trying to hide her emotions, desperately trying not to give anyone "a show," much like her mother would have done. As a result, she sat four rows back. With the whole front row empty, reserved for the immediate family, I thought her choice of seats was weird. I felt that for me to sit on the front row alone would be even weirder. I tried to get her to sit on the second row with me. She cut her eyes down and vehemently shook her head in the negative.

Greg dropped Dad off at the church, then went to park the car. This frail old man was standing at the back of the church, looking lost. Calley had been the one to care for them both, so I didn't want to overstep, but nobody was helping our father to his seat. I didn't know if Calley, feeling she had done the bulk of the care for our parents, might feel I was "playing the dutiful daughter" if I went to help him. As always, I doubted my decision-making skills concerning myself, but nobody was helping him to his seat. I asked if she wanted me to go to him. She nodded in the affirmative.

I walked around and took his arm, "Dad, are you ready to sit down?" He looked relieved to see me, saying he was, indeed, ready to sit down. Karly had been sitting with me on the second row, but I felt he was meant to sit on the first row. I decided to seat him next to the coffin, with the beautiful picture of his wife on top. Rather than leave him alone, which would have been completely inappropriate, I sat next to him and held his hand.

Dad said, "Why didn't she take me with her?" He began to cry, so I put my arm around him and snuggled him into my side. The service hadn't begun yet, so my daughter came with my purse and sat next to me, which was a great comfort to me. Holding my crying father in my arms caused me to start crying, as well. My Karly girl put her hand discreetly on my leg and handed me a box of tissues for my father and me. After a minute, Calley came and sat on the other side of Dad, with her husband, Mitch, beside her. When Greg came into the building, he and his wife, Dana, sat on the other side of Mitch.

At the end of the day, when Karly and I got back to our hotel, she told me about her experience.

Karly had been hanging around with her cousins, Greg's boys, before the service. When people came up to offer the boys their condolences, the boys would introduce Karly as Lois's granddaughter. Lois's church family all said the same thing, "I didn't know she had a granddaughter. I thought her only grandchildren were Greg's boys." Karly said it only confirmed for her that Lois did not consider me her daughter, nor did she consider my children her grandchildren. However, her grandchildren never considered my father to be anything but their grandfather. In fact, Greg's boys didn't find out my father wasn't their biological grandfather until they were practically grown. Those boys have always called me Aunt Jo, and I've always considered them my nephews. But for Lois, there was a definitive line between *her* children and her stepchildren. Her relationship with my sister Lisa, or lack thereof, notwithstanding, there was no reason for her to feel that way toward my children and me. We had done nothing to cause her to deny us.

Dad quietly passed away in his sleep in March 2017, eighteen months after Lois passed.

Dad continued to live in the little apartment he and Lois had been renting when she passed away. As a diabetic, Dad stopped watching his diet. Lois had made sure he didn't eat or drink anything that was not on his diet. Once Lois was no longer there to supervise, he began bringing unhealthy foods into his home.

Calley, being the only one of their children living in the same town with them, was responsible for keeping an eye on them. That became quite a chore with Dad. When his blood sugar was out of control, he would pass out. He was becoming combative and argumentative with Calley. Greg had moved a couple of hours away, so he was no help at all. Remembering everything Dad and Lois had done over the years for Calley and Greg, I decided that I was not obligated to be responsible for their care in their old age. In addition, I felt justified in that decision based on my children and myself being noticeably neglected by Dad and Lois.

Calley often called to discuss what was happening with our dad. At first, I was appreciative that she wanted to include me. After a while, Calley began to call me about every little thing, which caused my paranoia to kick in. If she didn't want to discuss the latest stunt Dad had pulled, she wanted to complain that Greg wasn't pulling his weight helping with Dad. I couldn't decide if this was her way of chastising me, that I wasn't doing enough, or if she just wanted to vent. I chose to believe she was just venting. How much could I do from 1,800 miles away?

Calley had gotten the state to provide part-time home healthcare. Two days a week, someone would come to check his blood sugar, make sure he was taking his medicine, and bathe him.

One day, Calley called me in tears. She said Dad had stopped leaving his bedroom, then stopped leaving his bed altogether. He wasn't even getting up to use the bathroom. She was overwhelmed. That day, not for the first time, she'd had to force him to get out of bed and let her bathe him. She said he had crapped himself in the bed. He refused to clean himself or his bedding.

Calley explained, while the help from the state was appreciated, the help provided wasn't enough. She was not trained for the care required, nor did she feel she could continue. Calley was feeling massive guilt. She no longer *wanted* to care for Dad's needs.

I told her, "Nobody should be required to care for a parent's hygiene." Calley and I felt Dad had given up on life, no longer wanting to participate in any way. She and I agreed the time had come to get him into a skilled nursing facility. She called the service who had been coming twice a week to ask what they recommended.

Calley told me, the service provider said, "We were just waiting for you to decide it was time. We have everything in place, and we can have a bed ready for him in the next day or two."

Dad was moved to Red Bluff. Calley still visited Dad several times a week, not wanting him to feel he had been abandoned by the family. Calley told me Dad no longer recognized her most days. On my first visit to see Dad in the facility, I experienced the same thing. He was well cared for; the facility smelled very clean, which is a huge indicator to me of a good facility, but he didn't know me. Dad was happy for the company; the opportunity to get out of bed and be wheeled down to a visitation room, but I could have been a complete stranger.

On my next visit, he was much better. The facility had gotten Dad's blood sugar leveled and his medications straightened out. He knew all of us. He was alert, but still very weak and unable to get around on his own. Greg's eldest son, MJ, brought his fiancé and their new baby to see Dad. Dad acted like he knew who we were, but he was having trouble with how the baby was related to him. He kept asking my nephew, "This is your baby?" Dad was captivated by the tiny little toes and would reach out to just barely touch the baby's toes.

Dad had an ulcer on his foot that wasn't healing. Calley had scheduled an appointment for Dad to go in for an angiogram, in order to diagnose atherosclerosis. I flew out for a visit and to help Calley get Dad to the hospital for the procedure. Calley and I loaded him into her car and drove him to the hospital. The doctor was hoping that he could remove any blockages keeping blood from flowing properly to the affected foot. Had that been the case, the foot would begin to heal. Unfortunately, the doctor said the blockage was so bad; he was unable to get the catheter through the artery.

While Dad was in recovery, the doctor told Calley and me, the only alternative was to amputate above the blockage. In this case, he recommended amputating above the knee to ensure good blood flow for better healing.

When Dad was awake and coherent enough to understand, Calley told him the doctor's recommendation. She and I explained that ultimately, the choice was his, but if he didn't have his leg amputated, he would die sooner rather than later. He told Calley, "It's all right, Sis. I'm okay with losing the leg."

Calley began making the necessary arrangements for the surgery. I couldn't stay for the surgery, so I stopped in one more time to tell Dad goodbye. I told him I had to be going, but I'd be back. I kissed him and told him I loved him. He said, "I love you, too."

Calley and I agree on this point. Dad didn't really want to go through that whole mess, having surgery to remove his leg. He just didn't want to tell Calley he would rather die. Dad stopped eating; he just refused to eat. Calley asked him if he had decided he would rather go be with her mother, Lois. He said he had. She called me, and between the two of us, we decided that palliative care was the next step. Greg did not agree, but he hadn't been around to see Dad's condition. She and I outvoted him.

We asked the staff to keep our father comfortable. We were assured he would be kept hydrated and pain-free.

Calley began to visit daily. Most days he slept through her visits, but she felt better spending that time with him. She called me often and sent pictures of Dad.

One day, my phone rang. Calley's cousin was calling. She said she and Calley had been on their way to Red Bluff to visit Dad when a nurse called to tell her he had passed away. The nurse said she had checked on Dad at 11:00 am, spoke with him, and asked if he was in any pain. He said he was not in any pain.

The nurse checked on him again at 12:00 pm; he was sleeping peacefully. When she checked on him at 1:00 pm, he was gone. No struggle at all. He didn't look any different than the last time she had checked on him. He had simply stopped breathing.

Dan and I made arrangements to drive out there right away. We left the next morning. Calley and I talked on the phone almost constantly, making decisions about the funeral. Calley had discovered, when she buried her mother eighteen months earlier, just how expensive a funeral is; not knowing until it was too late that the folks had let their insurance policy lapse. Calley and Greg paid for their mother's funeral, casket and burial, so while Calley was making the arrangements for Dad's funeral, she made sure to go a less expensive route.

Dad was cremated, and his ashes buried in the "double depth" companion plot which had been purchased for Lois and Dad to be buried together. Dad's ashes, in the original container, were placed in a nice wooden box, which was then buried on top of Lois's casket. Once Calley had all the arrangements in place, I asked what the total cost would be. I then told her I would be paying for Dad's funeral. She broke down crying. I'm sure she was stressing about the additional cost, but I didn't want to tell her I would be paying for his funeral until she'd made all the arrangements. Personally, I feel any money spent on a funeral would be better spent on a party to celebrate the deceased's life. I knew it was important to Calley, and it was what Dad would have wanted. Knowing she would attempt to keep the funeral as economical as possible thinking she might have to pay for it, I didn't tell her in advance. I know I sound extremely controlling, but let's face it, I'm not the most trusting person.

The graveside service was lovely. I wrote the eulogy myself and had it approved by Calley. I never saw Greg until we were at the grave, and he left as soon as the service was over.

There was some drama the night before. Greg had called Calley and told her to tell his ex-wife, the mother of his children, not to come to the service. Calley told him to tell her himself. Then, she asked, "Why don't you want her there? You know Mom and Dad loved her. She'll want to be there for her children, too."

Greg said, "She embarrassed me at Mom's funeral." After his mother's funeral, everyone was invited back to the church for lunch. Someone had set up a microphone for anyone wishing to say a few words about Lois. At some point, Lindy, Greg's ex-wife, got up and said something about how much she loved Lois.

Lois and Dad *did* care about Lindy. Greg had his own reasons for hating Lindy. After many, many years of denying her sexuality, and a decade of supporting him, Lindy left. The circumstances behind her leaving her children are not clear to me, but also none of my business. Lindy had always been there for her three boys, whether her ex-husband agreed or not.

Greg should be grateful to Lindy for leaving and for creating the opportunity for him to find, marry, and live happily with his second wife.

By continuing to hate his ex, I feel he is disrespectful to his current spouse. Everyone could benefit from exes letting go of anger and resentment. Making excuses to hold on to those feelings is not healthy and does a disservice to the children, as well as the new spouse. If I were Dana, Greg's second wife, I would be asking, "Why are you still so obsessively angry with Lindy? Shouldn't you just be glad she left, paving the way for you to marry me? Am I not reason enough for you to let go of your anger?"

I feel the same way about Dan's mother. Why did she continue to rage against Dan's father when she was able to marry the love of her life, thanks to being divorced?

I remain friends with Lindy. In fact, she is one of my best friends today. Talking about Greg and Lindy's divorce, I like to say, "I got Lindy in the divorce." Lindy and I don't talk about Greg, at all. I have nothing nice to say, so I choose to say nothing at all and Lindy refuses to speak badly about the father of her children.

As for Dad's funeral, Greg told Calley, "Tell Jo to tell Lindy not to come." My good pal, Calley, told him, "No! If you don't want Lindy to come to the funeral, that's on you!"

He went on to say, "If Lindy's going to be there, then I won't be."

"Well, none of us are going to tell her she isn't welcome. So, I guess you won't be coming," Calley told him. Greg hung up on her.

Greg was supposed to pick up Dad's ashes in Red Bluff on his way down, so, Dan and I gleefully volunteered, "We'll go get the ashes. We don't mind at all." Any excuse to avoid Greg.

Greg stopped answering his phone and responding to Calley's texts. Calley sent a text to Greg's wife and told her I was going to pick up the ashes since they wouldn't be coming to the funeral, to which, Greg's wife texted back, "What are you talking about? Of course, we're coming, and we're going to pick up the ashes on our way down." Calley told her to ask her husband.

A few minutes later, Calley got another text saying *it* was all straightened out, and they would pick up the ashes on their way.

I'm not sure what "it" was that got straightened out, but Lindy and her wife did not show up for the service or the luncheon afterward. This was a shame because Greg and his wife left the graveside as soon as the service was over and never showed up at the luncheon. Which meant, neither of the boy's parents was there for them. Calley stepped up again. Calley never had children of her own, but she has a wonderful relationship with Greg's boys. She goes out of her way for them every single day.

Greg's boys are lucky to have their Aunt Calley. Their father, Greg, is a classic narcissist. Most of the time, Greg is a Covert Narcissist. Unless he feels his illusion of superiority has been shattered, then his narcissistic rage exhibits itself in unreasonable, disproportionate aggression.

> People with narcissistic personality disorder (NPD)[7] are characterized by persistent grandiosity, excessive need for admiration, and a personal disdain and lack of empathy for others. As such, the person with NPD usually displays arrogance and a distorted sense of superiority, and they seek to establish abusive power and control over others. Self-confidence (a strong sense of self) is different from narcissistic personality disorder; people with NPD typically value themselves over others to the extent that they openly disregard the feelings and wishes of others, and expect to be treated as superior, regardless of their actual status or achievements. Moreover, the person with narcissistic personality disorder usually exhibits a fragile ego, intolerance of criticism, and a tendency to belittle others in order to validate their own

superiority.

The DSM-5 indicates that persons with NPD usually display some or all of the following symptoms, typically without the commensurate qualities or accomplishments:

- Grandiosity with expectations of superior treatment from other people
- Fixation on fantasies of power, success, intelligence, attractiveness, etc.
- Self-perception of being unique, superior, and associated with high-status people and institutions
- Need for continual admiration from others
- Sense of entitlement to special treatment and to obedience from others
- The exploitation of others to achieve personal gain
- Unwillingness to empathize with the feelings, wishes, and needs of other people
- Intense envy of others, and the belief that others are equally envious of them
- Constantly demeans, bullies and belittles others

Chapter 10

Cerberus, The Legendary Hell Hound

*I*n 1974, Mother, Lisa and I were living in a one-bedroom duplex, which shared a wall with Granny and Walter. Mother and Lisa had a double bed, and I had a twin bed, all in the same room.

At the back of the duplex was a narrow walkway. This walkway, as well as the entire property, was covered with desert sand. We rarely had cause to use the walkway, but Granny would walk the laundry back there to the clotheslines. There was a four-foot cyclone fence along the property line behind us. New neighbors moved into the house directly behind us and immediately added a six-foot-tall roll of bamboo to the cyclone fence, around their entire yard. The appearance was, they were trying to hide something. The next time Granny walked back there a giant English Mastiff dog hit the fence trying to get at her. She told us it scared her half to death, but Granny, being Granny, just started feeding the dog scraps.

We all started throwing food over the fence and talking to him. After a while, the big dog became accustomed to us. He would jump up on that bamboo and just lay it down across the four-foot cyclone fence. Once, when I was back there feeding him, he was lying across the top of the fence. I began petting his head, which was level with mine. As I was talking to him, he sneezed. Snot went everywhere, including in my mouth. He shook his hand and flung snot and slobber all over his own head. It was disgusting, but he looked so proud, I couldn't be angry. I had no choice but to spit and laugh.

Mother was working as a baker at a donut shop, although, "baker" is a misnomer, as there is no baking done in a donut shop, it's all deep-fried. At the same time, she was in the process of suing the company for whom she had been a baker in Cushing. The law stated there was a weight limit for women to lift. While working at the shop in Cushing, she had been lifting heavier bags of baking mix than she should have, by necessity. There was no one else to do the heavy lifting. As a result, Mother obtained internal injuries, so she sued the company.

There was a little beer bar down the street from where we were living in San Bernardino called *Norma Jean's*. Mother became a regular there, so, of course, Lisa and I did as well.

The owner, Norma Jean, was in her mid-fifties, and single. Her little beer bar had two pool tables. One was a bar size 7-foot table, and the other was a standard 8-foot table. There was a pinball machine in one corner and an electronic Pong table in the opposite corner. At the back of the bar, beyond the storage room, was a small one-bedroom apartment where Norma Jean lived.

I first picked up a pool cue in Hobbs, Arizona, while Mother was married to Tommy. I actually learned the game at Norma Jean's on the smaller 7-foot table. Then, I tried playing on the 8-foot table, where my game improved.

I played a lot of Pong, where I learned the basic geometry of angles, which translated to my pool game. My bank shots were perfection; I could almost see the line from the cue ball to the bank, from the bank to the ball, from the ball to my intended pocket. My problem was, I got into my own head. When I should have easily beat someone, I would over-analyze my shots. If I had the table to myself, just practicing, I did well.

Norma Jean held pool tournaments in her bar, having her own team which played against teams from bars all over town. These teams were all women. Mother, Lisa and I, all three, were team members, along with Norma Jean and a couple of other regulars at the bar. We played in pool tournaments all over town until late at night. My grades suffered.

In 1975, Helen Reddy came out with a song called, *You and*

Me, Against the World. Mother liked to say it was our theme song — the three of us against the world. Mother would tell us nobody loved us as much as she did. We would never be able to depend on anyone as we could depend on her. And we were lucky to have the world's greatest mom.

Mother often told us how lucky we were to have such a cool mom. She'd smoke dope with us, drink beer with us. Our mother provided us with cigarettes. Men would come over to our home, and we would all play card games until late into the night. Lisa and I didn't have any responsibilities or curfews.

The duplex we shared with Granny at the back of the property also had three tiny houses at the front, along the street. There was a large lot between the tiny houses at the front and the duplex at the back of the property. There were two driveways off the street, each running between two of the tiny houses. The lot was all sand, no grass, plenty of room to park around the perimeter, with room to back up and turn around. Each of the tiny houses was about three hundred square feet: one bedroom, a small kitchenette, a living room, and a bathroom.

Our little apartment had a laundry room off the kitchen. We weren't using it for anything but storage, so in 1974, Walter decided he could turn it into a tiny bedroom for my twin bed. He and I tore the room down to the studs and hung the drywall.

Walt installed a closet door on one side of the room and placed the bed on the other side. There was an exterior door I kept locked and blocked by a chest of drawers. The room was crammed tight, but with an accordion door leading to the kitchen, I had some privacy. I stayed back there listening to Michael Jackson, Donny Osmond and David Cassidy on my 45rpm record player, as well as my mother's headboard banging on the wall while she was having sex in the next room.

Mother having sex on the other side of the wall became a nightly ritual. She liked to laugh, saying her boyfriend was bald-headed because his head was continuously hitting the headboard. I felt silly for letting her sex life bother me so much. I thought that because I was sixteen years old and sexually active myself, I shouldn't be affected by the sounds of sex. I hated hearing my mother having sex. I hated hearing her descriptive detail about the sex. I hated sex. I didn't want to have sex. I only had sex, because I thought I was mature and supposed to have sex to prove I was a woman. Mother encouraged me to have sex, even going so far as to tell my sister and me we'd be foolish to wait. She said she was a virgin when she married our father, but he said he had no way of knowing if she was a virgin or not. If he couldn't tell, why had she waited? Therefore, we shouldn't wait.

There was a small, maybe eighteen-inch, square window on the outside wall of my room. The window had a simple casement latch with a lever handle and opened in, like a little door, with hinges on one side. One night, when I was fifteen, I was home alone, lying in bed when I heard a noise. I opened my eyes and looked at the window. There was a knife blade inserted below the latch, easing the latch up to unlock the window. Just as it registered in my brain what was happening, I heard the English Mastiff hit the fence and bark like he'd found his next meal. I like to imagine whoever was trying to open my window took off as though Cerberus, the legendary three-headed Hell Hound, was on his heels. I didn't know what to do, so I stayed awake, waiting for Mother and Lisa to come home.

Mother's reaction to the news of someone trying to come in while I was home alone was to show me how to use her .22 automatic. She said, "If anybody comes to the door when you're home alone, ask who it is. If they won't answer, slide this lever back on the gun and shoot through the door. If it's someone you know, they will answer. Otherwise, they deserve to be shot. It doesn't matter who it is. You're a child home alone. You won't get in trouble." She didn't see the irony in her advice.

Months later, after turning sixteen, I was home alone, sitting in the living room watching TV. I heard a noise at the front door and glanced over. The handle of the locked door was slowly turning one way and then the other. I ran to Mother's bedroom and got the gun from the side table. I couldn't get the lever to slide back, because my hands were sweating. I grabbed the hem of my skirt and used it to pull back the lever. My skirt got caught in the mechanism, so I had to yank it out. I went back to the living room and yelled, "Who's there?" The handle stopped moving. I was so scared, but I wasn't going to pull the trigger.

Our little breakfast nook had two windows. One faced out on the front porch, where I could see the silhouette of a man; the other window faced on to a patio shared by Granny's bedroom window. The windows were all opened a few inches to let in a breeze. I leaned down to the second window and started screaming for Granny. By the time she came running with Walter, there was no one to be seen. Granny called the police who found large footprints in the sand near our front door. I didn't mention the gun.

I can't say for certain, but I've often wondered if the man wasn't Jose, Mother's 4th husband. We were still getting calls from him, and we were back in San Bernardino. I'll never know for sure, but it didn't change anything at home. Mother still left me home alone.

In high school, I had a friend who was a year ahead of me. Marsha and I spent a great deal of time together. By the time she was a senior, we were very close. Mother had tried to teach me to drive her Maverick with "three on the tree." I was confused by the gears on the column. Marsha was driving a little standard transmission Dodge Colt with the gears on the floor. Her Colt was easier for me to learn. Once I learned to drive her car, I quickly learned to drive the Maverick.

A day came, in my junior year, when I asked Marsha to come over to my house. She said she couldn't, because she had made plans with another one of her friends. I was mad as hell. I said to her, "I thought I was your friend!"

"You are my friend. But I can have more than one friend," she casually replied. The fact that someone could have more than one friend came as such a surprise to me. In all my life, I never had more than one friend at a time. With all the moving around I did, I never had opportunities to make multiple friends. I'd had multiple acquaintances but never more than one person I considered my friend. I've never forgotten the lesson I learned that day. I had a genuine epiphany!

Shortly after Marsha graduated, she got married, and I rarely saw her. At about this same time, I got my fake I.D. and began staying out late with my mother and sister.

Early in my senior year at San Bernardino High School, seniors were told to make an appointment at a local photographer that the school had contracted with to take senior portraits. Each senior made an appointment to have his or her senior portrait taken at the studio. I remember going in and being impressed with how well the photographer directed me to pose for the best possible pictures. I told him I didn't want to show my teeth. He worked with me to achieve flattering photos without showing my stained and damaged teeth.

Not long after having my portrait done, I got a call from the studio. The photographer said my portrait turned out great, so good in fact; he wanted to use one in the studio. It was a profile picture that couldn't be in the yearbook, but he thought it was a special picture. Of course, I said he could use it. The photographer said I needed to sign a release, allowing him to use my picture for advertising.

I went in to sign the release, and there was my picture, hanging on the wall, bigger than my head. He asked if I was going to buy any of the pictures. I told him that I'd like to, and I agreed they were really good. I'd talk to my mother about buying some. I told her about the studio using my picture and asked if we could buy some. Mother said *no*, which came as no surprise to me. She never went to look at my portrait. What would be the point? I was not the pretty daughter.

When I got married, my husband had an 8" x 10" of his senior portrait. I wanted so much to have my own. When Dan and I got back to the States, I called to see if they still had the negatives. They did and said I could get a copy for twenty-five dollars. I sent them a check and got a copy for myself. It's packed away somewhere, but for a few years, we had both of our portraits framed and on the wall. I guess it was the first time I felt pretty.

Dan's senior portrait is a sore spot with his mother. He had let a girlfriend bleach his hair blond just before he had his portrait taken. Betty snarls and spits like an angry cat to this day when it comes up in conversation.

January 1976

Mother had "friends" who were more like assets. Mother would allow women to remain in her presence as long as they were useful. Judith was a tiny, bleached blond whose ego appeared to be the size of California. I was never able to account for Mother's relationship with Judith, other than an opportunity to knock Judith down a peg or two.

Judith had one child, a daughter my age. Judith told my mother she had entered her daughter, Karen, in the Miss San Bernardino Pageant. My mother immediately began hounding Lisa and me to enter the same pageant. There was no money to buy any of my senior portraits, but suddenly there was money for both of us to be in a pageant that neither of us was interested in being a part of. We had no desire, whatsoever, but she dared us. She pushed and cajoled until we finally just gave in. This pageant would be the first time two sisters had entered at the same time. The newspaper capitalized on our relationship, and we got quite a bit of press because of it.

We would sit with Karen at meetings and interviews. Lisa and I would hang out with Karen because she was the only contestant we knew. Also, she didn't want to be there any more than we did. We had regular rehearsals where we learned how to stand, how to walk, how to hold our heads up, and our shoulders back. They worked with us on our interview skills and taught us to use Vaseline on our teeth to keep our lips from getting stuck after smiling for so long and Band-aids on our nipples to hide them in our swimsuits. Then at one of the rehearsals, Lisa and I got called into a meeting with the pageant committee.

Judith and Karen were sitting in the room with them. The committee came *at us* like we were guilty of something. They said Karen had heard us telling one of the contestants the pageant was rigged. We were completely floored. I was scared by their accusations and their attitude. Lisa did not appear to be intimidated at all. She told them Karen was lying. Lisa suggested Karen's mother put her up to it. I just sat there with my mouth hanging open and silently crying. (My go-to reaction to anything that upsets me.) Suddenly, Karen said, "They didn't say any of that. My mother wants them out of the pageant. She made the whole thing up." The committee asked Lisa and me to step out of the room but not to leave. They would be calling us back in momentarily. After a few minutes, Judith and Karen came out and left the building. Karen looked at us and mouthed, "Sorry."

Lisa and I were called back in. The committee apologized to us and said Karen would not be returning to the pageant. They hoped we wouldn't let the incident ruin the experience for us.

When we got home, we told Mother what had happened. She was overjoyed by the news. Karen wouldn't be in the pageant, and Judith's plans had failed. There was no talk of how it had affected us; only that she, Mother, had "won." She had beat Judith. Her Narcissistic Glow was blinding.

I wanted to quit, and Lisa agreed. We felt disrespected, ashamed, and embarrassed, but Mother insisted we stick with it. We already had the designated swimsuits, and we each had a gown to wear during the formal part of the pageant, so we agreed to stay in the competition.

I was never a serious contender. I froze under the lights, even in rehearsal. I was barely coherent during the interview process. Lisa did really well.

Lisa and I had each bought a twenty-dollar dress, off the rack. Most of the other girls had dresses that were expensive and lavish. Lisa wore a form-fitting, cream-colored dress that set off her long, dark, curly hair, and went well with her olive skin tone. She was stunning.

I was ninety-eight pounds of a gangly, flat-chested tomboy. I picked a black dress and had my hair done up in a loose bun. I did not fit in with anyone else on that stage. I did not want to be there. Lisa was the pretty one. I was the one people said they mistook for a pool cue or a boy. "Don't stand too close to the cue rack. Someone will try to use you for a pool cue."

The year before, I had taken a class called Stage Craft in High School. That year I was part of the crew behind the scenes of the pageant. We all dressed in black and wore headsets to communicate with each other. I knew how the boys were talking about the contestants. I didn't want to be the object of their ridicule. I felt exposed, when all I ever wanted to do was hide in the crowd, or behind the scenes, dressed in black.

Before the final announcement was made of the winners, the host announced there would be a First Place Queen, a First Runner-Up (second place) and a Second Runner-up (third place). He said that there was a tie for Second Runner-up, and as soon as the judges got the tie straightened out, an announcement would be made.

Lisa got First Runner-Up. Mother was beside herself. She wanted the world to know, First Runner-up was her daughter. Lisa was very gracious, smiling, but keeping her pleasure low-key, letting Mother soak up her Narcissist Supply. I was thrilled for Lisa. I was very proud that my sister had gotten First Runner-Up. She got a huge trophy and her picture in the paper with the rest of the Queen's Court.

Mother immediately began telling everyone, both of her girls should have been in the Queen's Court. She said I had gotten cheated by the judges. She told everyone I had tied for Second Runner-Up, but the judges thought it best if the sisters didn't take second and third place; it might look rigged. I knew better, but I couldn't contradict her. *Never contradict Mother* was something I learned very early in life. If Mother was telling a story, it was our job just to go along. She was in her glory. One wrong word and all of that could change.

We never knew what might set off my mother's temper. Not just day-to-day, but moment-to-moment, we walked on eggshells. I remember a time when I came out of the kitchen to ask her something. I stopped in the doorway between the kitchen and the living room. She was sitting on the couch watching TV. I asked some innocent question, but *not* what she had heard. Whatever she heard really pissed her off. Maybe she was ready for a fight when I walked in. Maybe she really misunderstood me, but she laid into me like never before. She went on a thirty-minute rant about what an ungrateful bitch I was, how selfish and thoughtless I was being. She told me I never, ever thought about anyone but myself.

I was not about to try to explain what I had actually said. I wasn't going to say something like, "You misunderstood me." Should I tell her she was wrong? I couldn't stand up for myself; she would see self-advocacy as an argument. All I could do was stand there, silently crying. Snot was running down over my mouth. I couldn't breathe through my nose, and I couldn't open my mouth because of the snot. I was just beginning to panic when I realized there was a dishtowel in my hand. I used the towel and wiped my face.

Mother wasn't actually seeing me through her rage until I wiped my face. She screamed, "Stop crying! You always do this. Trying to make people feel sorry for you! You disgust me!" My heart races when I think about the fury and venom Mother directed at me. Any confrontation puts me right back there. I become the child whose tongue is frozen to the roof of her mouth, the tears pouring down my face.

As an adult, I'm learning to defend myself. With a racing heart and lots of tears, I stand up and say, "I have a right to my opinion," or, "I didn't say that." I tend to anger quickly. I feel defensive. My go-to reaction when I'm feeling defensive is anger, to which my husband shuts down. I'm unreasonable, but you can't talk to me when I'm feeling cornered.

Being overly defensive and easy to anger are some of my own narcissistic traits. It's like I'm on the look-out for an injustice done to me. I'm in a near-constant state of anxiety.

> *Women with Narcissistic Parents: Stuck in Worry*[8]
>
> Narcissistic parents lack self-awareness and can't take responsibility for how their behavior impacts their children. Their children stand *guard*, reading their parents' emotional temperatures. Growing up like *vigilant*, undercover CIA agents, it's not surprising that children of narcissistic parents become anxious adults.

Chapter 11

Predator and Prey

*A*s a child, and until I left my mother's home, I would suppress my anger. I learned not to give her any more ammunition. In Dr. Carter's book, *When Pleasing You is Killing Me,* one of Dr. Carter's patients discussed the need to present oneself as a pleasant, confident, easygoing, and carefree person. This easygoing attitude seems to please those around us. But beneath *my* happy veneer, I have a wave of simmering anger. My quick temper is not something I like about myself, and I work hard to control it. Sometimes I feel, in my attempt to control my anger, I am still suppressing my feelings. The struggle is to find a healthy balance. I've learned through counseling and research that anger is not the problem. My communication of anger is the problem. Much like the contents of a bottle of champagne under pressure, the top gets popped, and there is an explosion. I'm learning to communicate the anger more appropriately while remaining true to the purpose of the emotion.

I was raised to be a "people pleaser." It was ingrained in me to please my mother, and by association, others. I was naturally affirming of people, handing out compliments to make me likable. I was always cooperative, rarely saying *no* to anyone, men included. Some men, pedophiles in particular, recognized this and used it to manipulate me.

Mother pushed me toward men twice my age while reminding me not to have sex until I was on birth control.

I was fifteen when I met Barry at my mother's bar. He was thirty, a small man, with nothing going for him except everybody loved Barry. He was everyone's friend. Barry was *charming*. Barry began grooming me, with my mother's blessing; telling me, I was mature for my age. He could relate to me and loved spending time with me. He would caress my arm while looking into my eyes when I talked. Barry acted like I was special. I had never received such attention in my life. I was lapping it up like a kitten with a bowl of milk. When I decided to have sex with Barry, I told my mother. She told me to go to Planned Parenthood and get on the pill, so that's what I did. Mother didn't question my decision, nor did she go with me for my first gynecological exam. She didn't seem to care about the emotional ramifications of my decision, only that I do not get pregnant.

Barry took me to a little motel where he got us a room. There was no foreplay; no words of assurance — nothing to prepare my body for what was to come. Barry hurt me, all the while telling me it was uncomfortable because it was my first time. He assured me the pain would stop, and I would suddenly begin to feel pleasure. There was never any pleasure.

A woman's body needs to be sufficiently prepared for intercourse. Foreplay is meant to make the woman desire intercourse, naturally lubricating the vagina. Teenage boys need to know how to treat a woman's body so that both teens enjoy the act. Teenage girls need to understand their bodies so that they know what to expect and what needs to happen for both participants to enjoy sex. Men and women should get as much pleasure from *giving* pleasure as *receiving* pleasure. What passes for Sex Education in school is nothing more than what goes where, how to wear a condom and/or abstinence.

As soon as Barry finished, we got up, got dressed, and went back to my mother's bar. He loudly told everyone, including my mother, that I had enjoyed it so much I had scratched up his back. I felt violated, exposed, and maligned. If Barry truly cared about me, would he openly talk about our private moments? And to blatantly lie about his prowess! How did Barry know my mother would approve of him talking about me this way in front of all these people?

I remember walking out of the bar and going to sit outside to give some thought to what had happened, to figure out how I felt about it. My sister's boyfriend, Freddy, came out to check on me; not my sister. Certainly not my mother. Freddy asked me if I was okay. I told him I was fine. I couldn't tell him what I was really feeling. I was taught not to be a burden.

When I was seventeen, I met Mike at the bar. He began the same game. Mike took me to see *Jaws* at the drive-in. He stayed apart from me in the car, treating me like a friend. He asked me how old I thought he was. He was balding, so I thought he had to be at least thirty-five. I said I thought he was about thirty. He told me he was twenty-seven. After the movie, we drove back to the bar, where we sat in the parking lot talking. He said all the right things. He made me feel special, but he took it a step further, buying me gifts. I was getting what I thought was positive attention, and I liked it. So, I began sleeping with him. Unfortunately, sex with Mike wasn't any different than sex had been with Barry. I realize now; they didn't care if I received any pleasure.

From the ages of fifteen to nineteen, I was targeted by predators. The men who look for and groom the emotionally broken, the ones with low self-esteem and/or obvious insecurities.

> To establish a relationship with a child, and the child's family, child groomers might try one or all of these things: They might try to gain the child's or parents' trust by befriending them, with the goal of easy access to the child. A trusting relationship with the family means the child's parents are less likely to believe potential accusations. Child groomers might look for opportunities to have time alone with the child, which can be done by offering to babysit; the groomers may also invite the child for sleepovers, for opportunistic bed-sharing. They might give gifts or money to the child in exchange for sexual contact, or for no apparent reason. Commonly, they show

> pornography to the child or talk about sexual topics with the child, hoping to make it easy for the child to accept such acts, thus normalizing the behavior. They may also engage in hugging, kissing, or other physical contacts, even when the child does not want it.[9]

The summer between my junior and senior years, I went to visit my Dad in Chico for a couple of weeks. Lisa never went back after he refused to pay for college. When I came home from my visit, having ridden there on a Greyhound bus, Mother met me with the biggest grin on her face but not because she was happy to see me. She had met a woman who looked like me and had agreed to let me have her driver's license. Mother was so excited. "Now the three of us can go out, and you can stop whining about staying home alone," she said.

The truth is, I never whined about being left home alone. I knew complaining to my mother would do me no good. I may have complained to Lisa, but never would I say anything to my Mother. This was a common practice with Mother, telling me what I complained about. She used to tell me, and everyone else, that I was always complaining because the photo albums were so full of pictures of Lisa, but not me. That drove me crazy!

I always have, all of my life, made excuses for people, when I'm treated poorly. I justify their actions in ways to explain their reasoning, to convince myself they weren't deliberately trying to hurt me or my feelings. *For the first three and a half years, Lisa was an only child. Naturally, there were more pictures of her*. That's what I always told myself. The fact is, our mother didn't take as many pictures of me. Lisa was a beautiful child with long, dark, curly hair. There are people in my family who tell me still, what a beautiful child she was. I had thin, blond hair and freckles. And I looked like a boy. I'm not bothered by it, and I honestly don't even care. I've never been photogenic, so I'm not a camera hound. What *does* bother me is, Mother was always telling me that I complained about there being more pictures of Lisa than of me. It's simply not true.

Mother was forever telling me I was ungrateful, a complainer and overly sensitive. "Overly sensitive" is a favorite phrase of the Narcissist. A narcissist will accuse others of being too sensitive when they get their feelings hurt by the horrendous things the narcissist has said to them. Calling me overly sensitive is probably my biggest pet peeve. As though I shouldn't be hurt by the things insensitive people say. It's my fault if my feelings get hurt. Bullshit!

My husband said to me one time, and one time only, "You can be overly sensitive." I blew my stack! I explained, "I have a right to my feelings. Maybe *you're* too insensitive." Apparently, I had been holding onto that one for a long time, and he got the brunt of it.

Mother's friend, Joyce, gave me her old driver's license, went to the Department of Motor Vehicles and told them she'd lost it. The DMV gave Joyce a new driver's license, and all was right with the world, according to my mother.

I knew I wouldn't answer to Joyce, so I changed my name to Jo. If anyone looking at my new I.D. asked, I just said it was short for Joyce. I was seventeen years old when I changed my name to Jo. I feel like the name suits me. Besides, I've always hated the first name on my birth certificate. Don't ask.

By this time, Mother had won her case for the injury she had sustained while working at a donut shop. She bought Norma Jean's, the little beer bar down the street. Mother moved into the small apartment at the back of the bar. Lisa and I stayed next to Granny.

Now that I had a fake I.D., Mother was taking us to all sorts of bars, introducing us to some pretty unsavory people. She wanted "girlfriends," not daughters.

By Christmas break of my senior year, I was failing my Government class. The school called and said I'd have to come back after my senior year to take that class over again before I could graduate. I told them I wouldn't be returning to school after Christmas. I figured I'd go to work full time.

Mother found me a job as a cocktail waitress at a bar with my fake I.D., and I began helping to pay the bills. Lisa and I didn't keep our paychecks. They went in the "kitty," as Mother called it. Our mother agreed to give us an allowance, from our own paychecks.

My friends, kids who had also come from broken homes, or dysfunctional families, thought my mother was this Super Cool Mom. She let them smoke and drink in her home, never treating them like kids. She became a really screwed up mentor to them. Mother was a predator. She was grooming my friends to be her friends.

I remember how she kept telling us that if a man wanted to spend money on us, we would be stupid not to let him. My friend was at the bar with me one evening when some stranger came in and sat down. He drank a couple of beers and struck up a conversation with my mother and the rest of us. He said he was in town on business. He wanted to know if any of us knew a good place for a steak dinner. Mother told him about a restaurant we all liked and suggested he take me along to show him the way. I had other plans, so I wasn't available. He asked my friend if she would be interested. She accepted his invitation for a free steak dinner.

After their meal, he told her he knew some people in town and would like for her to meet them. He began driving down some back streets and ended up at the defunct train depot. He reached in the back seat and came out with a knife which he put to her throat and proceeded to rape her.

When the rape was over, she convinced him she had enjoyed it and suggested they go back to the bar for a drink. Pretty smart, considering what she had just endured. This lunatic rapist agreed. They pulled in the parking lot of the bar and started inside when he said he'd forgotten his cigarettes in the car. He turned to go back to the car, and she ran inside, screaming, "He raped me!" All the men in the bar, friends of ours, ran out the door just as he was driving away. They jumped in their cars and tried to chase him down, but he lost them. He was never caught, and a report was never filed. Mother told my friend that reporting the rape wouldn't do any good since she had gone out with a stranger willingly. Mother never took any responsibility for the situation.

Mother started a professional poker game in her apartment at the back of the bar. She ran it very professionally and had players every night, while an employee worked the bar. One night, Mother was a player short, so she came out into the bar and asked if anybody wanted to join the game. Some guy said, "Yeah, I'll play." The next day Mother got busted for running an illegal Poker Game. She had to go to court, but she wasn't worried. Mother walked into court exaggerating her disability, crying and begged the court for leniency, saying she didn't know it was illegal. Of course, she knew, but she got off with a warning.

I met Ron at the bar where I was working as a waitress. He was the drummer for the band and only a few years older than I. I moved in with him for a month but went back to living with Lisa pretty quickly. I thought to live with a member of the band would be fun, but it was not what I had expected. He was kind of a dork and let the band leader influence him too much. Ron would run around with this guy, wouldn't call to tell me he'd be late, or not coming home at all. I made it clear to him that I felt disrespected when he did that. I gave him the old, "I didn't know if you were lying in a ditch somewhere," line.

Of course, he reminded me I wasn't his mother. At which point, I reminded *him* I was not his mother, and since we both agreed on that point, I felt the time had come to move out.

Mother was involved in a traffic accident that eventually leads to all of us leaving California and moving to Oklahoma in October of 1976.

The sequence of events and dates are unclear to me, so I can't go into too much detail. Mother pulled her car out in front of some motorcycles, braked for whatever reason, causing one of the motorcycles to crash into the back of her car. The driver and his passenger went over the top of her car and were badly injured. Mother said the friends of the injured had sworn revenge. Apparently, she was worried enough to sell out and leave the state.

Part 2

Narcissist (n): A more polite term for a self-serving, manipulative, evil asshole with no soul.

Chapter 12

Losing Granny

*M*other drove the biggest U-Haul truck she could find, filled with our belongings, as well as Granny and Walter's. Walter drove their car with Granny. Lisa and I took turns driving our Chevette or riding with Mother in the truck. We had only one cat at the time, Toby. He was a great traveler, always riding in the Chevette.

I was following along on Interstate 40, keeping my eye on the U-Haul truck in front of me. I happened to glance up in my rearview mirror where I saw Toby's tail straight up in the air, quivering, a clear sign, my cat was peeing in the car. "Oh, Damn!" I quickly pulled off the side of the road, ran to the back, lifted the hatchback, throwing Toby out in the sand where he finished his business. Poor little guy! I couldn't remember the last time I had let him out to potty.

We all agreed, we would get through the higher elevations as soon as possible, for Granny's sake. When we got to Albuquerque, Walter said we had to stop for the night. He felt he couldn't go on. Mother reminded Walter we had agreed to get Granny out of the higher elevation as quickly as possible. Granny said she would be okay, insisting we get some rest.

My grandmother told us the next day she had slept sitting up in a chair because her chest hurt when she attempted to lie down. Mother suspected Walter might have had an ulterior motive: to cause Granny to have another heart attack. We all knew staying in the higher elevation could cause another heart attack.

We arrived in Fox, Oklahoma, the next day, November 1, 1976. Walter's sister and her family lived in Fox. They made room for all of us, including pallets on the floor for my sister and me. The next evening, we were all in the living room watching the Presidential Election results. Granny was asleep in a recliner in the corner. She sat up suddenly. Looking at me sitting on the floor, she said, "Where are we?"

Granny's confusion scared me. She was giving me a completely blank stare. Then, just as quickly, she laid her head back and sat back up again, seeming to be fine. During the night, an ambulance came to take her to the hospital. She'd had a heart attack.

We rented a house for the five of us in Fox, on State Highway 76, in preparation for Granny's homecoming. Granny never left the hospital. My grandmother died on Thanksgiving Day, 1976.

Before Granny's passing, two of her brothers who lived in Oklahoma came to visit her at the hospital. Her oldest brother was a pastor. He had spent twenty years traveling the country and attending revival meetings with his two eldest daughters. When he wasn't preaching, he and his daughters sang hymns in three-part harmonies for the congregation. He was a great comfort to my Granny near the end of her life, as he spent hours by her hospital bed praying with her.

Her other Oklahoma-based brother, whom she had practically raised after their mother died, was younger. He had lived a wild life after running off to join the Navy in his youth, but he worshipped his big sister. She asked everyone to leave her hospital room so that she could have a private moment with her baby brother. He later told his daughter, who relayed to me, what my grandmother said to him from her hospital bed.

She told him, "I am ready to die. I'm not afraid to die, because I know I will be in Heaven with Mommy and Daddy, as well as my husband. But it breaks my heart you won't be there, with all of us, to share in the reunion."

My grandmother's brother told his daughter those words shook him to his core; he was ready to be saved, right there, at her bedside. They prayed together, and he accepted Jesus as his Lord and Savior.

When he left her room, his children, his wife, and his brothers knew. He was a changed man. He was a Christian who looked forward to The Great Reunion in Heaven. He lived the rest of his life as a Christian, never wavering in his belief.

My sister and I were not allowed to grieve for our grandmother. Mother made her wishes clear. She was glad to be rid of her mother. Our mother appeared to be relieved of "the responsibility" of caring for her mother. If we showed any grief for the loss of our grandmother, Mother would feel we were disloyal to her. The lesson here was: when someone close to you dies, when someone leaves you, when you lose a friend or a pet, stuff your feelings deep down. Forget about them. *Feelings are not good. Feelings are bad. Feelings are not good. Feelings are bad. Repeat. Repeat. Repeat.*

Since we'd spent all our money on the move to Oklahoma, there wasn't anything left for a funeral. Mother and Walter went as cheaply as they could, having Granny buried in Graham, Oklahoma. The location of a donated cemetery.

Walter died the following April, in 1977. He was buried next to Granny. Later, his sister and her husband were buried on the other side of him.

I've never been one to visit graves. I don't think my loved ones are spending eternity sitting on a headstone waiting for visitors. However, I would have visited my grandmother's final resting place periodically, simply out of respect. She was in a place so far removed from anywhere I had any reason to be, visiting wasn't feasible. A two-hour drive with nothing else around, or "on the way" to anywhere. There weren't any other family members to visit in the area. There was no reason to be down there.

In 2016, my husband and I began making our plans for what we wanted to happen to our bodies when we died. When we discovered we were eligible to have our ashes interred in a national cemetery, we both decided to be cremated, having our ashes interred together at Fort Sill National Cemetery. We took a drive down to check out the cemetery, planning to continue on to the small, donated piece of land in which my grandmother was buried.

After having seen the beautiful, pristine condition of the National Cemetery, we were both disheartened to see where Granny's remains had been for nearly forty years. Weeds had choked out any semblance of grass, wildly overgrown scrub oak trees throughout. Walter, his sister, and her husband's headstones were all clean, recently decorated with flowers. Granny's was not. I understand Walter's family never had a chance to get to know my grandmother. They had no connection to her. My heart broke to see the obvious neglect. My wonderful husband said, "We should have her moved to Hugo." I nearly burst into tears.

"Do you really think we could have her moved? It could be pretty expensive," I asked.

"I think we should. I know how important she was to you; what a huge impact she had on your life. We could have her moved to Hugo to the family cemetery, where her parents and siblings are buried," he suggested.

We decided we were going to do whatever was necessary to move Granny's remains. My only concern at this point was, would my sister attempt to stop me, purely out of vindictiveness?

A full year went by to get all the necessary permits. We had to find the required licensed funeral director willing to be in attendance at the exhumation, as well as the re-interment. He had to find a backhoe operator with an assistant willing to make the 140-mile trip to exhume the forty-year-old casket. During the following year, I got in contact with a cousin who lives in Hugo. She spoke to her brother who, due to unforeseen circumstances, was willing to sell me his burial plot next to their daddy, their daddy being the very brother who had accepted Jesus as his Lord and Savior at my grandmother's bedside forty years earlier. What more appropriate place for her remains to be buried?

Dan and I took a trip down to Hugo about six months before all of this was to take place. I paid for my cousin's plot. His sister took us out to the local monument company where we ordered the new headstone. We had decided to leave the headstone in Graham, next to her second husband's headstone. We didn't figure his family would know the difference or even care. As Granny's last surviving descendants, I had to get my sister to sign off on my plan. I didn't ask for, nor did I want, any help from her. Lisa didn't give me any grief; she simply signed the paper and mailed it back to me in the SASE I had included. Everything was set. We scheduled it for after the summer heat had cooled down.

September 25th, Dan and I arrived moments before the funeral director and the crew to do the work. The funeral director said this would be the oldest exhumation he had ever attended. Forty years is a long time to wait, but I felt so good about our decision. When they got down to the casket it looked to be in great shape. The top looked almost pristine, but as soon as they tried to remove the forty-year-old casket from the ground, it broke in two. They stopped immediately and began to make another plan. Eventually, the casket came out in one piece. Only the lid was split in two. Rather than study my Granny's remains, I looked at the contents of the casket as a whole. I saw her blue glasses still on her face. Also, there was a blue and white afghan in the casket with her. After forty years, the afghan, which she had crocheted herself, was still blue and still had the pattern intact.

The casket, along with my Granny's remains, were placed in a large, plastic burial vault, completely enclosed and sealed for reburial. Dan and I left the cemetery to spend the night in Hugo. The casket, with my grandmother's remains, was taken to the funeral home in Hugo where it was kept overnight.

The next morning, September 26, 2017, we all met at the Hugo Cemetery for re-interment. My cousin came to see my Granny buried next to her daddy, Granny's brother. My heart was filled with joy for my Granny. Granny's nieces and nephews all agreed; moving Granny was the right thing to do. My grandmother was where she belonged, and I know she approved.

The new headstone was already in place. I had decided to put both her maiden name and her married name, my grandfather's last name. For genealogy purposes, headstones are a great source. I chose to list her birth date, the date of her death and added at the bottom a reference to when she was moved to Hugo. I honored my grandmother with this line. "Welcome home, Granny. 2017"

After Granny died, Walter decided to move in with his sister. Mother, Lisa, and I moved to Oklahoma City, to an apartment. We all three got jobs working in the same bar establishment. Mother managed the bar, while Lisa and I bartended. My fake I.D. allowed me to get a Club Card, which was required in the state of Oklahoma to serve alcohol. Mother sent me downtown, to the police department, where I had my fingerprints taken before I was issued a Club Card. I was eighteen by this time, so I knew if the authorities discovered I was using a fake I.D. I could go to jail. Mother didn't seem concerned.

For Christmas, that year, I asked Mother if I could get a ticket to see KISS in concert. Yes, I was working full-time, but I had to ask my mother if I could buy a concert ticket. She agreed that it would be my Christmas present. I certainly don't regret seeing my favorite band at the time, but I look back and just shake my head. I had to ask my mother if I could buy a ticket, although I was doing the work of an adult and bringing home a full paycheck.

The best thing about moving to Oklahoma was getting to know my mother's extended family: the people she had grown up with, and their children, our cousins. Dale was a year younger than Lisa. He took us to his favorite gay nightclub, *The Free Spirit*. I loved being there. Lisa and I could dance, with or without a dance partner. Nobody cared. I was in my element - disco music and dancing.

Dale introduced me to a friend of his, Shawn. She came to The Free Spirit for the freedom from unwanted attention from men.

Everyone knew she was straight, so neither the men nor the women attempted anything more than friendship with her. She and I hit it off and became close for the few months that I lived in the area.

Shawn was a Miss Oklahoma City or Miss Oklahoma; I can't remember which, I just remember she had been the queen of some beauty pageant. She was gorgeous. I remember when she would order a drink at the bar, the first thing she did was take out that tiny little swizzle straw and lay it next to her drink. I had previously noticed that prissy chicks liked to sip from the straw, but not Shawn. Finally, I asked her, "Shawn, I'm just curious. Why do you choose not to use the straw?" She became very serious like she was going to let me in on a secret. She leaned in and said, "One night I was really flirting with this gorgeous man, giving him my full attention. I reached over to pick up my drink, all the while looking him in the eye and hanging on his every word. I raised the drink to my mouth, and the straw went up my nose."

I just about spewed the drink that I happened to be taking a sip of at the time. "Oh my God, what happened?" Shawn, completely straight-faced, said, "I sat my drink down on the bar. Then I reached up and pulled the straw from my nose." That's when I actually DID spew my drink. That was a one-minute conversation that I have never forgotten. Hysterical!

Dale had two younger brothers: Don, my age, and Dean, who was about fourteen years old when we moved there. Shortly after we arrived, we heard Stephen King's *Carrie* had been made into a horror movie. The radio DJ said it was at *"a theater near us*." I loved the book. I told everyone we absolutely had to go see the movie. Dean wanted to go too, but his parents didn't allow him to see R rated movies, so we just didn't tell them the movie was rated R.

Dean sat next to me in the theater. The movie opened in the girl's locker room at a high school, with naked teenage girls showering and teasing each other. Dean whispered in my ear, "I think I'm going to like R rated movies." About 20 minutes into the movie, he hid his face behind my shoulder, never to emerge again. He didn't like that particular R rated movie. *Carrie* scared him.

JoJo Maize, Basic Training, Lackland AFB. April 1977.

Chapter 13

Leaving on a Jet Plane

*M*other had a girlfriend in high school, her best friend, Maureen. Maureen had a boyfriend in high school but ended up married to someone else. Mother married my father in early 1953 and had my sister in December of '54. Shortly thereafter, the family moved to California to find work. Mother and Maureen remained friends, writing letters back and forth, for 20 plus years.

In 1976, after Mother moved us back to Oklahoma, she and Maureen got to catch up again. We found out Maureen was having an affair with her high school sweetheart, Merle. She said she was in love with him and that she planned to leave her husband to marry Merle. Within days of their reunion, my mother called Merle to invite him to meet her for drinks. The next morning, Mother advised her friend, "Merle isn't a good guy. He didn't hesitate to fuck me." Mother thought Maureen was stupid because she wasn't grateful to my mother for proving Merle to be a player. Mother never mentioned Maureen again. My mother felt nothing at the loss of a lifelong friendship. Maureen wasn't important enough to ever think about again. As with most things, my mother felt no remorse. *A complete emotional disconnect.*

Mother had a number of girlfriends over the years but always slept with their boyfriends or husbands, without fail, unless she ran across a man with morals and conviction. I believe, in my heart, the motive was to prove Mother was more sexually desirable than her friends. For Mother, in all instances, she had to win.

In March of 1977, I left for the United States Air Force Basic Training in San Antonio, Texas. I had gone to a recruiter's office to sign up. He sent me downtown to take the entrance exam. They asked me some questions, then took me to a room to take a written exam.

A week later, I was back at the recruiter's office. He drove me downtown, where I joined a roomful of kids to get sworn in. He notified me I would be going to Technical School right out of Basic Training to learn to be a Missile Maintenance Technician. Then he told me when to arrive at the airport for my flight to San Antonio. I told him I didn't have a ride, as my mother would be working late the night before and would be unwilling to take me. He said he would gladly pick me up, driving me to the airport himself.

On the plane ride to San Antonio, I met Irma Gulley. She was also going to Basic Training. Our personalities clicked right away. We ended up in the same Flight Class, going all through Basic Training together. As *Forrest Gump* would later say in the 1994 film, "She was my Best Good Friend."

I got called in for a meeting while I was in Basic Training. I was told the Air Force needed to fill a quota of Airman Basics and females in the biomedical field. They wanted me to change from Missile Maintenance to Biomedical Technician. The People Pleaser in me thought, *Yeah, sure. Whatever.* I shrugged and said, "Okay."

I graduated from Basic Training in May of 1977. Irma and I got on the same bus which took us to Sheppard Air Force Base for Technical School. At our very first In-Service Seminar, we were told, "Never go anywhere alone. Any time you leave your dormitory, have at least one other girl with you. There have been several sexual assaults and rapes here on base. Be safe."

Forty-plus years later, I'm appalled, remembering the command staff had decided the avoidance of rape was our responsibility. The message we received pre-1980? As women in the military, we had volunteered to take on a man's job. We needed to be prepared for the consequences.

Though women served honorably in the war effort pre-1948, most notably as nurses, their work was often stigmatized and mocked. Sexual harassment was common, as were the implications women were trading sexual favors for their military ranks. The Women's Army Auxiliary Corps, WAACs, were not made eligible for Veteran's Administration Services until 1980, which meant they were not eligible for disability compensation, or any of the other various benefits men were receiving after serving. Furthermore, women were not allowed to serve in direct ground combat roles until 2013. For decades, the reason for refusing to integrate women into regular service was; if women were in the regular military, men would have to take orders from a woman.

Irma and I were both put in a dorm for women in the medical field. They tried to bunk girls together who had the same classes, so they could study together. I had a room to myself, as my field wasn't really medical - it was electronics. There wasn't a whole dormitory dedicated to women in electronics, as I was the only one in attendance that semester. Irma became friends with her roommate, as well as other girls in her field of study. This new arrangement left me alone and vulnerable.

We would all go to the chow hall for breakfast at 5 am, then line up for the march to class. I was told, at a certain point, I would break off on my own, heading to the electronics facility. Yes, before the sun came up, I was told to go off on my own to find the building where I would be taking my classes. They told me the building number and said, "Go find it." It was a mile-long walk along the flight line to the engineering facility. I was walking alone in the dark, exactly what I had been warned not to do.

By the time I arrived at the facility the first morning, I was a wreck. I feared a rapist was going to jump out of the dark at any moment. The thought had been put in my head during the first in-service seminar.

While waiting for the facility to open, I was the only woman standing in a group of a few dozen young men. I was approached and targeted by one of the instructors. He was a predator, and I was his prey. I was a lone figure in an unfamiliar situation. A Staff Sergeant, this man began asking me personal questions, which I tried to be as evasive as possible answering. I wanted him to walk away. At this point, I still didn't know if he was my instructor, and I was intimidated by his rank.

Ewa is a Polish American writer, independent researcher, transformational coach, and narcissistic abuse survivor. The following, taken from her article, *How Narcissists Use Sex to Exploit and Control You*[10], is spot-on. I wish I'd had access to information like this in 1977. I have it broken down into three segments.

The Chase[10a]

> Once a narcissist targets you as a particularly attractive nexus of supply, s/he will take the chase to the extreme. In fact, the better word for it is a hunt—as in a predator hunting its prey. It's primitive, instinctual and exhilarating.
>
> They savor breaking boundaries and using manipulative tactics to exert their domination and extract your submission. While you think you're dealing with a benevolent being to whom your happiness is of primary

concern, the truth is exactly the opposite. This is only a story used to soften and open you up.

Feeling entitled and above others, even the law (the antisocial types), narcissists get their power fix from exploiting the naïve. Some flagrantly say that they are fully justified in their actions because of how stupid people are for believing in their knot of lies.

For some, the more difficult the target is to tame, the drunker on power they feel once they finally gain control over you. This is why you feel the instant coolness and ambivalence set in once you entrust a narcissistic pursuer.

Now that they got you, the thrill is over. Unless they push you to do something you will later regret, or that's outside your comfort zone, such as participating in a threesome, a particularly humiliating sadomasochistic act, taking drugs, etc. If that is the case, you can be sure they will use it later to shame you and tell you that you've been *stained*, no one will ever want you.

The next day, Gabe, the Staff Sergeant instructor, approached me again. He asked me to go out with him for a drink after class. I declined. The day after that, he pushed harder until finally, I just gave in. I think he saw me as a lost, scared, little girl. As I said, I was skinny, with bad teeth due to the Tetracycline I was given when I had pneumonia. I was extremely self-conscious about the discoloration of my teeth. I had no self-esteem. Narcissists and predators have a sort of radar for the downtrodden. He wore me down. Then he began a methodical assault on my need to be loved and validated. We did not have a healthy relationship.

The definition of sexual harassment in education includes harassment by both peers and individuals in a position of power relative to the person being harassed. In schools, though sexual harassment initiated by students is most common, it can also be perpetrated by teachers or other school employees, and the victim can be a student, a teacher, or other school employees. Some have argued that even *consensual* sexual interactions between students and teachers, due to the inherent power over the student, "mutual consent" is impossible.

Before I met Gabe, I had been sexually active, but never had I been sexually satisfied. I had never had an orgasm. Gabe gave me my first orgasm.

In the book, *The Color Purple*, there is a scene where Celie tells Shug Avery what sex with Mister feels like to her.

Celie says Mister climbs on top of her and "do his business," making perfectly clear, Celie has never had a positive sexual experience. Shug decides Celie is, in Shug's opinion, still a virgin, since she has never had an orgasm.

Then Shug proceeds to teach Celie about her own body and makes love to Celie, giving Celie her first orgasm. From then on, Celie is obsessed with Shug. Later, Celie realizes, the orgasm is what she is obsessed with.

I became obsessed with the orgasm but confused this obsession with an obsession for Gabe. I was blind to the negatives. He was a Super Controlling Narcissist. Everything had to be done his way: I had to follow his rules and dress the way he thought was appropriate for any given situation. If I had an opinion, he reminded me I was too young to know what I was talking about.

Addicted[10b]

Narcissists use sex as a bonding tool to hook you on their energy. Sex can be an excellent instrument for inducing trance states, which is how they seize control of your attention.

Naturally, during deep sharing, all of your attention is on your partner. Using a method called bait-and-switch, they amplify the intensity and then quickly withdraw. It gives them a way to test how deeply invested you are in them.

If you are hooked, the emptiness that ensues as a result of their sudden retreat will make you crave more. This gives them huge bargaining power over you. Now they are free to start making demands and dropping suggestions. If you don't comply, you'll be starved of their sweet poison.

Many victims of severe mistreatment who stay in abusive relationships admit that the reason is that the sex was so good.

As I'm sure you are beginning to see, sex with a narcissist is a form of addiction, an escape from pain. What's 'crazy making' is that in abusive relationships, the oppressor serves both as the tormentor and the pacifier.

Instead of your drug of choice, in this form of addiction, we are dealing with powerful neurochemicals your own body produces, such as oxytocin, norepinephrine, dopamine, and cortisol.

Gabe told me what I would do and when. He made me attend functions with him that I did not want to attend. He took me to a couple of softball games he was playing in with his co-workers but told me not to talk to their wives. He also kept me from my friends. I never saw Irma again.

One weekend, Gabe took me camping to a lake where he raped me. He was forcefully trying to convince me to have sex with him in the water, surrounded by families with children. When he wouldn't take my attempts to dissuade him seriously, it became clear that I would have to scream and yell, or physically fight him off to make him stop groping me. I didn't want to draw attention to us, so I kept my mouth shut, hanging across my air mattress while he proceeded to rape me from behind in front of God and everyone on the shore. Of course, he didn't consider it rape. He felt he had convinced me that I wanted to have sex. A common misconception, when bullying someone to have sex, is that they've changed their minds. That is not the case. They've given in, which is not the same. At the time, I thought that was what had happened as well, even though I had tears running down my face the whole time. As a grown-ass woman, I realize now it was rape. *Not taking no for an answer is rape.*

Trauma Bonding[10c]

> A sexual relationship with a narcissist is characterized by intensity and almost otherworldly greatness. Especially when the heat is still on, and they use all the artillery in their arsenal to hook you in on their toxic juju. Trying to make an unforgettable impression, they pump you full of excitement and elation. It's like they are awakening something in you that's been dormant for ages.

But *intensity* is not *intimacy*!

To narcissists, the concept of intimacy is foreign. In order to have intimacy, there needs to be trust. That takes time to build. Both partners need to be empathic, listen clearly to the needs of the other, tune in, and immerse themselves into each other's world.

If you've been in a relationship with a narcissist, you know you can do that. But they cannot. The farthest they can go is to mirror you, pretend that they are there while their mind is completely elsewhere.

Instead of creating a bubble of security and trust, intensity introduces an element of danger. Danger, coupled with closeness creates a subconscious fear of loss, making your partner appear more attractive than he or she is. On a chemical level, coupled with oxytocin, cortisol makes for an extremely strong bonding cocktail.

The bond is rooted in trauma, not in genuine trust and respect. It is a one-sided affair meant to garner narcissistic supply.

By taking you on a roller-coaster ride, the narcissist is using you as a plaything. While it will vary from person to person, what they are after is to see reflected in your eyes the awe you feel as they raise you up and the despair as they drop you down. They crave the power they feel knowing that they've managed to blow your mind.

By week four or five at the Technical School, I flunked out. I was called in by a lieutenant who shamed me for flunking out of my class. The Air Force thought I had failed deliberately. What I didn't tell him was, one of the instructors at his school had kept me from even attempting to study. Gabe had made clear I wasn't to tell anyone we were in an exclusive relationship. The lieutenant asked me if I wanted to be discharged from the Air Force.

"No," I said. "I want to stay in the Air Force." So, he gave me three military occupations to choose from. I could go into road work, filling holes and working with hot asphalt. I could be a cook in the chow hall. Or I could go to work in the field of Transportation. I asked what Transportation entailed.

"Driving Generals around all day," he said.

"I want to go into Transportation," I told him.

Within the week, my things were packed and shipped to Montana.

At the same time, Gabe was reassigned to Chanute AFB, in Champaign County, Illinois. He *suggested* we get married, so I could join him at his new base. I agreed. I think I had known him for four or five weeks by this time. I couldn't tell him, *No.* I was never taught how to say *No* to anyone.

Before I left for Montana, he said to me, "We are both adults with needs, so until we are back together, we will have sex with other people. Just for the sex. There won't be any romantic attachment."

When I balked at the idea, he said, "I thought you'd be mature enough to agree." Wanting to prove I was a mature adult, at eighteen, I agreed.

Being sent to Montana probably saved my life. I dodged a bullet by not marrying him. I found friends who encouraged me, made me feel confident about myself and gave me the confidence to listen to my instincts, no matter my age. I had just turned nineteen.

When I talked about Gabe, my friends questioned why I would marry someone so controlling. One friend told me Gabe was the kind of man who would be physically abusive. I assured her he wouldn't. She asked what kinds of things he did to control me. She helped me to recognize where my relationship with Gabe was heading. She made it clear; physical abuse may well be in my future.

I was frightened of the confrontation, so I decided not to call him. I wrote him a letter telling him I had changed my mind. I had decided not to marry him. I told him I felt I needed to learn some independence.

He called. He was very nice. He seemed to understand completely. He said he had a trip to Seattle coming up. He told me he would be stopping in to see me.

I guess I hadn't made clear my intention. Not only would I not be marrying him, but I didn't want any relationship with him. Because saying *No* was not in my vocabulary, I agreed to his visit. When I told my friend about the call and his impending visit, she suggested I might not want to see him. The more I thought about the upcoming visit, the more I realized I was not confident in my emotional strength to face someone who was so emotionally demanding.

The day after agreeing to his visit, I called his new apartment; a woman answered his telephone. She put Gabe on the line. I didn't ask who she was or why she was answering his phone. I simply told him I didn't want him to come to see me on his way to Seattle. I told him I didn't think to see each other was a good idea, as I thought we should end our relationship altogether.

The phone line vibrated with his next words, "That's too bad. I was looking forward to a good fuck." He began yelling. His rage was extreme. I was so stunned and frightened, all I could do was hang up the phone and cry.

When I told my friend about the conversation, she thought I was crying about this other girl he'd already hooked up with. I told her I was crying because I had just realized how lucky I was to get away from him when I did.

Heinz Kohut explored a wide range of rage experiences in his seminal article *Thoughts on Narcissism and Narcissistic Rage*[11]

For Kohut, narcissistic rage is related to narcissists' need for total control of their environment, including "the need for revenge, for righting a wrong, for undoing a hurt by whatever means." It is an attempt by the narcissist to turn from a passive sense of victimization to an active role in giving pain to others, while at the same time attempting to rebuild their own (actually false) sense of self-worth. It may also involve self-protection and preservation, with rage serving to restore a sense of safety and power by destroying that which had threatened the narcissist.

Chapter 14

Not Fence Post! Not Fence Post!

When I first arrived at Malmstrom Air Force Base, I was picked up at the airport by SSgt. Meacham. He explained I would be attending several in-service seminars to familiarize myself with the base, as well as go over some of the safety issues concerning the extreme winter weather conditions exhibited in Great Falls, Montana.

The first thing I noticed about every single seminar I attended was that they all started with the same basic information. "Montana is called Big Sky Country for obvious reasons. In your off time, you will enjoy the best hunting and fishing anywhere in the country." Okay. I had very little interest in either of those activities.

One of the last seminars I attended was at the Community Center. The Director, a woman, began by saying, "I'm going to skip the part about fishing and hunting. No need to beat a dead horse." We all chuckled. Then she told us about the many forms of entertainment and services offered at the Community Center. Finally, she ended with, "If you have any suggestions for classes we might offer, or if you have a unique talent you would like to offer as a class, please feel free to let us know." I had met only a few of my co-workers and hadn't settled into Malmstrom as yet, so I offered to teach a class on shooting pool. I suggested we provide the service for women only, open to dependents as well as military personnel, alike. Free of charge, of course.

The director seemed to be happy; I had stepped forward to offer this service. We decided on Tuesdays and Thursdays, and I would have access to the pool room, which contained four 7-foot commercial tables. The coin mechanism was removed, so my students and I had access to the balls at will. The flyers were made and distributed by Community Center personnel. Flyers showed up at the Commissary, the Base Exchange, and at the gym and Chow Hall. I was surprised to see a flyer on the bulletin board at the entrance to my dormitory. They were all over the base.

I had about a half-dozen women in attendance at my first class. Coincidentally, they were all dependent wives. Most had no clue what a cue ball or cue stick was. None had ever held a cue stick, but what surprised me the most was the lady who said her husband had a pool table in the basement. He and their sons all shot pool together but refused to teach her how to play. She was the most motivated and became my best student. She picked up on everything I taught her. Having access to a table at home, she had plenty of time to practice. By the third or fourth class, she told me she had surprised her family by challenging them to a game. In 1977, her family had decided a woman couldn't learn to shoot pool. She proved them wrong.

None of the ladies dropped out of the class. In fact, by the second class, some of them had brought more friends. I can't remember how many weeks we did the class, but we had a lot of fun.

On my first day on the job, I walked to Warm Storage from my dormitory. Warm Storage was a large, metal building where they kept busses and large vehicles, specifically to protect them during cold weather. The building was the size of an airplane hangar, with plenty of room to maneuver large busses. There was even a place to wash the vehicles under cover from the elements. After meeting my co-workers, I discovered I would be washing buses for the foreseeable future while learning to operate anything from a forklift to a semi-tractor trailer, also known as an 18-wheeler.

My time in Ground Transportation was short. After learning to drive a 5-ton tractor-trailer, I made one delivery to the Commissary. I got licensed on a 44-passenger bus, which also got the 29-passenger bus automatically added to my license. I had only one lesson on a forklift. I never once chauffeured a General.

I accepted the offer of an office job — no more washing busses for me. I never again drove anything bigger than a 10-passenger van.

I was in Ground Transportation for only a few months before I got transferred to the Transportation Control Center. All of my vehicle training came to a halt for my new assignment. TCC was a fast-paced office, requiring a security clearance. The reason for the security clearance was for those times when missiles were being moved between sites.

Malmstrom AFB had two hundred Minuteman Missiles in the 1970s. The missiles got moved periodically, for reasons unknown to me. The security during a move was always on High Alert. The truck hauling the missile had several vehicles ahead, as well as following behind, providing security. The truck driver, or his co-pilot, checked-in with TCC every fifteen minutes.

The purpose of them checking-in every fifteen minutes was to assure us they were not under attack or experiencing any threat. On these occasions, the truck driver and his co-pilot had agreed on a code word to signal us of an imminent threat. At the end of each check-in, they would close by saying a random word, usually a word generated by something random they saw in the field. Any word would do, as long as it wasn't the code word for trouble.

The last time I was involved in one of these exercises, the driver notified us the code word would be Fence Post. At some point during the exercise, the driver told his passenger, a young recruit in training, to radio TCC. At the end of the young man's transmission, he looked around and nonchalantly said, "Fence Post." The driver began screaming, "No! Not Fence Post! Not Fence Post!" Too late. Air support was scrambled. The base commander was alerted. The City of Great Falls was alerted. We had to take action, all the while knowing that airman was having his little butt chewed up one side and down the other.

The winters around Malmstrom AFB were extreme. We had Winter Driving Seminars and Winter Safety Seminars. In 1980, two years after I left, Great Falls experienced a day when the temperature went from -32 to 15 above in seven minutes. Sudden *dropping* temperatures were common as well, and deadly. We were taught to keep food, blankets, and other safety equipment in our cars. Government vehicles were all fitted with safety equipment. Although twenty-foot drifts had been seen earlier in history, while I was there, we had six to eight-foot drifts. Great Falls is known for the Chinook Winds. These winds come down the East side of the Rocky Mountains at speeds up to 100 mph and raise the air temperature by 25 to 35 degrees in a matter of minutes. While this would melt the snow quickly, walking to and from work in those winds was challenging. I remember trying to get home one day, holding on to street signs and trees. I went from one to the next, any time the wind would die down enough for me to get to the next support.

When a military vehicle left one of the base facilities, the driver would check-in with TCC. Whether they were leaving the base heading to a missile site or traveling between missile sites, a travel ticket was created for their vehicle. The ticket was put in a position on our vehicle tracking board, showing they were in transit. It was all done manually, with pen and paper, old school style. On this ticket, was their ETA, Estimate Time of Arrival. Close tabs were kept on all the vehicles in the field, knowing how long it should take to drive between any two locations. Most, but not all, of the vehicles had a radio on which they kept in contact with TCC. When they arrived at their destination, they would radio-in. If they didn't have a radio, they would use one of the phones at the site to check-in. When TCC didn't hear from them within a few minutes of their anticipated arrival time, we called them on their radio, or we called the site to see if they had arrived but hadn't had a chance to call us yet. Because the weather was so extreme, it was critical we knew where they were at all times. The drivers were responsible for checking-in, at which time they would get a code-key matching their Travel Ticket to prove, if for whatever reason it became necessary, they had checked-in.

There was only one time while I was on duty, that I had to initiate a helicopter safety check. The driver didn't check-in, and his truck didn't have a radio. He was supposed to have called when he arrived at his destination. The crew at the missile site said he hadn't shown up. We called for air support. A helicopter was sent to find the driver and his vehicle, flying along the route. The temperatures were so cold, and the driver only had a limited amount of time before he would freeze to death. The helicopter found the truck, with the driver inside. The truck had broken down a few miles from his destination. There was nothing for him to do but hunker down and wait. Luckily, the rescue team arrived within thirty minutes of his estimated time of arrival. Airmen depended on us. We needed to know where they were at all times. Knowing was literally a matter of life and death.

One morning, I got a call from a second lieutenant. Second lieutenants, the lowest commissioned officer rank in the U.S. Air Force, are known to be brash. Something about them being so young and fresh out of the Academy made some of them feel the need to go on a power trip. Not all second lieutenants, of course, but enough that it's a standing joke. This particular second lieutenant said, "I'm leaving the base. Give me my code-key." Very abrupt.

I asked him, "Sir, what is your destination?"

"You don't need to know my destination," he told me.

"Sir," I said. "I need to know your destination before I can give you your code-key."

"Listen here, Airman. I don't have to tell you a damn thing. I'm ordering you to give me my goddamn code-key, so I can leave, or I'm going to be late for my meeting."

"Sir," I repeated. "I need to know your destination before I can give you your code-key." The lieutenant hung up on me.

I reported the incident to my supervisor, who said, "No problem. I'll take care of it." He went into his office, closed the door, and made a phone call. A few minutes later, he came out of the office with a smile on his face. He said I should be expecting a call from the lieutenant. Shortly thereafter, the lieutenant called. He apologized for his abruptness and gave me his destination. I gave him his code key.

My supervisor explained to me, when one of their troops is rude or inconsiderate, a superior officer is embarrassed. In fact, if a complaint goes higher up the chain, the captain or major can get their butt chewed for not keeping their troops in line. Being rude to an airman is similar to being rude to the wait staff at a restaurant, which is considered unacceptable.

When I first began working in Warm Storage, I was introduced to everyone on the crew. On Monday of my second week, a guy came in I hadn't met because he was on leave when I arrived at the base. I was across the building with another female airman, who later became a good friend. When I saw the young man, who was returning from leave, enter the building. I asked Barbie, "Who's he?"

She looked up at about the same time all the other airmen around the office began yelling greetings and clapping this guy on the back. They were obviously happy to see him.

"Oh, that's Dan. He's been home visiting his family," she said.

I remember thinking, *Wow, what a good-looking guy, and what a great laugh.* His laugh was one of the first things I noticed about him and the way his face lit up when he laughed.

We walked over to the office, which was a corner of the building, separated from the vehicles by four-foot-tall half-walls. Within the walls sat a couple of desks, some file cabinets, a sofa or two. The crew was all standing around, drinking coffee, talking, and getting ready for our day to begin. Barbie introduced me to Dan. We each said hello before beginning our day.

Friday, after work, they all decided to go to a small local lake to go swimming. I was invited to join them. Larry, one of the guys, offered to pick me up, along with the other two girls from our dorm. When we arrived at the lake, everybody else was already there. Dan and Larry decided to swim out to a little island in the lake. We all thought they were crazy, but off they went. They made their way to the island okay, where they sat down for a rest. I found out later. Dan had asked Larry if he and I were together. Larry told him I wasn't with anyone.

We all swam for an hour or so; then somebody suggested we all get cleaned up and head to a little bar in town.

Now, I was in my environment. There were a couple of pool tables, some pinball machines, the usual. I stepped up to the table nearest me, placed my quarter on the side, and challenged the winner to a game. A couple of guys from town were playing. They seemed surprised but agreed I would play the winner of their game. My co-workers all looked surprised and asked me if I could play. "My mother used to own a little beer bar," I told them.

I was never as good as my sister at shooting pool, but I have definitely won my share of games on a pool table. I won my game against the townie. Dan jumped up, suggesting he and I team up as partners against the two townies. I think Dan's suggestion was partly to keep the guys from feeling like a bunch of "Airheads" had come to town and taken over their table, which was always a concern when airmen go to town. Also, I think he wanted to make a move on me. As I was getting ready to sink the eight-ball, he came over and said, "How about a kiss for luck?"

I said, "Well, I think I'm going to need some luck to make this shot, so yeah, a kiss for luck." Dan gave me a little kiss; I called my shot and then sank the eight-ball for the win.

Chapter 15

I Forbid You to Get Married

*W*hen we first got to the bar, I ordered a beer and a shot of Southern Comfort. Yes, I was trying to impress them. After all, I had just turned nineteen. I thought I needed to impress. They questioned me about my drink choices. I told them that Southern Comfort was my favorite hard liquor, so then they called my bluff. One of the guys asked if I liked Everclear. I had to be honest. I said I'd never heard of Everclear. He ordered a shot for everybody. Most of the guys did their shot; the girls did half a shot. I did my shot, as well as what was left of somebody else's half shot. *I was an idiot, thinking I was cool.* Typical teenager, I got so wasted!

Dan offered to drive me back to my dormitory. Larry offered to ride with us. I sat in the middle, between the guys. Larry had his window down, so I leaned against Dan, threw my feet across Larry, sticking them out the window. As we started to pull up to the gate to get back on base, Dan suggested I sit up. I'm sure I made a great impression.

Later, Dan got in the habit of spending the day with me at work. Then, he would call me in the evening to see if I wanted to go out, which I always did, but I realized I didn't like the message that was sending him: that I was always available when he called. Why didn't he ask me at work? Was he waiting to see if a better offer came along? Maybe I was over-thinking his motives, but I wanted to have some self-respect. This was new to me, so I had to give some thought to how I would proceed. I went to my friend's room to ask what she thought I should do. Barbie agreed we should make plans to go to Ladies Night at a club in town. If he called, I would just tell him I had other plans. Sure enough, he called.

I said, "I'm going to Ladies Night at a club with some girls, then we're heading to the Red Barn. Maybe I'll see you there."

We did as we had planned, then headed to the Red Barn. As soon as we walked through the door, I spotted Dan at the back of the room playing pool. He had stopped to see who was coming through the door. He laid his cue down, coming right over to me. From then on, he made sure to make plans with me before I had a chance to make plans with someone else. I made sure our plans usually included our friends, too. I didn't want to be with someone who would try to keep me from my friends. Been there, done that!

Dan and I had been dating for a few weeks before we decided to take our relationship to the next level. Dan asked his roommate to let us have the room for the night. When we got to the room, we removed our clothes and got under the covers. We spent the next hour or two, just talking. We talked and talked. We laughed, we cuddled, and we kissed. Everything was perfect. For the first time, someone had not just climbed on, going for the gold. I felt significant. I felt like I was a real person to him, not just a piece of ass. No one had ever made me feel respected before. Then, we actually made love.

Dan held me like I was important to him. We didn't know each other well enough for the sex to be great. We were so young, but in time we found our groove. For the time being, what we had was more than just sex. I've never felt more important to someone than I did with Dan, the first time we were together. That feeling intensified as time went on. Dan told me that he felt making love was as emotionally close as two people could get. That should be the definition of Making Love, as opposed to sex without an emotional connection.

Dan got an offer to transfer from Warm Storage to the Food Distribution Warehouse at about the same time I got transferred to TCC. They had a small crew, just four guys, plus a supervisor. Every morning, they would load up a five-ton refrigerated truck to deliver supplies to the individual missile sites. He loved making those runs to deliver food to the off-base sites. Dan made some good friends on the crew.

Dan would call me at TCC to get his code as he was leaving for the drive to the missile site. When he arrived, he would call me again. One day he called from a little bar out in the sticks. He said their truck had broken down. They had walked back to the nearest business to use the phone. The weather was nice, so they were safe. We just needed to send a mechanic out to get their truck going again. I was very glad we weren't in the middle of winter, or their little adventure could have gone terribly wrong.

When I first arrived at Malmstrom AFB, Dan had been home on leave visiting his parents. While he was home, he talked to a friend of his from high school. The father of his friend had some pull with the Coast Guard. Dan asked him if he could help get him transferred from the Air Force to the Coast Guard. Leaving for the Coast Guard was the plan when Dan got back to Malmstrom. However, when he got back to work, he found out he had orders to go to Germany. Dan told his Coast Guard connection he would be staying with the Air Force. Dan was going to Germany.

By the time I got to know Dan, he already had plans in place to go to Germany. I told myself that I wasn't going to fall in love with this guy. In fact, I told him I wasn't going to fall in love with him because I wasn't looking for that. He agreed that it was probably for the best. We would just have some fun until he left for Germany, which was in about five months.

Robert Burns said, in 1785, "The best-laid schemes of mice and men, often go askew." Truer words were never spoken. As we neared the time of Dan's departure, I realized I was crazy about this guy. I did not want him to leave me, but when you join the military, you agree to do what they tell you to do. You go where they tell you to go. You can't say, *meh, that doesn't sound like something I want to do*.

Dan was due to report to his next assignment on Monday, the second day of January 1978. He had decided to spend the whole month of December at home, with his family. By now, we had been together for five months. Dan sold his car to one of his friends. All of his belongings, which all fit in a small crate, were shipped to Hessisch Oldendorf, Germany. We had made plans that I would drive him to the airport, where we would say our goodbyes. That was tough, but we said goodbye without any tears.

As I drove away from the airport, I thought, W*ell, that's the last time I'll see him. Buck up! You're going to have to get over him.*

All evening, I moped around my room. I was nineteen years old. This couldn't be the end of the world. Then the phone rang. Dan was calling me. He asked me if I would like to come to Tacoma to spend Christmas with his family. He said he had discussed the possibility with his parents. They were looking forward to meeting me. Of course, I said, "Yes!"

A couple of days later, I got a letter from Dan. The next day, I got another letter from him. His handwriting is wretched, to this day, but he was writing to me. That had to mean something. I was writing to him just as often. We were making plans for when we both got out of the Air Force. His assignment was for only eighteen months. We both knew how to drive trucks, although I would need a lot more training. We planned to get our CDL licenses when we got out of the Air Force. We would become a cross-country truck-driving team. I knew we sounded like two little kids trying to plan for a future together, but I was enjoying the fantasy.

Then, I just stopped — reality set-in. We were silly. For one thing, I didn't want to be a cross country truck-driver, so in my next letter I told him we were making all these big plans; they were never going to happen. I told him he would probably fall in love with some little Fraulein and get married while he was in Germany. He wrote back that he didn't want that to happen. He said in his letter, "What if we get married while you're here for Christmas? Then you can join me in Germany." I believe I mentioned his terrible handwriting. I went to my friend for confirmation. I asked her, "Does this say what I think it says?"

She read that portion of the letter and said, "He's asking you to marry him!"

"That's what I thought," I replied. "What should I do?"

She didn't give me any advice, except to say, "Call him."

I went back to my room. When I called his parent's house, Dan answered the phone. I said, "I got a letter from you today."

"You did?" he said.

"Yeah, but I'm not sure I read this paragraph right," I hinted at the proposal.

"What do you think that paragraph said?" he asked me.

I hemmed and hawed, "I'm not sure. Sounds like a proposal."

"You read it right," he said.

"Maybe you should clarify?" I asked him.

He laughed that distinctive, full body laugh of his. He said, "Will you marry me?"

"Yes!" I said, "I will."

Dan replied to my teasing with some of his own, "You will, what?"

My turn to laugh, "I will marry you!"

I put in for a week of vacation, which got approved. I left Great Falls on December 20th. Dan picked me up at Seattle-Tacoma Airport. We headed to his parent's home, the house in which he had grown up. As he turned into a neighborhood, I began to notice there were large, elegant homes. I looked at him in a panic. I asked, "Is this how you grew up? Is your family rich?"

He began to laugh. "No. This is a shortcut to my neighborhood." He made a couple more turns, at which point we entered a neighborhood that made me more comfortable. We arrived at a small, neat little ranch-style house. When we came through the door, his parents were there to meet me. Betty, his mother, and Lee, his stepfather, both met me at the door with open arms. I immediately felt comfortable. They made me welcome in their home. Dan and his brother, Glen, were the only kids at home. Dan's two sisters, who were married to Navy men, were living out of state. Glen, who was in the Army, had come home for Christmas as well. Dan and his brother shared their childhood bedroom. I got the third bedroom, which had once been the room his two sisters shared.

That evening, Dan's mother served spaghetti for dinner. We were happily chatting away when Dan's Dad made some smart-ass comment to me. I turned to Lee, without missing a beat, throwing his smart-ass tone right back in his face. My humor and my lifestyle were both far more "adult" than that of most teenagers. My mother owned a bar, my home away from home since I was fifteen years old. I had been waiting tables, serving drinks in bars, since I was seventeen. Adults, I could handle. Dan's mother choked on her dinner, laughing out loud. She said, "Oh, you are going to fit right in here. Anybody that can give crap back to Lee can hold her own in this family."

Dan and I went shopping for Christmas gifts the next day, December twenty-first. We also went to the courthouse, where we applied for a marriage license. We were told that our license would be ready on Tuesday, the twenty-seventh, as Monday the courthouse was closed for the long holiday weekend. We told her that I had to be on a plane headed back to Montana on the twenty-seventh. We were obviously panicked. She said she had another couple with similar circumstances. She had agreed to meet them at her office on Monday the twenty-sixth at ten that morning. She said if we were there on time, she would give us our license as well. We assured her we would be there on time.

I met Dan's friends, as well as their girlfriends. Dan had been friends with Dave since the fifth grade. Dave was going to marry Sherry in January. Dan had originally agreed to be the best man, but since his orders came in, he wouldn't be able to attend their wedding, let alone be in it, so Dan asked Dave to be *his* best man. I asked Dave's fiancé, Sherry, to be my maid of honor. They both agreed.

I had planned to buy a dress when I got to Tacoma but forgot to pack my checkbook, and I didn't own a credit card. I refused to ask Dan's parents to help out, so I just decided I would wear my brown corduroy slacks with a cream color pull-over blouse I had packed. Very casual. Dan's folks had gotten married just ten years earlier, at a small community church. Lee suggested it might be fun if we got married in the same church. Dan called to make an appointment to speak with the pastor of the church. He asked us a few questions before agreeing to officiate. The date was set. We were getting married on December twenty-sixth, the day after Christmas.

On Christmas day, I called my mother to let her know. I began by wishing her a Merry Christmas. I told her what I had gotten for Christmas, ending with the drip coffee pot Dan and I had received from Dave and Sherry as a wedding gift. She asked, "Why would someone give you a drip coffee pot for Christmas?"

I said, "Well, actually, that was a wedding gift. Dan and I are getting married tomorrow."

She blew up, "No! You are not getting married. I *forbid* you to get married!"

I was prepared for just such a reaction. I kept my cool. I didn't get excited or cry like I normally did with her. I simply said, "I'm over eighteen. I'm an adult serving in the Air Force. I don't need your permission. I was just calling to tell you."

That shut her up. Mother blew out a breath. She simply said, "You're right. Okay. Well, if you decide you've made a mistake, you can always get divorced."

Thanks, Mom.

Next, I called my father. Dad was never one to get angry, so I wasn't afraid of that, but what he did say shocked me to my core. "Are you pregnant?" That was my father's only question because I hung up the phone. He had no way to call me back. And I didn't wish to speak to him any longer.

I wasn't a virgin, but I hadn't been with every Tom, Dick, and Harry. Granted, I had made some bad decisions. I had slept with a few men. Men who had taken advantage of me. Used me, then threw me away like used toilet paper. His question, or accusation, hurt deeply.

Some years later he apologized.

December twenty-sixth was upon us. Our wedding day. We had ordered corsages for the girls, and boutonnières for the guys. I thought it was a silly tradition, considering what I was wearing. Dan would be in brown corduroy bibbed overalls. But Lee, Dan's stepfather, insisted. He said it wouldn't be a proper wedding without flowers.

Dave and Sherry drove us to the church, which was still decorated for Christmas with a couple of hundred Poinsettias. Dan's parents and his brother, Glen, attended the ceremony. Dan's other best friend, Steven, was our photographer. Steven's family moved to the area when the boys were in sixth grade. Dan and Steven played sports together. All three boys were tight.

After the ceremony, we went back to the house, where the parents of Dave and Steven, all joined us to celebrate. They had watched Dan grow up. He was like another son in each of their homes. Some of Lee and Betty's friends came to the reception, as well. We had ordered a small cake and a single bottle of champagne to toast the occasion.

We had a small, quiet little wedding, but we loved it. We talk about our wedding to this day, forty-plus years later. Ours was unique, like no other, and, we didn't start out married life in debt. *Bonus!*

We left the house to spend our wedding night at the Holiday Inn, driving a car the guys had decorated. The back window said, *Just Married.* A car full of teenage boys pulled up beside us. They started spraying us with a fire extinguisher. They were laughing and saying, "Congratulations!" They were having some innocent fun with us.

The next morning, Dan took me to the airport. I believe I did cry at that time, but I knew we'd see each other again. I just didn't know when.

Part 3

Reprieve. noun

re-prieve - ri-ˈprēv

A temporary respite as from pain or trouble.

I moved 5,000 miles away to avoid the pain.

Dan's parents, Lee and Betty, with Dan and me, shortly following our wedding. December 26, 1977.

Chapter 16

Roots at The Chow Hall

*B*efore I left for Tacoma, I had told our friends we might be getting married while I was there, although it was in no way, a "done deal." As I had learned growing up with my mother, nothing was a "done deal" until it happened.

When I got back from Tacoma, a married woman, I chose to change my name, which meant getting a new military identification card and driver's license. There were new name tags for all my uniforms to be ordered, and I had to put in for an assignment change. I could only hope the Air Force would approve a Compatible Assignment. Dan applied for a Compatible Assignment on his end as well, which meant his Unaccompanied eighteen-month assignment needed to be modified to an Accompanied Assignment. My new Accompanied Assignment, as are all A.A.s, would be for three-years. Dan had to extend his assignment time at Hessisch Oldendorf to cover my time in the country.

We got really lucky. The people on Dan's end actually created a job for me. They had a one-person office: Driver's Training, Education and Licensing. The office did all of the testing and licensing of all military as well as dependent drivers on base. Hessisch Oldendorf Air Station wasn't even big enough to be called a Base. One person had been enough. Luckily for me, they decided they could use a second person in the office, an airman to work for the NCOIC, non-commissioned officer in charge.

Dan and I had known each other for five months when we got married. We were separated for the next four months. My goal in writing this book is to show all of my own flaws, as well as how all the narcissists throughout my life affected me. I admit to all the bad choices I have made, as well as the mistakes based on my upbringing. I was not taught great morals. In fact, my education at home was lacking in so many life lessons that I was not prepared for a world without my mother making all of my decisions for me. I was trying to be a functioning adult, but I lacked the skills. Over time, I learned these things through my husband, the people I went on to meet throughout my life, Life Coaches, and therapists.

During the four months that I was separated from Dan, I began to question my decision to get married. Mother was writing to me. Knowing my new husband was in another country, she questioned my decision. Had I rushed into marriage? Had I made a mistake? And then there were all the single guys on base, and all my friends were single. Maybe I should just get an annulment.

I received my first letter from Dan, with a return address I could write to, a month after he arrived in Germany. Once his first letter arrived, they were coming almost daily. This was in 1978. Each letter took four weeks to arrive at its destination.

I also received my orders to join him at Hessisch Oldendorf Air Station. His letters were so encouraging, filled with love and impatience to reunite. I began to remember why I had married him in the first place. I never did anything to be ashamed of during that time, although I did think about it. That's hard to admit, but it's the truth.

I decided I was going to join him and give our marriage one hundred percent of myself. I'm so thankful I did.

I flew to Germany in April of 1978. I landed in Hamburg, where my husband was waiting to drive me home. We hadn't actually seen each other in four months. Other than all the letters we had written, we didn't know each other very well. We had a two-hour drive.

Germany is a beautiful country, so green, so clean. There wasn't any trash on the sides of the road. However, there were billboards with pictures of topless women, advertising who-knows-what. Later, I discovered they were promoting nude beaches at vacation resorts.

Dan was working in the 600 CSS Transportation Division at Hessisch Oldendorf Air Station. One of their duties was to send a driver, in a military vehicle, to the Hamburg airport when new airmen arrived to be assigned at Hessisch Oldendorf, Germany, also known as the HOG. The day I arrived, they gave the assignment to Dan. Luckily, I was the only one flying in that day, or riding in the car with us might have been terribly awkward for the unlucky airman.

Dan drove us directly to the Transportation office. I met everyone in the Transportation Unit. Then we walked over to the office where I would be working. I met my new Supervisor, a Technical Sergeant, Sergeant Walt Howard. He was the most welcoming person I have ever met.

After introductions, we got in the car Dan had bought for us, a dark green Audi. The Audi was a great looking car, with four-on-the-floor. We soon realized there was a problem the previous owner hadn't disclosed; the transmission kept slipping. The lever in the car connects to a control shaft, which pivots on a ball fulcrum. The problem we began to have was where the shaft pivoted on the ball fulcrum. The shaft began popping off when we downshifted. We'd have to pull over, pop the hood, reach in and put the shaft back on the ball fulcrum. As the problem began to persist, we got rid of the car.

Dan took me to our first home together. My supervisor, Sergeant Howard, was married to the woman who ran the Off-Base Housing Office. Being fluent in the language, because German was her first language, she was the perfect choice to run the office. She had helped Dan find a place just a few blocks off base. We rented a space in a large single-family home. The owners had closed off some rooms at the back of their home, creating a small apartment. The apartment had one bedroom, a small living room, an even smaller kitchen, and a private bathroom. We parked on the street and came through the gate, where we were greeted by three long-haired Dachshunds. They were always so happy to see us. Personally, I don't think those dogs understood a word we were saying to them.

At the back of a lovely garden and courtyard, there was a set of stairs, carved into the hillside, going up to our apartment. Ours was a perfectly lovely, comfortable little apartment in which to begin our married lives. Dan had gotten furniture from the base at a deep, deep discount. You can't beat Free. They let us keep the furnishings for a year, which gave us time to save some money to buy our own furniture. We bought a used couch, chairs and end tables from the German civilians who worked on base with us and ordered bedroom furniture from AAFES, the Army Air Force Exchange Service.

The best thing about living in Germany at the time, as a young married couple, was learning to depend solely on one another. I can state categorically; if my mother had been there to influence me, my marriage would not have lasted. We didn't have the internet and making a phone call to the United States was so expensive, the only time we did call home was when our daughter was born.

Dan ended up getting really sick shortly after I arrived, in fact, so soon after I arrived, I didn't even have a driver's license. Dan had come down with Mononucleosis. After receiving treatment, his whole body turned purple. The doctor on base, of which there was only one, insisted Dan had to come in every day if he wasn't going to go to work; it was an Air Force policy. Dan went in when he first got sick, but the first morning he woke up purple, he literally had to crawl on all fours to get to the bathroom. He was so weak; there was no way to get out to the car. Even if he could get to the car, he would have to drive us to the base.

I walked up to the base, went to work, and told Sergeant Howard what was going on. I told him I'd have to go to the Aid Station to report just how sick my husband really was. Sergeant Howard went with me, making my husband's condition abundantly clear to the doctor on staff. We told the doctor what had been happening since Dan had begun taking Ampicillin. The doctor said Dan was having an allergic reaction to the Ampicillin and gave me another prescription for him. Then, he gave me a note for Dan's supervisor, saying Dan would be out for a week.

During this time, the base was showing an episode of *Roots* every evening at the Chow Hall. During the week, Dan was stuck in bed, unconscious, and I walked up to the base to watch the show. I hadn't met too many people yet, so I always sat alone. This was my initiation to the little air station in Germany.

Dan and I rarely stayed home when we weren't at work. We loved exploring the little town of Hessisch Oldendorf, as well as other little communities in the North of Germany. We visited a small town by the name of Hameln, located just twelve kilometers from our home in Hessisch Oldendorf. The English name is Hamelin, well known for being the home of the legendary rat catcher. *The Pied Piper of Hamelin* has gone from legend to folklore.

> "The earliest known record of this story is from the town of Hamelin itself, depicted in a stained glass window created for the church of Hamelin, which dates to

around 1300. Although the church was destroyed in 1660, several written accounts of the tale have survived."[12]

Every Sunday, from May to September, townsfolk reenact the story in the town square. Like most towns in Germany, the architecture dates back hundreds of years. Hessisch Oldendorf and Hameln are located on the River Weser, a truly beautiful part of the country.

One day, we decided to drive to Ellrich, Germany. We had been told about an interesting memorial to Nazi-era crimes in a forced labor camp. We were able to walk around the outside, but of all the days to go, they were closed on the day we went. To be perfectly honest, what we did see was so depressing, I'm not sure I could have done the underground tour. We drove as far East as possible, where we got out to hike the rest of the way. When we saw the barbed wire fence and the guard tower on the East German side, we turned back. The people in the tower had binoculars with which to watch us. Of course, they were armed as well. This was, after all, The Iron Curtain.

The Cold War, which followed World War II, began between 1946 and 1947 when the United States challenged the Soviet power. The Berlin Blockade (24 June 1948 – 12 May 1949) was one of the first major international crises of the Cold War. The Soviet Union blocked the Western Allies railway, roads, and canal access, cutting off all supplies getting into Western Berlin. Western Allies including the United States Air Force, the Royal Air Force, the French Air Force, the Royal Canadian Air Force, the Royal Australian Air Force, the Royal New Zealand Air Force and the South African Air Force organized the Berlin Airlift. Over 200,000 sorties were flown in one year, providing the West Berliners with necessities such as fuel and food.

With the concrete wall separating West Berlin from East Berlin and other parts of Soviet Occupied Germany, there was also the longer Inner German Border, which came to symbolize the "Iron Curtain."

The Eastern German government announced on 9 November 1989 that all German Democratic Republic citizens could visit West Germany and West Berlin. The "fall of the Berlin Wall" officially took place on 3 October 1990.

We also enjoyed driving forty minutes to Hannover for their Old Town Flea Market, which is held on Saturdays. Located along the River Leine, both sides of the river have improvements including paved paths and garden walkways. The vendor's set-up along both sides of the river, as well as along the walking bridges crossing the river at regular intervals.

Dan and I discovered two movie theaters showing English speaking movies. One was located in Hamelin, near a British Military Installation. The other was near another British Military Installation in Buckeburg. This one was a much nicer theater that we liked to frequent. We never knew what would be playing, but tickets were inexpensive, and we discovered we both enjoyed watching movies.

My supervisor, Sergeant Howard, and his wife, Mary, had decided to take a Night Train to West Berlin. They asked us to join them. Dan and I consider our trip to West Berlin to be our honeymoon. Just like our wedding, our honeymoon was uniquely "*Us!*"

We all boarded the Night Train in Bremerhaven. Our Military I.D.s or Passports and necessary Russian-translated papers were taken by U.S. Army Personnel as we boarded the train. As we crossed into Communist East Germany, the train stopped. All the papers were inspected by Soviet officials in Marienborn. We peeked out of the curtains, which had all been closed. The train station at which we were stopped looked like an old black and white movie: people mulling around in uniforms, carrying weapons, looking like a newsreel from 1945. Finally, we had begun the 110-mile journey through Communist Eastern Germany.

After going through the same procedure before returning to Free Germany, we were returned our I.D.s and Passports. We continued through to West Berlin. A short bus ride later, we arrived at our government-issued hotel rooms, where we got cleaned up and began our tour of West Berlin.

Walt and Mary went one way; we went another. Dan and I walked our butts off throughout the day. We were specifically looking for the Berlin Wall. At one point, we stopped to take pictures of a beautiful old building with bullet holes all over the surface. Dan was leaning back against a concrete wall looking up to take pictures when I asked, "What is *that* you're leaning against?" We realized he had been leaning against *The Wall.* Nothing like what we were expecting, the structure came as a shock, just a plain, concrete wall. A tower with stairs was nearby for tourists to climb. These towers made it possible to look over the wall, into East Berlin. The first thing we noticed about all of these observation towers was there were towers on the other side, at exactly the same intervals. Every time we climbed to the top of one, there were Soviet soldiers in the opposing tower watching us. For fifty yards beyond the wall, on the Eastern side, there were mines and then a batch of cross timbers lined with barbed wire. The buildings just beyond the barbed wire timbers were empty. These buildings resembled two and three-story apartments, but we were told people were not allowed to live on the side of the building with windows looking out toward freedom. As usual, everything seemed to be in shades of gray.

We walked down brick-lined streets, where the houses butted up against the street and had windows and doors filled in with bricks.

Thus, the windows of these houses, which had previously looked out at the street, now became part of The Wall. The pamphlet we carried told us these homes had all been bricked up in one day. If family members weren't home at that time, they were never allowed to return. Husbands were separated from wives, mothers separated from children.

There were several memorials along the streets. Family members had erected them for other family members who had tried to escape to Free Germany. Families on the western side installed three six-foot-long 4" x 4" timbers into the ground, standing upright in a triangular pattern. The timbers were then wrapped in barbed wire and a placard attached which bore the name of the deceased, their birth date and the day they died. Each person had been shot down by Soviet soldiers in his or her attempt to join their family. We saw a memorial with dates, showing that one woman had tried to escape the Soviet Zone on her 40th birthday.

The next day, after a good night's sleep, Walt and Mary suggested we all take a bus tour, which was great and so much better than walking. We saw all the famous sights: The Brandenburg Gate and Check Point Charlie. Grosser Tiergarten and Victory Memorial, Charlottenburg Palace, and The Kaiser Wilhelm Memorial Church.

Later in the evening, I convinced Dan we needed to go to a burlesque show, since when would we ever get another chance to see a burlesque show? I didn't know, but he swears I purposely got him to this particular burlesque show, a show one hundred percent drag. The show was outstanding! We had a ton of fun, and Dan was Baptized in the Church of Drag.

Contact with my mother during our time in Germany was limited to letter writing, which was a good way for us to communicate, as she wasn't able to intimidate me. She still had a great deal of influence on me, but she didn't attempt to push too much.

Lisa got married in July of 1978. She asked if there was any way I could be there, to be her matron-of-honor, but, of course, we couldn't afford for me to fly to Oklahoma.

Dan and I spent the first three years of our marriage in Germany, where we learned to depend on each other with no outside influences.

Chapter 17

Mother Gets Her Revenge

*A*fter about six months, we found a single-family house to rent in Schaumburg, just ten minutes from the base. On the hill, just above our house, was Schaumburg Castle.

The house had two bedrooms and one bathroom. The kitchen had a small refrigerator, but we didn't keep too many groceries at once. All of the meat at our commissary came up from Sembach AFB, in the south of Germany. When they got fresh meat, the older meat was frozen and shipped to us. Most people on our base bought preparations for a meal or two at a time. In the Wintertime, I could keep our drinks on the ledge outside the kitchen window, freeing up space in the refrigerator.

Something we never got used to was The Schaumburg Witch. That's what we called her. Now and then, when we drove home in the evening, we would turn the corner, and our headlights would hit this little old woman, stooped and wearing all black. She would raise her cane over her head and shake it at us. We just knew she was putting a curse on us.

In the winter of 1978, we experienced the first ice storm either of us had ever witnessed. A warning had come into the base of the impending severe weather, and some offices were closing early to let their people get home before the ice hit. But our office manager, MSgt. Stiles refused to let us leave. He lived on base, just minutes away, so I suppose he wasn't too worried. When he finally gave us the word to go, it was too late to avoid the ice.

Dan and I had gotten about halfway home when we came upon a pile of cars. The pavement, covered in ice, had a slight incline and curved to the left. Every vehicle trying to get up and around would slide sideways down into the pile of cars at the lower side of the road. Dan got off on the edge of the road, in the dirt, and he was able to get traction. We made it up and around the pile of cars only to be stopped again when we got to a tiny little hamlet in the road.

Although we were in the middle of an ice storm, the outside temperature was right at freezing. Without any wind, the air temperature felt warm. There were cars pulled off to the sides all over the streets of this tiny little village. An airman from our base was standing outside, helping drivers get their vehicles safely maneuvered off the road. He insisted we park our car and come into his place.

When I say *the house was filthy*, I may be understating the fact. We're talking the middle of winter, and the insides of the windows had live flies. They were breeding somewhere in the house. The children were super friendly, wanting to hug and kiss on us, but the snot on their faces made me want to gag.

I asked to use the bathroom shortly after we arrived. I went down the hall and walked into a nightmare. The bathtub was full of clothes, soaking in water covered in a scum so thick, there might have been a body under the surface. And there were flies nesting all over the expanse. I could not get out of there fast enough. How much time had gone by since that bathtub was used for its intended purpose?

I told Dan we had to get home. I had left the slow cooker on when we left the house earlier in the morning. So, we got the hell out of there and walked the rest of the way home. We might have had a four or five-kilometer walk to the house if we had stayed on the road. Instead, we walked across the plowed fields. The ice cracked and crunched under our shoes, but neither of us fell, and we made good time getting home. When we got to the top of our street, we squatted down, sitting on our heels, and slid down the street on the leather soles of our shoes. As we came alongside our walkway, we reached out and grabbed the bushes to stop ourselves. Then we crawled to the front door and let ourselves inside to the warmth. Holy Smokes! What an adventure. We were so happy to be home, and we did have a roast waiting for us in the slow cooker.

Our friends, Bob and Terri, had a baby boy while we were living in Schaumburg. Before we got married, I told Dan I didn't want children, which is what my mother had drilled into me. He said he was okay with not having children. But, after Bob and Terri had their baby, I got the fever. We discussed the possibility of having a child, and Dan said, "Whatever you want is okay with me. It's your body, and you have to make that decision. Just know, I'm okay with whatever you decide." We decided to have a baby. Like rabbits, we worked to get pregnant. After the third month without getting pregnant, we decided to stop *trying* and just let nature take its course. Of course, I got pregnant immediately.

I had written a letter to my sister, Lisa, telling her we were trying to get pregnant. I asked her not to tell Mother. I said, "I'll tell her when, and if, I get pregnant."

At about the same time, Mother had some foot surgery and was in the hospital when Lisa got my letter. Lisa told me in her next letter what had happened. She said she and her husband had gone to the hospital to visit our mother. Mother asked if she'd heard anything from me recently, and Lisa said, "Yes. I got a letter from her today." She went to hand the letter to my mother when her husband asked if she should be showing Mother the letter. Lisa yanked the letter back from Mother. This, of course, infuriated Mother. We were keeping a secret from her, which did not sit well with Mother. Lisa apologized but said she had been asked to keep this particular information to herself.

The next thing I know, I'm receiving letters from both of them. Lisa was apologizing for her part. And Mother giving me hell for keeping a secret from her. By this time, I knew I was pregnant. I wrote to Mother and simply said Dan and I had decided to have a baby and I didn't want to *worry her* until we knew for sure. I lied. The truth is, I didn't want to hear all her reasons not to have a baby.

When I heard from her next, she didn't mention the pregnancy, *at all.* She had written to say she booked a flight to come to visit us. Let the anxiety begin. I literally, and I do mean *literally,* told my husband not to let her near me when we got close to any stairs. I think he thought I was kidding, but I made my point very clear, it was no joke. When I use the word, literally; I literally use it in the most literal of terms. I didn't trust her, and the timing was questionable.

Years later, I was proven right, when I needed Mother's help to prevent a miscarriage of my second pregnancy. She refused to help me.

Dan had never met my mother. I remember one night while lying in bed, and I was telling him some stories from my childhood. When I was telling one of the many things I experienced as a child, he said to me, "You are so full of shit. All the things you tell me cannot be true. That much stuff doesn't happen to one kid." First of all, I was pissed at being called a liar. Then I realized I really had lived an unusual life. I didn't know anybody who had moved around as much as I. I had gone to seventeen different public schools. My mother had been married six times by then. She had been married to five men, one of them twice. We lived in far too many towns and houses to count. I'd had a fake ID when I was seventeen and worked in a bar waiting tables. It was no wonder he didn't believe me.

After I thoroughly explained what my mother was like, he began to believe me. With a good amount of skepticism, perhaps, but he gave me the benefit of the doubt. And I think he began to understand why I did things the way I did or said things the way I said them. Why I reacted to things unnaturally, and why I got angry so easily. I was pretty screwed up. By the time Mother came to visit, Dan had a pretty good understanding of what I had been through, and what to expect when he met my mother. Of course, when Mother stepped off the plane, she didn't appear to be the Devil Incarnate. Her performance was intended to mollify any suspicion he may have about her intentions.

Mother was flying in the next day. Dan and I went to bed prepared for the drive to Frankfurt, four hours south of us. We had just gotten to sleep when the doorbell rang. We opened the door, and there stood, Charlie, a friend of ours from Montana who was stationed at Rhein-Main Air Base, near the Frankfurt Airport.

I had written to him and told him if he ever got a chance, he should come up and see us. He had decided to surprise us. He jumped on a train to make his way to Hessisch Oldendorf but got lost and took all day to find his way to our little base.

Charlie managed to reach Ray Crane, who was working the night shift in the Transportation office where Dan worked. Ray was a friend of ours. He knew where we lived, but of course, we didn't have a telephone. Ray offered to drive Charlie to our house. And now, here they both stood, on our front porch.

We thanked Ray, and Charlie came inside. I explained to him we were heading down to Frankfurt in the morning to pick up my mother. His leave ended at the same time we would be taking Mother back to the airport. Charlie decided he would stay for her entire visit if we didn't mind. I had the guest room set-up for my mother, and Charlie slept on the couch.

The next morning, we all drove to Frankfurt Airport. The three of us were standing at the gate, by 12:00 noon, waiting for Mother to get off the airplane. When she finally did deplane, she had two or three German men in love with her. They all wanted her contact information, and all, including my mother, were tipsy. She was on Cloud Nine, soaking up the Narcissistic Supply, and not the least bit interested in my new husband or me. She said her goodbyes to her men, finally turning to me. I introduced her to Dan and then told her our friend had decided to surprise us with a visit so that we would have a full house. She turned her Narcissistic Glow on Charlie, and never did it dim, the entire visit.

We had a great time while they were both visiting. Dan and I took them out to eat at our favorite restaurants, establishments that welcomed Americans. We took them to Tony's, the little bar off base where all the airmen went. Mother had her first beer in a boot. A biersteifel, or glass boot. The young airmen in the bar were all willing to teach her how to drink from the boot to avoid the bubble pressure effect, thus dousing herself in beer.

Another night we decided to drive to Buckeburg to see a movie. Mother and I were happy to discover the movie showing that night was Grease, a musical. The guys weren't thrilled but graciously went along. Just before the movie began, the manager made an announcement. A sneak preview would follow the movie and any of us with paid admission to Grease were welcome to stay to see the premiere of Superman. Now the guys, as well as Mother and I, were all thrilled.

Their last night in town the four of us decided to go dancing at the NCO Club. The nightclub for airmen and Non-Commissioned Officers. Disco was still all the rage in 1979, so I was all for it.

Later that evening, Mother leaned over to me at one point and said, "Charlie sure is a good-looking guy."

I turned fully around in my chair, looked her in the eye, and emphatically said, "NO!" I knew my mother, possibly better than anyone. I knew what she was thinking.

She looked offended and said, "Oh, come on! I didn't mean that." I made it clear to her, I in no way wanted her to pursue him. She assured me, again, she had no plans to pursue our young friend, who was six months younger than me.

My mother had decided to come to Germany, I believe, to get me back under her thumb and to punish me. She knew she had *lost* control when I got pregnant, and such an offense could not be allowed to slide. She always needed to feel in control in order to "win". I don't know what her plan was when she decided to come to Germany, but when she discovered Charlie was there as well, she had to adjust her plans.

We'd had a good time, the four of us: the restaurants, the sight-seeing, the movies. The visit was going great. Then Mother decided to humiliate me. She took Charlie to one of the bathrooms and had her way with him. Immediately after telling me she wouldn't, and then made sure I knew about it. When they came out, she was hanging all over him, and then they began making out on the dance floor. Everyone in the building knew what was happening. That night we could hear them in her bedroom having sex, again. She got her revenge by humiliating me. My new husband had discovered who my mother was.

Mother talked as though she hated men, but she acted like she loved the power she felt when she used sex to get what she wanted.

Chapter 18

Her Fat Ass Will Not Be Harassing You Anymore

*T*he owners of the house we were living in decided to build a Gasthaus on the back. The English translation is "guest house." Work began at 7 am and didn't end until 8 pm every night; exactly as their laws were written for construction hours. They even installed a door in the wall between our home and the Gasthaus. As soon as the work began, Dan and I got on the list for an apartment on base. It was a nightmare living there during the construction; but they had the rooms rented immediately, and the guests treated us like we were their hosts; coming to us with their complaints.

We moved out in November of 1979, one month before our baby's due date of December nineteenth. We got help with the move from some friends, thank goodness.

Our new home was a two-bedroom, one-bathroom apartment in a third-floor walk-up. I wasn't much help. Although our apartment building wasn't considered Base Housing, it was within steps of the base. We were paying rent, so we were still getting HOLA and COLA, Housing Allowances and Cost of Living Allowances, which came in the form of extra pay for living on the economy. Our apartment was right outside the back gate of the base, German-owned.

The doctor at the Aid Station wasn't interested in me or my pregnancy. One of my friends asked if I was taking prenatal vitamins.

I didn't know I was supposed to. On my next visit with the doctor, I asked him if I should be taking them, so he gave me a prescription for prenatal vitamins. He didn't seem to care that I had gained fifty pounds. He didn't warn me about my weight. I had no clue what was happening to my body or any possible complications associated with my weight gain.

Dan and I had decided we were making enough money living on the economy and that I could get out of the Air Force and stay home with the baby. The original plan involved me staying in the Air Force, but when I saw the options for childcare on base, I hated the thought of leaving my baby with any of those strangers. There wasn't an actual Daycare. People found dependent wives who were willing to babysit for some extra spending money to watch their kids. I agreed with Dan. I received an honorable discharge on November 30th.

On November 4, 1979, fifty-two American diplomats and citizens were taken hostage in Iran. The hostages were held captive for 444 days in the U.S. Embassy in Tehran. All European U.S. military bases were put on Alert Status.

All military personnel on the base were put through gas drills, rehearsing the proper use of a gas mask. I was exempt due to my pregnancy. During a practice run, everyone in the Transportation Division was assigned a vehicle to take off base and hide, to ensure enemy troops didn't take the vehicles.

Then we began "War Games." The Base Commander and his staff, along with all the Division Commanders, were put in a "Command Post," which was a conference room with a table large enough to seat them all. The Base Commander was assigned a Driver. I was assigned a twelve-hour shift, where I sat in the corner of the Command Post awaiting orders to drive the Base Commander where he needed to go. All offices were on twelve-hour shifts while the base was on Alert Status. I was told, "Anything you hear in this room, stays in this room." There were procedures already in place for possible scenarios in the event of war. Every base has them, in a book on a shelf somewhere, specific to each division. Each division played out the contrived event specific to them. The Commanders kept tabs on how these situations played out via radio.

At one point everyone on base was told the front gate had been breached by enemy forces. Listening to the radio, we heard about personnel being killed, as well as a tank that had driven into the Base Post Office. I remember it sounding so realistic. I could picture bodies lying around the base. I could "see" a tank in the side of the Post Office. Then a call came from the enemy demanding the Base Commander be delivered to them at the Post Office. The Base Commander looked at me and asked, "Are you ready to drive me to the Post Office? Should we concede to their demands?"

Holy Crap! He caught me off guard. I said, "Sir, I will follow your orders if you think that's a good idea." My eyebrows must have been in my hairline, and my eyes as big as saucers.

He stared me in the eye for a moment, then said, "I don't think so." He winked at me and got on the radio, telling them he would not be caving to their demands. I won't say what happened next, or how he decided to handle the situation.

There were plans made for the Civilian Dependents. They included the spouses and children of the military personnel on base, as well as those assigned to the two mobile radar units. Plans were in place for what would happen to the civilians, how busses would remove them in the middle of the night. They would not have any warning, and they would go in the clothes on their backs. Again, those plans were not to get back to the civilians. The Command wanted to be sure enemy forces would not take the civilian dependents and use them as hostages. So, even the dependents who would most be affected weren't to know in advance what would happen to them in case of a war breaking out. My discharge came through a week later. I knew what to expect and had time to prepare. Just in case. But I was a nervous wreck thinking about the possibility. I kept a packed diaper bag at the door.

By the time December rolled around, I was going to bed every night hoping my baby would make his/her debut. Dan was helping me at the laundromat on December twenty-fourth, when I felt what I thought might be labor, five days past my due date. He stayed and finished up the laundry, and I walked to the Aide Station. It was Monday of the long holiday weekend. The doctor wasn't at the Aid Station, there was a physician's aid, or maybe he was a nurse. He couldn't tell me if it was labor or not. Besides, he didn't want to be working on Christmas Eve and made it clear he didn't want to be bothered. He suggested we go out to the British Military Hospital and let them decide. Dan and I drove out to the BMH, the hospital where all the babies on the base were being born. I was a week overdue. We thought for sure our baby would be born on Christmas day. Our friends, Bob and Terri, had had their baby on Christmas day, the year before. They had left The HOG to be stationed in Oklahoma. I was so excited our babies would share the same birthday since Terri and I had stayed in contact.

Labor stopped. They kept me overnight, in case it started up again. But they refused to induce. I begged, but they said, "Your baby will come when it is ready." We went home and began the long wait.

A full night's sleep was out of the question. I began sleeping on the couch, so I could stay up reading, or "people watching" my neighbors in the apartments across from us, which technically was "spying." I saw a doozy of a fight one night. I thought they were going to kill each other. But, by staying in the living room, I didn't disturb Dan, who had to get up for work the next morning. Every night when Dan went to bed, we said, "Maybe tonight."

My water broke at two o'clock in the morning of January 18, 1980. I labored for twenty-three hours. Our beautiful baby girl was born a full month past her due date, on January 19 at 12:55 am. She weighed ten pounds.

We had a midwife, who was a member of the British Military, although she hailed from Canada. The hospital kept a doctor on call, but usually, the on-duty midwife delivered the babies. By the time we got to the delivery room, they had called for the doctor. He said our baby girl was the biggest baby he had personally ever delivered.

Melanie was born in a British Hospital, on German soil. She was delivered by a British Military Doctor, with the help of a Canadian Midwife, to American parents. We called her our International Baby. She had both an American Birth Certificate and a German Birth Certificate. Duel-citizenship until she turned eighteen.

Melanie and I stayed in the hospital for a full week, which was their policy. I discovered while I was there, I had undiagnosed Gestational Diabetes. This hospital was by no means a hotel. We Moms would get out of bed, flip our sheets to the "clean" side, and then the next day put a set of clean sheets on the bed. The following day, we again flipped the sheets. Our meals were served in a dining room down the hall, family-style. I will say the food was incredible. Our babies were kept in the nursery overnight, but we were woken at 2 am to go to the nursery and feed them. In the morning, we walked to the nursery, got the bassinette with our baby, and rolled it to our room, where they stayed all day.

I was having a terrible time just walking to the bathroom, let alone all the other walking I was expected to do, back and forth to the nursery and dining hall. On my first day there, after having a ten-pound baby, I was making my way, gingerly, to the bathroom down the hall. A large woman, in a British Military nurse uniform, said something to me to the effect of, "Stand up straight and walk right.

You do not have a disability. You had a baby, for God's sake." I wasn't able to talk back or stand up for myself.

In the afternoon, the doctor who had delivered Melanie was making his rounds with some students, as well as the rude nurse, who was taking notes. After showing them "the giant baby" he had delivered, he asked if he could check my stitches. I told him I felt like my legs had been sewn together. He said I had torn pretty severely, even after the episiotomy. Finally, he asked if I had any questions. I bucked up and said, "Could you tell her to stop harassing me about the way I'm walking?" He turned and looked at the nurse.

"I don't think her fat ass will be harassing you anymore after this," he said. I never saw her again.

Dan made the only two phone calls either of us ever made during our time in Germany. He called his parents and my mother.

For the next eleven months, I enjoyed my baby and my husband, and my life to the fullest. We had bought a nice baby carriage, known as a pram. I had made a miniature comforter to use in the pram, for those cold winter days.

Every couple of days, I would get a basket of dirty laundry ready by the front door. When Dan left for work, he would carry it downstairs and leave it next to the pram which stayed in the foyer. I could load up my baby, cozy as a bug in a rug, then place the laundry basket across it. She and I would walk up to the base laundromat. When I finished doing the laundry, we would go back home. I left the pram and laundry basket in the foyer. When Dan came home after work, he would carry the basket upstairs. It was a good system.

When Melanie made a poopy diaper, we would fold it up and leave it on the stoop outside our front door. The next time one of us went downstairs, we took the dirty diaper to the dumpster. No Diaper Genie for us, it hadn't been invented.

Dan liked to come home every day for lunch. While I got his lunch ready, he would give Melanie her bottle. He loved his time with his baby girl. He learned to remove his uniform shirt before giving her a bottle after she spewed all over him a couple of times.

She was such a good and happy baby. I was never bored or sorry I had stopped working. Melanie and I stayed busy. Once she got big enough to use a walker, she followed me around the apartment while I cleaned. Sometimes we would go for walks, for some fresh air. Melanie and I had other young mothers and babies with whom we got together. And there was a little place off base where Dan and I could leave her for a couple of hours so we could go out once in a while. We did it only a time or two. Melanie would be asleep when we picked her up. After putting a clean diaper on her when we got home, she would be wide awake. So, we stopped going out.

We lived by Dr. Spock. Neither of us knew anything about babies. Other than the little bit of babysitting I did when I was thirteen, I hadn't spent much time around them, and neither had Dan.

I had half a dozen reference books about babies, long before *What to Expect When You're Expecting*. Gosh, I wish I'd had that book. Every pregnant woman needs *What to Expect When You're Expecting,* followed by *What to Expect the First Year*. Dan and I were committed to becoming the best parents we could be. We were a great team. We made mistakes, but Melanie survived.

Shortly after Melanie was born, Mother offered to pay for the three of us to fly to Seattle to visit Dan's family for a few days, and then to Oklahoma City to visit my family for about a week. We had to get Melanie a passport, but then we were ready to go. Melanie was three months old when we left Germany. We flew on a large commercial airplane across the ocean. Shortly into our flight, a flight attendant took Melanie from us, saying she wanted the others to see her. Melanie had white-blond hair and the brightest blue eyes you've ever seen. Dan has blue eyes, but Melanie's eyes were just like Dan's sister's eyes. Her eyes are like blue diamonds. Every few minutes, we would see another flight attendant walk by carrying our baby. I've never seen anything like it. They didn't give her back to us until she needed to be fed, or her diaper changed. If they weren't serving food or drinks, they were carrying our baby. By the time Melanie was three months old, she had looked six months old.

When we arrived in Seattle, I called my father. I hadn't spoken to him since I called to tell him I was getting married. Although I had been writing letters, I never mentioned our last phone call. So, when I called him, he was surprised to hear from me. I told him where we were, and he asked if we could come down there for a visit. I told him Mother was paying for it, so if we made plans to come down there, he'd have to pay the extra. He said he was happy to do so. We cut a day from our visit with Dan's family, and postponed our arrival in Oklahoma City by a day, to spend two days in Chico. Mother was not happy, and I felt guilty, which is what she wanted. But we had a very nice visit with Dan's family and my family in Chico.

I can remember specific details of our visits with them all, but I can't remember anything good about our visit with my mother. The only thing I remember is feeling trapped, suffocated, and suffering a great deal of anxiety. She was constantly telling me what to do and how to do it. Treating me like the stupid, incapable girl she'd always told me I was. She made a concerted effort to manipulate and influence my decisions. She was setting a precedent.

After we arrived back in Germany, Mother began making plans for us to move to Oklahoma. She said there was an oil boom happening and jobs were plentiful. The cost of living in Oklahoma was certainly lower than in the Seattle area. Dan was always ready to do whatever made me happy, so we decided we would be settling in Oklahoma when he got out of the Air Force.

Mother wrote she had bought a van for us. She said we could pay her back when we got there; or not if we decided we didn't want the van. Dan was not at all happy about her manipulations. He made it clear we would not start down that road, letting her make life decisions for us. I just told her in my next letter that we would give it some consideration.

She offered to let us stay with her in her apartment until our things got delivered. We were informed our household goods would take about a month to arrive. She said we could have the master bedroom, where she had already put a crib for Melanie that she'd bought from a friend. I know it makes her sound generous, but there was always an ulterior motive. If I weren't grateful enough, she would play her trump card. We did need a place to stay, so we were truly grateful for the offer to stay with her. But it made me sick to my stomach thinking of what life would be like living with my mother again.

Dan was scheduled to be discharged in January of 1981. He took some leave time, and we left Germany in December of 1980. Melanie was eleven months old when we arrived back in the United States. She walked off the airplane. Mother was at the airport waiting for us with her live-in boyfriend. Surprise!

Part 4

End of my reprieve.

Even when things are great,
I'm always waiting for the other shoe to drop.

Chapter 19

I Didn't Tell You to Get Pregnant

*M*other had been taking trips down to Hugo and camping out on her grandfather's property. The property was uninhabited. The house itself was rubble. The property was still in the family, and she had permission from her cousin to use it. Of all her cousins, she was probably closest to him, even though he was living in another state at the time. The property, which we called *Papa's Place*, had great memories for her from her childhood, and she loved primitive camping. She had bought the van, supposedly for us, but she was using it for camping at *Papa's Place*. She would pack the van before leaving for work on Friday, and then she would drive down to *Papa's Place* after work. She would come home on Sunday evening to get cleaned-up before returning to work on Monday. She spent her days relaxing in a lawn chair and reading her books. Evenings she would hang out at local bars, which is where she had met Warren.

I'm not sure how their relationship grew to him moving to Oklahoma City. Did he follow her after one meeting? Did she return to Hugo two, three or four times before he moved to Oklahoma City? I don't know. She had mentioned him in a letter, but we had no idea he was living with her until we arrived from Germany.

Warren was six months younger than me, her youngest child. Quiet and unassuming, Warren had lived in Native American Housing his whole life. Mother felt he could do nothing right, and he was completely malleable to her direction and training. And for some crazy reason, he said he loved her. He was the perfect foil for my narcissistic mother.

Dan joined the Oklahoma City Police Department soon after we arrived in Oklahoma City. He had just finished at the Academy and was riding with a Training Officer when he saw my mother and Warren coming out of the courthouse downtown. He pulled over and introduced them to his T.O. Mother told him they had just gotten married. Her sixth husband said, "I do," in her seventh wedding ceremony.

In the meantime, I had gone to work for the State of Oklahoma as a purchase order typist. A low-level, get-your-foot-in-the-door position, with great benefits. In the beginning, I was not a good employee. I was a great employee in the Air Force. I took pride in my job and my ability to do well. But now, I had Mother in my ear, giving me advice about how to show the people around me I was not to be expected to do more than my share, or possibly even my full share. Mother believed everybody was trying to take advantage. "Screw unto others before they screw unto you." So, I admit, I was not a good employee, and I was disrespectful to my superiors. I regret, to my very core, taking my mother's advice.

Once I made the connection, in my head, I realized if I was going to advance in this job, I needed to be a better employee. I needed to be a responsible and respectful adult, and once again, take pride in my work. I stayed there, advancing until I got myself into a position with so much pressure, it was more than I could handle emotionally. After ten years, I left to become a stay-at-home Mom — the best decision I ever made.

Mother and Warren bought a little, two-bedroom house. Then she began pushing us to buy a house near them. We found a cute little two-bedroom house that had been built in 1952, which had recently been remodeled. We paid $32,000 in 1982. The house had two bedrooms and one very original bathroom: pink tile, pink sink, pink bathtub, and pink toilet. The garage had been converted to an eat-in kitchen, filled with Avocado Green appliances. Mellie was two years old when we moved into the house on 44th Street.

Our little 925 square foot house was outside the Oklahoma City limits. When the City started the "Take Home" program, we decided to move back into the city limits. The Take-Home program meant, if an officer was living in the city limits, he or she could have a black and white patrol car to drive to and from work. It was a real game-changer for young couples. The pay was lousy, so having a city car to drive and use city gas, really helped. And the communities benefitted from having a visible police presence.

Talk at the department was about a new housing development going in on the west side of the city, right at the edge of the city limits. We could be as far out of the city as possible and still have a Take Home car. And, as a bonus, the schools were great.

After walking through the model homes and thinking of the money we would save with the Take Home car, we decided to sign a contract to have a house built. Construction began on a 1350 square foot house, with three bedrooms and two bathrooms. The builder took our current home in trade for the down payment. I don't recommend making a similar deal without doing your homework. In the end, we got screwed, to the tune of several thousands of dollars.

Mellie was getting close to turning three, and I wanted another baby. Dan agreed, so we began trying, and I got pregnant right away. I was thrilled, thinking our children would be the same age difference as my older sister and me. Mother was not so thrilled, especially when she found out Lisa was pregnant and due one month before me, in July of 1983.

I felt Mother was angry for the same reason she was angry the first time I got pregnant; she was losing control of my sister and me. She never wanted to discuss our pregnancies at all. If either of us brought it up, Mother would leave the room. She would constantly remind us that she had told everyone she knew that her daughters were too smart to get pregnant. By getting pregnant, Lisa and I embarrassed our mother. She was, quite literally, ashamed of us. We had let her down. The first time I got pregnant, it just proved I was the stupid child she had produced. But when Lisa got pregnant, Mother was disappointed. She honestly thought Lisa was "too smart" to get pregnant.

Lisa and I, on the other hand, were thrilled to be having our babies so close together. Of course, we couldn't discuss it in front of Mother, but we were used to keeping our joy about anything to ourselves.

At ten weeks, I began to spot blood. I went to see my doctor, who said spotting is not unusual. She suggested I go home and lie down. She specifically said, "Find someone to take your toddler home with them. I don't want you trying to keep up with her. Come back tomorrow, and we'll check you again."

Just sitting at my desk, writing this, makes my anxiety level skyrocket. I think it was the most traumatizing experience I ever had involving my mother. I called her, told her what was happening and asked if she would pick up my daughter from daycare and keep her, just until Dan got off work. He was working until midnight. She said, "No. I didn't tell you to get pregnant. I'm not going to help you keep it."

Sit back and let her statement sink in for a moment. *She didn't tell me to get pregnant*. I had gone rogue, again. Now, I didn't feel I could ask anybody for help. I had never been able to ask anyone for help. She taught me I was selfish and spoiled when I asked someone to do something for me. And now she had reinforced the notion I shouldn't ask anyone for help.

I drove to the daycare and picked up my daughter. I went through a drive-thru and got her some dinner, then went home. I laid on the couch and tried not to get up. Mellie was so good. She brought toys in and sat on the floor next to me. She played, and I talked to her. Later, I got her ready for bed and made sure she was taken care of before lying back down on the couch. The bleeding had gotten worse, but I just put on a heavier pad. When Dan got home, at midnight, I told him everything that had happened. He consoled me, got me set up with a drink and some food next to the couch, where I said I wanted to stay. He told me to get him if I needed him, and he went to bed.

It's hard to believe, but I couldn't, simply could not, ask for help. It was not an attempt at being a martyr. It was psychologically impossible for me to ask for help. I stayed on the couch all night except when I was in the bathroom, changing my pad. When I ran out of pads, I began using folded up washcloths. And when they soaked through too fast, I began using folded up hand towels. I was in actual labor, and the pain was just as you would expect. As the night wore on, I just kept saying to myself, "I have to make it at least until the daycare opens so we can take Mellie there before going to the hospital."

At six o'clock I finally went in and woke Dan. He made a valiant effort to remain calm, getting Mellie out of bed and into the car. I was trying so hard to keep from crying out, because when I made any noise at all, Mellie wanted to know what was wrong with Mommy. Dan drove straight to the Emergency Room. I have vague memories of what happened there, but I can't distinguish fact from dreams. I know at some point Dan took Mellie to daycare and returned to be with me.

I have some memory of a nurse walking me into a room and saying, "Get up on the table." And then a gush of blood came out of me, a huge puddle on the floor, running down my legs and soaking my stocking feet. But I don't know if it happened or not.

Dan called my office to let them know what was happening, which is how our friends, Chip and Monica, found out. I worked with Monica. She was and still is, my dearest friend. She called her husband, and they both took off from work to come to the hospital. Monica later told me they found Dan sitting alone while I was in surgery. She said he looked sick and frightened. He told them, when he got back from taking Mellie to daycare, I was already in surgery. He didn't know what was happening. Someone finally came out and told him I had hemorrhaged. They were doing a D&C, as well as a blood transfusion, and that I would be spending the night at the hospital.

Mother didn't come to see me in the hospital. She never asked about it, and I never mentioned it. It was a sick and twisted relationship, but it was all I had ever known. It would not occur to me until years later, that I didn't have to have a relationship with her at all. Coming to the realization would require years of therapy.

We got moved to our new house but didn't try for another baby for over a year. In the meantime, Lisa and Marvin had a baby boy and named him Dillon. And our friends' Chip and Monica had a baby girl that they named Kimberly.

In 1984 we decided we were ready to try for another baby. By July, when my nephew Dillon was turning one, I told Lisa and Monica I was pregnant. However, I didn't tell anyone else until I got past the ten-week mark.

This was also about the time Dan and I had gotten invited to a party. We asked my mother if she and Warren could keep Mellie overnight. Warren was great with Mellie, and she adored him. He was Pawpaw to her. He carried several pictures of her in his wallet, pulling them out every chance he got to show people his blue-eyed, blond grandbaby. He loved the reaction he got from people. Not only because of her coloring, but also because he was barely old enough to have a child her age, let alone a grandchild.

Mother and Warren agreed to let her stay the night. Mother loved to countermand anything I said to Mellie. If I told Mellie she couldn't have a cookie, for whatever reason, Mother gave her a cookie. If I told Mellie she couldn't go outside to play, Mother took her outside to play. It was a constant battle.

Well, the morning after Mellie spent the night, I got a phone call. It was Mellie calling. She was four years old, so I knew my mother had dialed the phone.

"You have to come get me," Mellie said.

"Tell her why," I heard my mother say.

"Because I'm bad," my baby told me.

I told Mellie I was on my way; I would be there as soon as possible. It was a twenty-minute drive, but I pushed the limit. Not so fast I would get stopped for speeding because I couldn't afford to lose time getting to my baby.

When I drove up in front of my Mother's house, Mellie was sitting on the front porch, alone and crying, waiting for me. I held her for a moment, told her she wasn't bad, and I wasn't mad at her. Then I told her to wait just a minute while I went inside.

"What the Hell?" I asked my Mother. She huffed around in her kitchen for a couple of beats.

And then she said, "She woke us up at seven o'clock demanding breakfast. When I told her to go back to bed, she fussed and cried, saying she was hungry. I told her she didn't make demands of me. She had to do what I said, not the other way around. But she kept demanding breakfast and cartoons."

"Are you kidding me?" I practically yelled. "You have taught her she can have anything she wants when you're around. What did you expect? You can't have it both ways." She began to puff up like a blowfish. But I wasn't having any of it. For the first time in my life, I was standing up to her. I walked out the door, picked up my little girl, and got in the car. I wish I could say I never saw or spoke to her again. Sadly, I backed down and allowed her to continue manipulating and abusing my children and me for several more years.

April 1985

Mellie was five years old when her baby sister, Karla, was born. Where Mellie was a blue-eyed blond at birth and looked just like Dan, Karla had brown hair and hazel eyes. She looked like me.

Mellie loved her baby sister. She would talk to Karla and sing to her. Karla tried talking back, making little cooing sounds and giggling. We had a complete family. The only issue I have looking back at the pictures of those times is my hairstyle. It was the 1980's; a bad decade for hairstyles, and flashy clothes.

Mother was never a great housekeeper. But for some reason, she was able to shame me about every little thing I did; in my house to how I raised my children. And about the fact that I was a "government employee." Mother taught me shame. In her opinion, every mistake I made was cause for shame. If I tripped and fell in public, I felt shame. If I dropped my fork, I felt shame. Imagine if every little flub in your day-to-day life caused you to feel completely ashamed of yourself. I still had not learned the difference between *utter shame* and plain old *embarrassment*. If my mother called me out about something, to me, it felt like another character defect. For this reason, my house had to be spotless. People were not allowed to come to my house unannounced, because I had to be sure everything was perfect. I didn't want to give anybody the impression I was a less-than-perfect housekeeper.

When Pleasing You Is Killing Me, Dr. Les Carter, Ph.D.[13]

> "The people pleaser is quite distinct from the narcissist and is commonly the foil in that person's efforts to manipulate and exploit. The pleaser, in fact, can harbor guilt, insecurity, and shame when it is hardly warranted. (This is a truth not lost on many narcissistic predators.) For instance, to a pleaser, a mistake is not just a mistake; it's a character defect. Or a distinct preference is not just a unique way of viewing life; it's an indicator of disloyalty. All that is needed for a pleaser to succumb to false guilt is to have a controller cry foul, and the downward spiral into doubt and guilt begins."

On the subject of People Pleasers and Pride, Dr. Carter points out, people pleasers often are prideful. We don't normally think of ourselves as prideful, but after he explained, we people pleasers feel the need to be appreciated for our thoughtfulness. It stands to reason we take pride in our efforts. We feel because we are always trying to think of others first, shouldn't we be considered thoughtful? Should we not be treated in kind? But why are we considerate of others? Is it selfless? Do we put others first with humility or pride?

When I offer a compliment, I always say I wasn't looking for a compliment in return, but if I don't receive some form of appreciation for my consideration, am I not hurt?

Often, my nice behavior may be accompanied by my assumption; I deserve to be treated better because I'm nice. As if being treated well in return, is the reason I'm nice. And let's be honest, wanting people to be nice to me is a great deal of the reason I am nice. I want to please others, so they will like me.

How about when we falsely agree with someone? We just say we agree, so they will think we are smart. "Hey, she's smarter than I thought if she agrees with me." It is pride based. But if we stand in our truth and simply say, "We'll have to agree to disagree," then we are being true to ourselves and taking the humble stance. They may not think we are as smart as they are, but at least they know who we are and what we stand for — no false pretenses.

I had to go back to work when Karla, whom we now called Karly, was six weeks old. Dan was working on the graveyard shift. I would drop the girls off at daycare and head for work. Most mornings, I met Dan in passing at the intersection right outside the daycare. We would wave, and I always got such a charge out of our little moment, seeing my Sweetie in his police car, heading home.

Dan's partner at work and his wife attended a church known for not only welcoming police families but encouraged them to attend their church. So, Dan and I began attending their church.

Within a few weeks, the church split. There was a rift with the pastor, he was asked to leave, and he took the police family with him. Being new to the church, and not members, we didn't hear what had caused the rift. The pastor and his loyal followers rented a couple of office spaces to conduct their service and hold Sunday School for the children. There was a nursery for the babies, and church members were asked to sign-up for turns working the nursery.

A few things about this new church community began to bother me. First, I was being *assigned* to work the nursery every other week. Nobody asked me if I wanted to work the nursery, I hadn't signed up to work the nursery every other weekend, it just became a thing. And then it was every week. I started to complain to Dan. I felt like I was being used. And to be frank, I felt they wanted him at their church, but not me. So, the following week, Dan came to the nursery and worked it with me. Some of the congregation came up to him after church service and said they'd missed him.

There was also something happening at church which completely floored me. The pastor called for a meeting of the members after service one day. The pastor announced his teenaged daughter had been having an affair with one of the married deacons in the church. The pastor's best friend and his daughter. She was pregnant, so the deacon was going to divorce his wife, leave his children, and marry the pastor's teenage daughter. The pastor explained how God had forgiven the deacon and felt we should all follow God's example. *Are you freaking kidding me???*

We left after the meeting, and I told Dan, "I will get the girls ready on Sunday mornings, and you can take them to church with you if you want. But I will not be returning." He said he wouldn't be returning either.

It was then I began to question organized religion. After a couple of years, I gave myself permission to question, or doubt, the existence of God. From there, it was a short trip to agnosticism.

> *Agnosticism*[14]
>
> Being a scientist, above all else, Thomas Henry Huxley presented agnosticism as a form of demarcation. A hypothesis with no supporting, objective, testable evidence is not an objective, scientific claim. As such, there would be no way to test said hypotheses, leaving the results inconclusive. His agnosticism was not compatible with forming a belief as to the truth, or falsehood, of the claim at hand. Sir Karl Raimond Popper, (Austrian Philosopher and Professor) would also describe himself as an agnostic. According to Philosopher William L.

Rowe, in this strict sense, agnosticism is the view that human reason is incapable of providing sufficient rational grounds to justify either the belief that God exists or the belief that God does not exist.

Chapter 20

Sitting on The Bottom of The Deep End

*A*s children, our mother had convinced my sister and me that our father and his entire family had decided they would pretend my father was Greg and Calley's father; my sister and I did not exist. Mother said it was easier for them to justify my father's relationship with his dead brother's wife. I was never able to discuss any of this with my father because I became too emotional about the subject, and I was not comfortable with those emotions, so my mother's twisted reasoning became my reality.

> In Dr. Les Carter's YouTube video titled, *When a Narcissistic Parent Coaches a Kid To Reject You*[15,] he recognizes a narcissistic parent will "brainwash the children against their non-custodial parent." More often than not, this brainwashing against the non-custodial parent will include the grandparents, aunts, and uncles.

I remember a time when my father said something about when I would one day have children of my own. I quickly objected, saying, "I will never have kids."

"That's your mother's brainwashing," he replied. Again, I objected. I was probably fourteen years old, but he was right. She told us over and over again. "Don't have children; they will suck the life from you." "Don't have children; they take away all of your freedom. Don't have children. Don't have children. Don't have children." Mother's harping on the evils of having children was the number one rule she drilled into us.

To give my father some credit. He never spoke against my mother to me again.

> In the same YouTube video, Dr. Carter goes on to say the non-custodial parent really doesn't have any recourse. The only real option is not to argue the point. Dr. Carter says, speaking to the non-custodial parent, "Don't poke the hornet's nest. At least, be committed to your own good character."
>
> Dr. Carter continues, "The narcissist may succeed in taking over the child. The relationship may become less full than desired. You have to adjust your expectations. This is a broken world, and narcissists are broken people. Sometimes, they're so broken, they're willing to risk a child's personal development, so they, the narcissist, can have control and be the ultimate sphere of influence. Sometimes they win, in a sense, they actually do bring the child over to their demented way of thinking. As best as you can, you want to show yourself to be the other, meaning; you don't get caught in the control game. Sometimes, it works out well and, as the child ages and matures, he or she catches on and can see it for what it is. The child may make the proper adjustments. Sometimes it doesn't work out. But your task is to make certain you remain true to your good character, good integrity, and

good intentions towards the children. And then, hopefully, something good can be found through that. No guarantees, though."

Over the years, Dad and Lois would take road-trips in their Recreational Vehicle, a motorhome, usually to Oklahoma to visit his children and his many cousins. Sometimes just stopping in Oklahoma on their way to other vacation spots.

One year, Dad's brother, my Uncle Charlie and his wife, Aunt Nancy, followed Dad and Lois in their own motorhome. We had a travel trailer at the time as well, so we all agreed to meet at a local lake. A few of my Dad's cousins were bringing their RV's as well, so we reserved one group site, with hook-ups for each RV.

In addition to that trip, Dad and his brother came back for a couple of family reunions.

Otherwise, family visitation was left up to my family and me. We took the same vacation every couple of years. We would drive out to California, visit Dad, Lois, and my stepsiblings. Then we drove to Washington to visit Dan's parents and any siblings who may have been living in the area at the time. Finally, back home, all in two weeks, sometimes driving up to twelve hours a day. It was very costly and became a chore none of us looked forward to because of the time spent in the car and the expense. We couldn't take our children to Disneyland, or even Branson, Missouri because we felt obligated to visit family.

When Pleasing You Is Killing Me, Dr. Les Carter, Ph.D.[16]

Responsibility can be overlearned. As a people pleaser, you have developed a keen positive presence in a sometimes-negative world. This is a sound philosophy, yet it is also one that can lead to stress and tension if carried too far.

I needed my extended family to love me and want me in their lives. I made it my mission to insert myself in a way they could not resist. I gave up my identity and became what they wanted me to be. After a while, it became too much work. I began to resent them for making me work so hard. When in truth, they didn't owe me anything they weren't willing to give, and I was not *obligated* to keep trying.

We still hear, "When are you coming for a visit?" but we've been making ourselves the priority. Now, as a couple of retirees, my husband and I have time to travel and see things we never had time for before. And we've taken more time for our grandchildren. If there is time for our extended family, and if it fits in with our plans, we stop in. Since my father passed away, I've stopped going out of my way to visit Chico, California.

When my father, stepmother, and my father's siblings had passed away, except his one youngest brother, Uncle Rusty, I realized; if I'm ever going to find out the truth, I had to talk to my uncle before it was too late. Not wanting to have to talk to him directly, because I wanted to avoid confrontation and any sign of emotions, I texted his wife. I asked if they knew if the family had come to a consensus in which they would pretend my father had always been married to my stepmother. Had they all agreed; my father, Donald Maize, was Greg and Calley's father, choosing to pretend my Uncle Jack, Lisa and I had never existed? Which is what our mother had told us. What I got back was a quick note, saying, "Call your Uncle. He has too much to say for a text." *Well, crap. That backfired.*

My Uncle Rusty was born in 1949, nine years after his next youngest brother. He told me his parents moved around a lot, usually, because his father was in trouble with the law. He would get drunk, destroy something, or someone, and the law would be after him. They would pack up, and off they'd go to another state. By 1959, when Rusty was ten years old, his three brothers and his only sister were all living in California, from Irvine to San Jose and places in between. He and his parents moved around, living near one of his siblings or another.

During summer breaks from school, Rusty would go to stay with one of his siblings. He said he often stayed with us. Uncle Rusty told me many stories of staying with us, including one about my mother hitting my sister. Lisa would have been about seven years old at the time. Mother kept hitting her and yelling at her to "Stop crying!"

Rusty was about twelve-years-old. He told my mother, "She can't stop crying if you keep hitting her!" He said she reacted like a light bulb came on in her head, and she suddenly realized the truth of his words. She held Lisa and told her she was sorry. She comforted my sister until she stopped crying. I don't remember my mother ever striking either of us, so I assume this was a pivotal moment in her life.

Rusty loved my mother. He said she was very good to him when he would visit. He had great memories of her taking him places, like the beach and on picnics. My father was always working, so Rusty spent his days with my mother and the two little girls. One of the houses in which we lived had an inground swimming pool. Rusty recalled the time when he came out to the backyard and saw me, having just turned four, sitting on the bottom of the pool, at the deep end. He seemed to remember my mother had come into the house, possibly to use the bathroom. She'd been gardening, and I had been out there with her. The fact he came outside when he did was very fortunate. He ran around the pool and dove to the bottom, grabbed me, and brought me to the surface. Mother was just coming out of the house when he brought me up from the bottom. I'd heard the story from her as well, and they both said I couldn't have been there long because I wasn't even coughing or upset when I came to the surface, and I wasn't traumatized in any way. I was taught to swim over the summer.

Finally, I asked him directly; why did the family never talk about Jack? I had never heard anyone speak of Jack after he died. Rusty said the family was uncomfortable with their emotions, and talking about Jack made them all very sad, so they didn't talk about him. He said there was never, at any time, a suggestion they would forget him or us. They never thought there was anything wrong with my father marrying his brother's widow. To do so wasn't unheard of, and in fact, was considered an honorable thing to do in history, to take responsibility for the widow and her children. Uncle Rusty said the only reason they never saw me, or my sister was because we either didn't live close by, or our mother made it difficult.

Rusty further said, years later, my father told him about my mother. Dad told him about her jealousy and emotional outbursts. He said she was irrational and controlling. He didn't feel like he could live with her anymore. Dad leaving Mother had nothing to do with me or my sister, nor did it have anything to do with Lois, his brother's widow. It was just time to get out. Dad and Lois getting involved was simply a product of them spending time together at his parent's home. She would bring the kids over to visit their grandparents. She and Dad were both going through some heavy emotional stuff; her husband and his brother had died, and his subsequent divorce. They were drawn to each other for comfort and support. They remained married for fifty years, until the day she died. He never recovered from losing her. He became a shell of the man he once was. He had no will to live. He passed away seventeen months after losing the love of his life.

Medical neglect of a child is defined as a failure to provide necessary medical or dental treatment of a child for whom the adult is responsible. Whether that be a parent or legal guardian, this would involve serious physical injury or illness.

Serious physical injuries may be defined as my sister's injury sustained while riding a Ferris wheel or a broken arm. Mother finally had to take Lisa to a doctor when the broken bone in her arm dislodged and attempted to break through the skin.

If my grandmother hadn't insisted, would Mother have taken me to the hospital when I had pneumonia? Or would she have allowed me to die?

I was fifteen years old when I got a kidney infection. When I first began to get sick, I probably had a urinary tract infection. Mother never took my sister or me to see doctors. Instead, she told me to walk the two blocks over to a grocery store to buy some cranberry juice. After several days, the symptoms got worse, and then the pain became excruciating. That evening I begged her to take me to a doctor. She said, "They're all closed."

I asked her, "Can you take me to the emergency room?"

"I'll take you in the morning when they open."

"Can't you call an ambulance?" I was nearly screaming, in agony.

Mother turned her full attention on me and gave me *that look.* She said, "That costs money. You'll be fine until morning. Go to bed." *That look*, Lisa and I knew well. It said *You're walking on thin ice. Tread lightly.* Then she went to bed.

In the morning, she took me to an emergency room. The doctor told my mother I should not have gotten that sick. He told her I should have seen a doctor for the UTI. Mother told him my father had refused to pay for me to see a doctor.

I spent the next few days in a hospital bed on a clear liquid diet, with intravenous antibiotics. My sister sat with me for an hour or so each day. I never saw my mother.

At seventeen, I finally had the tonsillectomy doctors had been telling my mother I needed for years. I had tonsillitis two or three times a year since I was nine years old. Mother kept telling me, "Doctors don't take tonsils out while they're swollen." Then she would say, "Well, you're not sick now. What's the point?"

When I was seventeen, I was on my fifth case of tonsillitis that year. I called my father and begged him to please pay for me to have my tonsils out. He agreed and told my mother to take me to a doctor and have them out.

For the next couple of years, Mother told me she kept getting bills for the tonsillectomy. She said Dad was refusing to pay.

To this day, I would rather have a root canal than a sore throat.

Chapter 21

Oh, I Peed on Your Floor

*W*e loved our new home. We had our beautiful little Melanie, whom we now called Mellie, and our little Long-Haired Dachshund, Dachsey. We both had jobs and a nice little income. I just wish we had moved to a completely neutral state, away from any family. Unfortunately, I had allowed my mother to determine where we would live when we left the Air Force. And now, Dan was in a career he loved, and we were well entrenched. Which is not to say I didn't pester him to move, all the time! I wasn't used to staying in one place. Dan always managed to keep me grounded. He had grown up in one house. He went to school for twelve years with all the same friends. I knew it was what we both wanted for our children, so we stayed. We lived in that house for eighteen years.

October 1983

Dan was working the graveyard shift the night Mother and Warren showed up at my house. Warren was tipsy, but Mother was drunk.

She said, "We both drove our cars to work and met up at the bar when we got off. I'm too drunk to drive my car home, so we thought Warren could take you back with him and you could drive my car home for me. Then Warren can bring you back here, and I'll go home with him."

I was completely taken off guard. She did this to me all the time. I never knew how to respond to her insanity.

I told her I didn't want to do that, but she kept insisting, she didn't want her Cadillac left there overnight.

"I was getting ready to put Mellie to bed, and then I was going to watch some TV." I was panicking. My brain wasn't functioning. I always got this way. I would panic, and then I couldn't think straight. I lost all common sense when talking to my mother. She could talk circles around me.

"I'll stay with Mellie. I can get her to bed and then I'll just watch TV until you get back." She argued.

I hated to leave my little girl with that woman, but, I'm ashamed to say, I did exactly that. I did not have the courage, or the fortitude, to tell my mother No. So many occasions come to mind.

Mother called me a couple of months earlier and said, "Wayne is not treating Lisa right. She told me that he shoved her into a towel bar and left a bruise on her arm. I have an idea. You call her and tell her you need to see her. Make her think you're having problems with Dan and that you need to talk to her. She'll come running, thinking she's going to help you. Then you can tell her the real reason you called her to meet you. Tell her that I have an extra bedroom and she should come live with me." She told me this as though I would be in on a conspiracy. I tried to weasel my way out of it, but in the end, I did what she wanted me to do, as usual. Lisa was not happy with me. I can't say that I blame her.

I realize now what Mother was doing is called Gaslighting. She was forever causing my sister and me to do or say things to each other that brought doubt about our relationship. I suspect what Mother told me about Wayne shoving Lisa was total bullshit.

On the drive to pick up Mother's Cadillac, Warren began easing into a topic that I still can't get my head around. He asked if I would ever consider having an affair with him.

"No!" I said. What the hell was he thinking? Could this night get any worse?

"You know, you're a younger version of your mother. How could I not be attracted to you?" He continued as though I had not spoken. "Remember that time I went on a ride-along with Dan? He took me to his girlfriend's house. He's been cheating on you when he's supposed to be working." He was babbling.

I told him that I did not believe that to be true. "You're making shit up, and you need to sit there and be quiet. Just shut up and sit there. Not another word." I had no trouble talking to him. In fact, I was so used to my mother talking to him like a child, and I usually found myself doing the same.

After getting in the Cadillac, I drove straight back to my house, rather than their house. I parked my Mother's car in front of my house. Warren didn't get out of his car. He just sat there waiting for Mother.

When I walked in the front door, Mellie was asleep on the couch. Mother was sitting on the floor watching TV. She asked where Warren was, and I told her he was waiting in the car.

"He knows I'm not happy about any of this. He's waiting for you to come out to the car. You can come and get your car tomorrow."

She got huffy, as though I had corrected her, or told her that she was wrong, or, God forbid, that I'd said No to her. "Why didn't you leave it at my house as I told you to?" I didn't answer her. As she left my house, she said, "Oh, I peed on your floor."

"What? Why?" I couldn't understand what she was saying.

"I just didn't get up in time to go to the bathroom. It was an accident for God's sake." She was bent out of shape that I had the gall to be angry at her.

Early the next morning, her car was gone.

I had to tell Dan about the whole evening and everything that was said. However, I always worry about the reaction I may receive. It's not just my mother. It's everyone. I always anticipate the worst. How will he react? Will he be angry that I left Mellie with my drunken mother? And, worse, will he figure out what a terrible mother I am because I didn't stand up to *my* mother and refuse to leave my child?

My anxiety kept me awake most of the night. When he got home, I had to tell him. He made no judgment about me or how I handled the situation. He has never tried to get me to approach her, or to demand better treatment of her. He just never allowed her to bulldoze me if he was present. That was the thing she disliked most about Dan; he refused to be intimidated by her. He didn't fall for any of her narcissistic crap.

Dan understood that every decision I made was based on my need to please and my difficulty saying No.

As far as the accusation Warren had made, I told Dan about it. But I made it clear I knew it was bullshit. Dan has always come straight home after work. Even in the Air Force, when most guys would stop for a beer after work, he was always eager to get home. As a police officer, he had a partner that I knew very well — a good man whom Dan respected and loved and considered a mentor. Dan's partner was not a man who would go along with Dan cheating on his wife.

It occurred to me that Warren saying all that stuff about my husband cheating on me was probably something my mother put him up to. Another attempt to Gaslight my marriage. The other stuff, about him wanting to sleep with me was his own doing.

The bad decision I made was in not telling Dan about Warren wanting to sleep with me. I chose to overlook it, rather than face all the blowback that would come with telling my husband and my mother. Eventually, years later, I did tell him. By that time, neither Warren nor my mother was in our lives.

Naturally, I worried about him leaving me because I didn't feel worthy. That was very early in our relationship. I also experienced some jealousy, simply because I feared he would realize what a loser I was and find someone better.

Over time, and with a whole lot of patience, he convinced me that was not going to happen. For many years I needed assurances. I doubted that anyone could really love me. I didn't feel that I was enough.

He loves me, and it shows. His actions convince me that I am good enough. Doubting my self-worth is something I still struggle with, but I've had enough counseling and received enough positive feedback from the other people in my life, that I have gained a modicum of self-assurance. It's a daily struggle, to believe in myself. I believe healthy-minded people continue to work on themselves daily. Whereas, Narcissists never think there is anything wrong with them that needs work.

Granny had sold the properties she owned in San Bernardino before we left California to live in Oklahoma. The last piece of property, the duplex in which we lived, was sold to an acquaintance of Mother's. He was a Real Estate Broker, and Mother said she trusted him. He wrote the contract, which Granny signed, agreeing to pay her two hundred dollars a month until it was paid off. When Granny died, Mother was the beneficiary. Twenty years later Mother called to tell me she was tired of fighting with him for payment. She said he was paying only every few months or so. Then she made me an offer. If I would fly out to California with her, go to the courthouse to see if she had any legal footing to take the property back, get back payments, or get him to pay her outright, then I would get whatever money was made off the deal. She would put the property in my name.

This all sounded suspicious to me, and I was skeptical of her motives. I told her we couldn't afford for me to go to California. She insisted she would pay for everything, including meals and incidentals; it wouldn't cost me a thing. Again, I was unable to tell her No. What was I getting myself into?

She and I flew to Ontario, rented a car, and drove to the San Bernardino County Courthouse, on a Saturday. I expressed my doubts, before we left home, that we could get anything done on a Saturday, and suggested we wait and go on Monday. We could take care of business and return home on Tuesday. She insisted someone would be working on Saturday. Naturally, the courthouse was closed for the weekend. She changed our airline reservations to fly back home on Tuesday.

I suggested we visit my high school friend and her family. I called Marsha and asked if we could stop by for a visit, and she said we should come right away. Mother and I rented a hotel room nearby before heading over to Marsha's so that we could stay as long as we liked and not worry about finding a hotel. When we arrived at my friend's home, we were welcomed by the whole family; Marsha, her husband, two kids, and her mother, who was living in their garage-conversion. Our mothers hit it off right away. They decided to go out for a few drinks, just the two of them.

I visited with Marsha and her family for a short time but felt an uncontrollable need to get out of there. It had nothing to do with

Marsha and her family. I was having an anxiety attack. I recognize it for what it was now, but at the time, I just knew I had to get to my hotel room and be alone before Mother got back. Marsha tried everything to get me to stay, but I made an excuse to leave. I know I sounded like a crazy woman. It hurt her feelings, I'm sure. I regret that, but I had absolutely no control over my anxiety. When I got home from California, I called and tried to explain it all to her, but I didn't do a good job expressing myself and haven't had the same relationship with her since.

When I was in my mother's presence, I had to be constantly aware of my actions, as well as what was happening around us. I had to be on high alert. I had to keep her happy, or my life would implode; which is why I tried to keep my time with her to short bursts. Normally, an hour here or there, but I was now looking at three full days watching my P's and Q's. And this was just the first day. I needed to prepare for the next seventy-two hours. So, I left Marsha's house, bought a six-pack of beer and a pack of cigarettes. I cannot say, to this day, what made me do that. It was a compulsion. I rarely drank, and I'd quit smoking years before. I went to my room, turned on the TV and began drinking the beer and smoking the cigarettes, perhaps hoping they would calm me. Instead, I stayed on alert. Car doors were constantly closing outside my hotel room, and every time I worried that Mother was returning. For three hours, I was a ball of nerves. Finally, I turned out the lights and tried to sleep. When Mother did come in, I feigned sleep.

Generalized Anxiety Disorder[17]

(GAD) is a psychiatric disorder characterized by a constant sense of worry and fear that interferes with daily life. People with Generalized Anxiety Disorder may experience feelings of dread, distress, or agitation for no discernible reason - psychiatrists refer to this unexplained, triggerless anxiety as "free-floating anxiety."

Those with GAD may constantly expect the worst, and worry about things like work, money, their family and friends, or their health, even when there's no real cause to be concerned. The anxiety experienced with this disorder may occur for a specific reason or be triggered by an event but be disproportionately great or unrealistic for the situation.

General Anxiety Disorder can turn into a cycle of excessive worrying. Though many people with GAD realize that their worry is unrealistic or unwarranted, feelings of anxiety persist and seem unmanageable, leaving sufferers feeling out of control. Some of those afflicted can still lead normal lives with productive jobs and active social lives but be constantly internally struggling with worry and distress.

Symptoms

You may suffer from GAD if you experience the following symptoms:

- Excessive anxiety about everyday things
- Inability to control your constant worries
- Free-floating anxiety
- Distress or worry that you feel is disproportionate to the situation
- Inability to relax
- Difficulty concentrating
- Feeling on edge and startling easily
- Trouble falling asleep or staying asleep

- Fatigue
- A tendency to worry about or jump to the worst possible conclusion
- Headaches, stomach aches, muscle aches, or other unexplained pains
- Difficulty swallowing
- Shakiness or twitching
- Irritability
- Profuse sweating
- Light-headedness and/or breathlessness
- Frequent need to urinate

Symptoms of GAD vary in intensity - the anxiety experienced can get better or worse at certain points. Sometimes symptoms may decrease, allowing those afflicted to lead normal lives, and then suddenly pick up in severity, preventing normal functioning.

Sunday morning Mother told me to figure out what we could do for the day. "Anything at all," she said. "We may never have an opportunity like this again, just the two of us. Let's have some fun!"

I gave it some thought and then suggested we go to Universal Studios. I told her that they have a tram that takes you around the studio. I told her what I thought Universal Studios was all about. We would see TV and movie sets, maybe see some Stars. Whatever was involved, she could do from the comfort of a tram. I had to be cognizant of her handicap. As she got older, it became more of an issue for her to spend too much time on her feet.

She thought that sounded like a great idea. Off we went to Universal Studios. I have been back in recent years, and Universal has changed dramatically. Today they compete with Disneyland. Universal Studios has roller coasters and other rides that rival all the big amusement parks, but at the time, the attractions were more low-key. Nevertheless, when we paid at the gate, we were told our tram would be leaving in a few hours. I couldn't believe it. I asked the girl in the booth, "What are we supposed to do until then? My mother is handicapped. We can't be walking around for four hours."

"Oh, you've never been here before, have you?" she said, smiling. "Park your car, then catch one of the shuttles. They'll drive you back up here. Go through these gates," she pointed to some twenty-foot tall gates that looked like they were made of Gold, "and enjoy all we offer. You'll find plenty to do and eat, before time for your Tram to depart. Just make sure you're there on time. Oh, and go to the head of each line and let them know you have a handicapped individual. They'll let you right in. You won't have to stand in line."

Mother and I ended up having a great time. There were attractions around every corner. Shows, mostly. The indoor shows had theater seating, while the outdoor shows had benches. The weather turned cold that day, and we were spending a lot of time outdoors, so Mother suggested we go to the gift shop and find something warm. We each got a sweatshirt, and Mother insisted I get an umbrella, as we had already experienced some sprinkles.

We had lunch, saw a few more shows, and got ready for our Tram ride. It was a full day and was the perfect solution to accommodate Mother's disability.

Monday morning, we went to the courthouse, where we were told there was nothing we could do. The contract had been completed in his favor. We were at his mercy.

Mother called him and asked him to meet us for lunch. She convinced him to pay her off at a discounted price. She accepted seven thousand dollars to pay-off the property. He told her he would get the paperwork drawn up and send her a check in the mail.

Tuesday morning Mother and I got ready to fly home. The previous night she told me she had run out of her pain medication. I asked if she wanted to stop at a pharmacy and get a refill.

"No, I'll be fine. I have more at home," she said. Apparently, she had never run out before. Neither of us knew what we were in for.

Chapter 22

No Contact with My Abuser

*O*n the flight out to Ontario, California, we had a stop in Phoenix to change planes. Mother was able to have a cigarette, before boarding the next flight. The flight home, from Ontario to Oklahoma City was non-stop. Apparently, when she changed our return flight, she didn't consider the fact that a non-stop flight would be No Smoking.

Mother heard the announcement that we were on a No Smoking flight and she became extremely agitated. She stopped a flight attendant and asked for clarification. I was sitting on the aisle, with Mother in the middle seat next to a stranger who was sitting in the window seat.

She was told that she had, indeed, heard correctly.

"And I can't smoke in the bathroom? Can't I just stand at the back of the plane and smoke a cigarette?" She was beginning to raise her voice. The flight attendant very politely told her that she could not do either of those things; it was against Federal Aviation Administration regulations. Mother became abusive. So, the flight attendant simply walked away.

I was not given the opportunity to just "walk away," nor was the gentleman in the window seat. We were stuck on a fully booked flight. Mother took out her frustrations on me. Now she was having withdrawals from her drugs, as well as cigarettes.

A few minutes later the Captain made an announcement, "Couple more minutes and we'll be released to fly. We appreciate your patience." Holy Shit, Batman! She lost her damn mind! "Patience, my ass!" she screamed.

She cursed and carried on the entire flight home. None of it made any sense. I couldn't keep up with it. As I sat there beside her, I began to cry from the humiliation of it. I was not imagining all the people turning to look, and giving the evil eye, which I perceived was directed at me. I realize now; the looks were not directed at me. If anything, they pitied me. I was curled up as tightly as possible, trying to be invisible. In fact, at one point, a flight attendant came by and gave me some tissues and a bottle of water. Mother began attacking her again. When the flight attendant walked away without acknowledging her, Mother began screaming at me for crying, "Stop crying! Stop your F***ing crying! You are weak, spineless, etc., etc., etc."

Today it would not have been acceptable. Flights have been known to make emergency landings to remove unruly passengers. I don't know what I would have done had that happened. The flight itself was bad enough; I cried the entire time. But if we had been asked to leave the plane, I'm not sure what she would have done.

A Short History of Pain Management[18]

> In an article by Roger Collier, he says pain "teaches us to avoid fire, poison, sharp objects and many other things that could cause us harm. It alerts the body to injury and disease. But it is also unpleasant and, depending on intensity and duration, can have a drastic

impact on the quality of life. Another thing about pain: We have always had to deal with it, and we always will."

"Pain is a constant companion for humanity," said Marcia Meldrum, an associate researcher in the department of psychiatry and biobehavioral sciences at the University of California, Los Angeles.

The topic of pain management has been much discussed in medicine of late because of the opioid crisis. For a short period, opioids seemed to be the answer to the long-standing problem of how to relieve pain without putting patients at high risk of addiction. It turns out, that was wishful thinking.

"The thing about opioids is they are very effective in interrupting and shutting off pain signals in the brain," said Meldrum. "They are very, very effective. But they are also very dangerous."

The struggle to manage pain in patients effectively and safely has long been an issue in medicine. In her paper "A Capsule History of Pain Management," published in the *Journal of the American Medical Association*, Meldrum wrote that pain is the oldest medical problem, but has been little understood by physicians throughout history.

I have seen my mother, on numerous occasions, lash out at complete strangers who got on her bad side. One time we were in a barbershop with one of her husbands, who was getting his hair cut. We were living in Los Angeles at the time, and there was a deaf woman who was well known in the area. She walked from business to business, showing a card that read something to the effect, "I am deaf. Anything you could give me would be appreciated." We had seen her before, and Mother had commented that it was "pathetic the way some people use their handicap to get money out of complete strangers." It was the 1960s, and there were not Government Agencies for, nor were people as understanding of, the handicapped. At that time, the attitude was "out of sight, out of mind."

This day, Mother was extremely agitated. Nothing was going right; everything she saw was wrong; everyone around her was an idiot. It was a bad day to be with my mother. Suddenly this woman came through the door. She stopped at the first person in the room and held her card in his face. Granted, she was always very pushy. She always "shoved" the card in the face of the person she was soliciting for donations. He gave her some money, and she started down the line of the barbershop patrons. When she got to us, Mother pushed the hand, holding the card, away. The deaf woman made a grunting sound and *shoved* the card at my mother again. Mother stood up so fast, with her hands out in front of her and shoving back, that the woman went over backward and landed on her butt. Mother got in her face and told her that it wasn't our responsibility to pay her way in life. The owner of the place helped the lady up and walked her to the door. Not a word was said by anyone else in the place. Mother sat back down, looking very proud of herself and protesting the donations given by the others in the room.

Mother talked about that moment for days. She was so proud of herself. And, being a child, I thought it was neat. I was proud of my mother for not taking any crap off anybody. I didn't know better.

When our plane arrived in Oklahoma City, Warren was at the airport to pick us up. He asked me what was wrong. My face was swollen and blotchy from crying. Mother said, "Oh, they wouldn't let me smoke on the plane. I complained, and she got all pouty. You know how sensitive she is." She told him what a great and successful trip we had. She just went on and on about what a great help I was, taking care of her, making sure she had everything she needed and that she hadn't had to go out of her way for a thing. To hear her tell it, we had the best time, and I was her favorite person in the whole world.

Two days later, I got a bill in the mail for expenses I had incurred on the trip. Expenses she said she would pay for. Dan said, "Just send her a check and be done with it." I never got the money from the sale of the property, but I hadn't counted on it either. After all, I was dealing with my mother.

She must have had an ulterior motive for asking me to go with her to California in the first place, but I never figured out what it was.

September 1988

I had been working, for months, on a birthday present for Mother. I called to tell her I had a birthday gift for her. I wanted to know when a convenient time would be to bring it by. She said she would be at a certain bar and I should bring it there. I told her I had my girls, then 3 and 8 years old. Mother said they could come in the bar as long as they sat at a table and not at the bar. I told her I'd rather not bring them to the bar, and it could wait. She said I was ridiculous and a prude; I should bring her gift at once.

I loaded my children into the car, and off we went to the bar. I gave her a large package that she then carried over to a pool table, her stage, complete with "spotlight." She opened the package to find a large University of Oklahoma afghan that I had been working on for months, specifically for her birthday. She made a huge deal, calling to her friend, "Patty! Look! She made it herself, just for me. Isn't it incredible?!" All the people in the bar, fans of OU, made her feel so special for this wonderful gift. I told her I thought she might like to display it along the back of her couch. The next time I went to her home, I asked where it was. She had sold it for $50.

There were only a few times that I allowed my mother, or my mother and Warren, to keep my girls overnight. Very few. The last time, something happened that finally gave me the impetus to go the No Contact route with my mother.

Karly was four, and Mellie was nine years old the last time they spent the night at my mother's house. The next day, after the girls got home, Mellie told me something that finally made me see just how dangerous my mother was, and that I had to protect my children from her.

It was 1989. Televisions were big, heavy components, usually sitting on top of a TV Stand. This was the case at my mother's house. Mellie said that she had asked my mother about something that was on the little shelf under the TV.

"Grommy, why do you have a sheet folded-up under your TV?" Mellie was always very aware of what was happening around her and very inquisitive.

Without skipping a beat, my mother said, "That is for those times when PawPaw and I rent porn, we can have sex in front of the TV."

My nine-year-old then asked what porn was, and my mother gave her a graphic definition of Pornography and sex.

I'll just give you, dear reader, a moment to let that sink in.

It was the kind of thing I had grown up with, and I pretty much allowed my mother to continue to abuse and degrade me, but not my children!

My husband and I agreed that was the end. We would not allow her to have any more contact with our children, nor did I want any contact with her. I spent the next few days on pins and needles awaiting her next phone call, at which point I would have to confront her. Anxiety, thy name be Mother!

Fortunately, I had an appointment to visit my therapist a few days later. I told her what had happened. She pointed out that my mother was “toxic”. A word I had never heard used to describe a person. Suddenly, I saw all these signs flashing in my head concerning my mother. Danger! Poison! Caution! Warning! Beware! After thirty years of knowing there was *something* wrong with my mother, suddenly it all clicked. Being around my mother was *unhealthy*.

My therapist told me that my mother would never change, and it was my responsibility to protect my children from her toxicity. I completely agreed with her interpretation of the situation, and we both agreed that I did not need my mother in my life. But how did I go about that? I could NOT confront her. My heart could not take that. Just thinking about it brought on palpitations.

My therapist suggested I write my mother a letter. She said that I should ask for some time to work out some issues.

“She will call me, or she will show up at my house and skin me alive. I won’t know how to handle it,” I told her.

My therapist simply stated, “Ask that she not call, or contact you in any way, for an unspecified amount of time. Tell her you just need to sort out a few things. This way, she won’t feel like you have completely broken contact with her. She’ll feel that there will be future opportunities for her to reel you back in at that time.” I was rapidly scribbling notes.

She continued, "Don't give excuses, don't justify your decision, don't make accusations. If you make her feel like she is being attacked, she will strike back."

As soon as I got home, I mailed a carefully worded letter to her. I did ask that she not contact my children either, as I felt she was not a good influence on them. That may, or may not, go over well, but I felt the need to be specific about that. I did not want her contacting them.

A week later, I received a letter from my mother in which she said she would honor my decision. She stated emphatically that she disagreed with me about her being a bad influence on my children, but that as their mother, she respected my decision to protect my children from any perceived threat. Maybe not in those words, but that was the gist.

She had said things like that to me before. I recognized it for what it was. If I let her back in, she was setting me up for another fall. "I respect your decision. I'm just sorry you're so overly sensitive."

She stated in her letter that she didn't want my girls to think that she had abandoned them, so she asked if it would be alright for her to send birthday cards. I wrote a short note telling her that she was welcome to send birthday cards, but that any correspondence my children received from her would first be read by me. Over time I had witnessed my mother use badmouthing to poison other relationships my sister and I had. With our father and his parents, to name a few. She had overtly demeaned me to my children in the past, telling them I was not very bright, and that I was overly sensitive. I was not going to let that happen ever again.

I went for eight years with No Contact. It was then that I began referring to her as Mother.

Eight years. It was the best eight years of my life, which is not to say I didn't continue to deal with Mother Issues. The emotional scars continued to show themselves in some inopportune moments. I continued to require therapy, just to cope with the unfortunate lessons I had learned, and to recognize the appropriate vs. inappropriate actions. I had to learn, and continue to learn, what society expects and considers "appropriate." It's a daily struggle with self-esteem, constantly second-guessing my decisions even twenty years after her death.

Part 5

Love doesn't die a natural death.

Love has to be killed,

either by neglect or narcissism.

Frank Salvato

Chapter 23

Starship Officers Only

*I*n the summer of 1997, one year before graduating high school, Mellie came to me and said she'd like to see my mother. After a discussion of how that might go, and in what way I would need to handle it for my self-protection, we agreed that I would call and make that happen. I got my mother's phone number from my sister and gave her a call. By this time, Mother had divorced Warren and was living alone in the country. I asked when a good time would be for me to bring my girls down for a short visit. We went the next weekend. It was a very pleasant visit. It had been eight years since I'd had any contact with her. She was on her best behavior.

We continued to stay in contact after that, on my terms. I explained to her that for us to have any kind of relationship, she would have to show me some respect and some common courtesy. I told her that I felt burned and would naturally have my guard up. I flat out told her, "I don't trust you."

Normally, experts agree, a narcissist will never change. And maybe she was playing me, just until I let my guard down, but she never gave me any trouble after that. On the other hand, she only lived a year after we resumed our relationship. It's impossible to say what our relationship would have looked like in time.

Later in 1997, Lisa called to tell me that she had won a radio contest. Grand Prize was a trip for two to Las Vegas for the Grand Opening of The Star Trek Experience at the Las Vegas Hilton, scheduled for January 2, 1998. The trip included round-trip airfare with two nights at the Hilton, and a limousine from the airport.

Lisa told me that her husband wasn't at all interested in going, so she had offered Mother the opportunity, but Mother suggested she take me instead. I was thrilled. She told me that some details needed to be finalized and that I should take over that duty because it involved some long-distance phone calls. So, of course, she left those up to me. I was happy to do it for the opportunity to go to Vegas for this great honor. The young lady that was our liaison was so excited for us. Every time we spoke, she told me about all the new science fiction actors who had contracted to attend the event. It sounded more and more like a Hollywood Red Carpet event. She stressed it was a Black-Tie Affair.

We had a whole month to get ready. I bought a fabulous suit to go with my flat-black ballet slippers. I wanted to be comfortable, and heels do not work for me. It was a very nice, Tuxedo-style pantsuit, black with just a touch of multi-colored pinstriping. Lisa asked if my neighbor across the street might be willing to loan her something since they were about the same size. So, that job got left up to me as well. Fortunately, my neighbor happily lent us a dress for Lisa. I, of course, had it dry cleaned before returning it to my neighbor.

When we arrived in Las Vegas, there was a limousine waiting for us. The driver, a woman, told us to help ourselves to the drinks and snacks. Lisa and I each put one wine cooler in our purses for later. Neither of us was comfortable in an elegant setting.

When we got to the Las Vegas Hilton, Lisa had to get us checked in, since everything was in her name. Before I left home, Dan told me his strategy for picking the best slot-machine. I don't know where he came up with it, as neither of us had ever touched a slot machine. But I followed his directions and found a machine that I thought he would approve. I put in two quarters and BAM! I won one hundred twenty-five dollars. I didn't even know how to retrieve the money from the machine.

That night I offered to buy dinner for both of us with my winnings. I had been to a *Medieval Times* restaurant before, and I thought Lisa would enjoy that. So, I made reservations at Excalibur for their dinner theater. We both enjoyed it immensely.

The next day we took a shuttle to The Strip. We walked for miles, sightseeing and taking a bunch of pictures. We were sitting on a bench in front of *New York, New York*, when Lisa spotted one of her favorite actors from the *Star Trek* series. Armin Shimerman, who played Quark on *Deep Space Nine*, was walking by us with his wife. Lisa got his autograph, and I asked if they were in town for the *Star Trek Experience* opening. He said they were and hoped to see us there. They were both very gracious. I think he was more than a little bit flattered that anyone even recognized him out of costume and make-up.

We got back to the hotel and got our clothes changed. When we went downstairs, we ran into Michael Dorn, who played Worf on *Deep Space Nine*, walking with Marina Sirtis, who played Counselor Deana Troi on *Star Trek, The Next Generation*. After getting their autographs, Lisa and I went looking for the party. It was a madhouse down there.

Finally, we decided to get in line for *The Experience*. The line followed a narrow, possibly 10' wide, raised walkway, up and around the entire casino. It was considered a walk-through museum, along the *Star Trek* timeline. It was fascinating, to Trekkies and Trekkers alike.

We probably should have gone to the party first, but we didn't know that at the time. We were in that line for well over two hours. Not only did we have all that memorabilia to enjoy, but we had a great view of all the stars as they came in below us. At one point we saw Jeri Ryan, who was playing Seven of Nine on *Star Trek: Voyager* at the time, walking in wearing five-inch stilettos. She started toward a long set of stairs going down to the Promenade and Quark's Bar. I was really concerned about her in those heels, but she just trotted down those stairs with more grace than I could have done in my bare feet.

Eventually, after following the Star Trek timeline, we ended up in a hallway designated for Employees Only. For just a second we wondered, *How did we get here?* Other signs informed us we had entered a passageway for Starship Officers Only. Actors, dressed as Starship personnel, began asking why we were there, where had we come from? We were taken to a shuttlecraft loading pad, where we were loaded and transferred to The Enterprise.

After being loaded on a ride meant to resemble a shuttlecraft, screens all around us began showing images of space, and we were being rocked around as though our craft was avoiding obstacles. Suddenly there were enemy spacecraft firing torpedoes at us. The lights began to flash, and the sounds of battle were all around us. We landed on The Enterprise and disembarked the shuttlecraft, where we saw Starfleet crew members rushing about. We were quickly loaded onto a large Turbolift, where we began the ascent to the Bridge. The lights went out, and it was suddenly pitch black. We continued our assent in the dark.

The sounds were continuous throughout this whole adventure, including people gasping and some even screaming. The floor under our feet was never still. When the lights came back on, we were escorted off the Turbolift and onto the deck of the Enterprise-D. And Boy! It was magnificent!

A Starfleet officer arrived to tell us that we had been transported to the future. One of the people in our group is an ancestor of James T. Kirk, but there was no time to determine which of us was his nine-times great grandparent. It was imperative that we all survive the war to ensure his ancestor be saved, or Captain Kirk will never be born.

We were taken to the transporter room where we were transported back to the past, our time. We were then loaded on another shuttlecraft where we were to be taken to our original location. The Las Vegas Hilton is below our shuttlecraft, we can see it, but aliens have followed us. Our shuttlecraft takes a direct hit, and we crash land on the roof of the Hilton. It was all very exciting. It was unbelievable. We loved it so much, and I couldn't wait to share it with Dan. Three years later, I had the opportunity to take Dan and Karly.

Lisa and I finally made it to the party, but it was nearly over. Most of the celebrities had left. I saw Chase Masterson, who played Leeta on *Deep Space Nine*, at the dessert table, all alone. I jumped up and went over. I asked her if she had enjoyed the Experience and inquired about what she thought of the deck of the Enterprise-D. She got so excited, and she said it was better than the studio set. I didn't want to be a pest, so I went back to my table. She followed me to our table and told me why it was better than the studio set. She said the set is only that little bit that you see on the TV screen. Unlike "what they have upstairs, which is a 365-degree replica of the *Bridge*," she told us. She was so friendly.

After we ate, Lisa and I went to get our pictures with a Klingon. They had a professional photographer set-up with a green screen and an actor in costume. Our Klingon was a woman. As we all know, Klingon women are warriors. Lisa is five feet, ten inches in her stocking feet. In heels, she was six-feet tall, right up there with this Klingon warrior. The actress, who was playing the Klingon Warrior, had some fun with us. She pretended to be trying to kill me, while my sister was fighting the warrior to save my life. The photographer was having some fun, too. We ended up with half a dozen photos.

The next day our limousine picked us up and took us back to the airport. When I got home, I called Mother to tell her all about it. I told her about winning a hundred and twenty-five dollars and taking Lisa to dinner.

"So, with the two hundred I gave Lisa to help with your meals, you two probably weren't out any money at all on meals," Mother said.

"What two hundred dollars?" I asked her.

She said she had given Lisa two hundred dollars to help pay for some of our meals. I told her, Lisa never mentioned that. Mother was not surprised, and neither was I.

Lisa had her issues, being raised by our mother. The most obvious manifestation was her secretiveness. She was never one to confide in others. But, if she were going to, it would have been me. Lisa had one friend that I am aware of, and that lasted less than a year while we lived in Arizona.

Lisa was cheap. Like no one I have ever known. She bought birthday gifts from Garage Sales. Even greeting cards all came from Garage Sales. I don't have a problem with that, except that I know Lisa. Since a very early age, if she got a dime to go to the corner store, she would find something for a nickel and save the other five cents. She has always been a big saver. So, when she went to Mother for a new washing machine, it wasn't that she didn't have the money tucked away somewhere, she just didn't want to spend her own money. Lisa was so cheap, (How cheap was she?) she would keep a birthday card in her car until the next time she was near your house, then leave it in the mailbox, to save the stamp.

In 1988 there was a Maize family reunion coming up in Pawnee, Oklahoma. Lisa had decided to go with her then five-year-old son, Dillon. She asked if we could meet them at a McDonald's on the way and let them ride with us from there. Of course, she offered no money to help with the gas, but we didn't expect it, either.

During the reunion, our father asked us to pose together so he could take our picture. We both took a seat on a stone wall, and I put my arm around her. Lisa pulled away and said, "I didn't say you could touch me." She was serious.

I know I went through a phase where I didn't want strangers to hug me, like the first time I met one of my sisters-in-law. I put my hand out and said, "I'm not a hugger," but smiled and welcomed her into our home. Just a few years later, I began to feel more comfortable with being hugged, and have since grown to like it. But I'm Lisa's only sister, as far as she is concerned. She doesn't count Lois's kids as her siblings.

I'll never forget the first time she met Mellie. We were visiting from Germany, so Mellie was three months old. As I handed Mellie to my sister, I said, "Go to Aunt Lisa." My sister pounced on that. She said, "Don't call me that! I don't call her Niece Mellie!"

Chapter 24

The Month That Wouldn't End

*D*an got a pay raise that allowed me to quit working and stay home with our children, full time. Karly started Kindergarten as Mellie began fifth grade. We stopped paying for daycare, which took my whole paycheck anyway, and Mellie began catching the bus to school in front of our house. I dropped Karly at school for afternoon classes, and she rode the bus home with Mellie.

I learned to budget and cut coupons. I cooked at home every night, rather than eating out. I even tried making clothes for my girls, but that ended up costing more than buying off the rack.

Once Karly started school full time, I took some college courses. In the past we had gone overboard on Christmas presents; that stopped. I had quality time with our girls, as opposed to just buying presents for the sake of buying presents.

Eventually, we bought a travel trailer that needed some renovating. Dan rebuilt the entire front wall, making it sturdy and waterproof. We spent our free time at the lake. We swam, played cards, dominos and dice games. We installed a small TV with a VHS player to watch movies after the mosquitos came out at night. Dan grilled while I made side dishes on the stove. We got our money's worth out of that little trailer.

In the meantime, over the past eight years, my sister had remained in constant contact with Mother, allowing Mother to continue her old ways in their relationship.

When Mellie turned fifteen, she no longer wanted to hang-out with us. She said camping was boring, so of course, Karly agreed with her big sister. Karly needed braces, so we sold the trailer and got Karly braces.

When Mellie turned sixteen, we bought a little Ford pick-up truck with a standard transmission. Dan had it painted black and put some nice wheels on it. It was our truck, but we bought it for Mellie to use. She had to keep her grades up and pay for her own gas. She got an after-school job and continued to do well in school.

The past few years Mellie tried to avoid her little sister, but once she got her driver's license, she began taking Karly and Karly's friends places. They all went to a few concerts together, or the mall. Oklahoma City has an amusement park, Frontier City, that they had Season Passes to, so they spent some time there. Mellie and Karly became very close during this time. It warmed my heart to see them spending time together.

The following May of 1998, ten months after resuming contact with my mother, Mellie graduated high school. We had a party to celebrate, and Mother attended, at Mellie's request.

A week later, Mother had an "episode." She had collapsed at home, alone. She was living out in the country, far from medical help, so it scared her. She immediately decided she needed to move to the city, maybe closer to my sister. She found a new apartment near Lisa that was handicap accessible. She made a doctor's appointment and decided to quit smoking. She went to a local store to buy "the patch" to help her quit. They didn't have Step-1, so she bought Step-2. She never opened the package and never smoked another cigarette.

This was a woman who had smoked a minimum of a pack a day since she was 18 years old. Her beer consumption was probably a 12-pack a day. She loved her beer. If she didn't have a cup of coffee in her hand, she had a beer. She began telling us when we were very young that she wasn't a happy person and would be glad when her life ended. She smoked, drank, and ate unhealthy foods, all in an effort to hurry along the process. But when it came down to it, she got scared.

In the handicap accessible apartment near my sister, she was closer to doctors and hospitals; an hour away from me.

Now that she was closer, we explored a new relationship, that I am happy to say, was very cordial. She told me that she had learned a lot over the past eight years. She respected me, and my decision to do what I felt was right for my children. I believe she also saw a change in me; a stronger, more confident person. In my opinion, she realized that if she was going to have any relationship with me, she would have to be respectful. I could not be bought. She didn't have anything I wanted or needed. And I was on High Alert to her bullshit.

Mother told me that she knew Lisa didn't necessarily want to have a relationship with her. She felt Lisa stayed in it for what she could get. That was the impression Mother had of their relationship. However, Mother said she would never give Lisa cash. Mother bought her what she needed, but never gave her cash. Mother said that giving Lisa cash didn't do any good. It just disappeared, with nothing to show for it. That was their relationship, according to Mother. Having said that, Mother may have been feeding me a line of crap in an effort at continued gaslighting of my relationship with my sister. No telling what Mother was telling Lisa about me.

Mother's primary care physician was concerned enough to send her to a cardiologist. Mother had some medical tests done to figure out what was going on with her heart. When an x-ray and a CT

Scan were inconclusive, the cardiologist decided Mother required an exploratory procedure, via laparoscopy. Lisa dropped Mother off at the hospital, and I stayed with her for the "out-patient" procedure, agreeing to take Mother home afterward. The doctor told me that the results were inconclusive. She needed a "tilt-table test." He said their hospital didn't have one, so she would need to contact her Primary Care Physician and get him to refer her to another hospital for that procedure. I drove her home and made her promise to call her doctor. In our old relationship, I would have taken on that responsibility, but in our new relationship, I left it up to her to follow-up with her doctor.

Near the end of June 1998, Dan, Karly and I were leaving on vacation. Mellie was working full-time and agreed to stay home with the dogs. A few days before we were due to leave, we woke to a flooded house sitting in two inches of water. A twenty-cent "O" ring under the kitchen faucet had rotted and failed. Fortunately, our house was on a slab. We called Steam Masters to come out to the house to properly clean the mess. They got all the water out and set-up dehumidifiers. After they left, the insurance adjuster came out and said that all the flooring would be replaced. The adjuster said we could leave it for now, and the installers would pull it out when they came. However, because we were leaving town and would be gone for two weeks, she suggested we might want to go ahead and pull the carpet in the living room, where it had soaked up most of the water. Since we were leaving Mellie home with the dogs, we thought it best to go ahead and pull the carpet out.

The day before we left, I talked to my mother on the phone for a good, long hour. She assured me she had put a call into her doctor for the referral to have the tilt-table test done. I told her about our house flooding a couple of days earlier. Then Mother said, "I have a small Life Insurance policy in your name through my old job at AT&T." I told her she should leave it to Lisa.

"She has stayed by you all these years. She deserves it," I said. And quite honestly, she had nothing I wanted.

Mother said, "It's not much. I want you to have it. Lisa will get everything else. My car, furniture, AT&T stocks, and Granny's whole coin collection. She'll get more than her share, don't worry about her."

I told her I wasn't going to argue with her. I just didn't want to talk about it. If she wanted to discuss it more, we'd get together when I got back from vacation.

A week later, July 6th, Dan, Karly and I were at his father's house in Tacoma when the phone rang. It was Mellie. She said that my mother had died. I needed to call my sister. Poor little Mellie, she was hysterical. I asked why she was taking it so hard. She told me she wasn't crying because Mother had died, she was stressed about having to be the one to tell me. Also, she'd had a hard time finding the phone number to Grandpa's house; Dan's biological father. Mellie had called her Grandma Betty, Dan's mother, and asked if she could help find the number. Mellie knew Grandma Betty was very bitter toward her ex-husband but said she couldn't think who else to call in her anxiety. Just about an hour later, my father called to see how I was; which I considered extremely thoughtful. I told Mellie, "We all knew she'd been sick, and there was something going on with her heart. I'm not surprised." I felt horrible for Mellie, but, in truth, I was more than a tiny bit relieved. That part of my life would not be causing me any more anxiety, or so I thought.

I called Lisa and asked if she needed me to come home. She said no that Mother was being cremated, so there was nothing for me to do. We had her Will, and we knew she didn't want any kind of service, but we had some decisions to make when I got back.

Mother had contacted the University of Oklahoma Willed Body Program. Upon her death, my sister was to call them. They would be responsible for procuring the deceased, storage of the body, issuing the cadaver to a class for medical education and/or research. The body would then be cremated, and the ashes returned to the family.

When Lisa called The University of Oklahoma, they said they had no use for her body in that state, having been dead for two days before being found. So, Lisa had her body taken to a funeral home for cremation.

Earlier in the week, Mother had made plans with her cousin to pick her up on his way to Hugo for a Fourth of July family reunion. He told me later that he had been trying to reach her on the morning of the fourth, to get directions to her place. But she never answered, so they went on to Hugo without her.

On the morning of the sixth, Lisa went over to check on her. She said she knocked on the door. When she didn't get an answer, she used her key to open the door. Lisa said that a horrible stench hit her as soon as she opened the door. She closed the door and went to the office to use the phone. She called her husband, who came and went in the apartment. He found Mother in the bathroom, on the floor. She had obviously been dead a while. One of the perks of the handicap accessible apartment was that there was a Call Cord on the wall in the bathroom for emergencies. It was hanging right next to her body. The Medical Examiner said she must have had a massive heart attack and been dead before she hit the floor. Exactly the way she wanted to go, like her father before her.

There were some members of our extended family, a couple of Mother's cousins, who felt I should have come home right away. They also had opinions about how we handled disposing of her remains. They thought we should, at the very least, have a funeral for everyone to get closure. But Lisa and I had, in writing, her wish to "not have a funeral, not have a grave." Because she had donated her body to science, she didn't anticipate there being a body with which to contend. And let's face it, she was our mother — the biggest narcissistic, controlling force in our lives. We had every right to handle it in our own way. And who, if not us, would know exactly how she would have altered her plans, had she known it would be necessary?

How to Memorialize a Loved One Who Asked for No Funeral[19]

A dying person's request for no funeral can be conflicting and painful for the family. For many, it just doesn't feel right to bury someone you love without taking the time to remember them. Others may see the request as a great way to avoid expensive funeral costs as they mourn individually. But for those families that feel they are missing out on something, "no funeral" is a very big ask.

A Person's Final Wishes Should Be Honored

As a society, we attempt to alleviate fear of death by ensuring people that their final wishes will be honored. In order to do that, people leave verbal and written wishes with their most trusted loved ones on all types of considerations. We assure our loved ones that we will protect their assets, take care of their dependents, and honor their memory once they are gone.

These are promises that are easy to break, because the person to whom the promise is made is not alive to hold anyone accountable. It is morally and ethically important to keep our promises to the dead, so long as those promises are possible, reasonable, and won't cause harm to anyone.

Find a Private Way to Honor Your Loved One

From planting a memorial tree to honoring your loved one on their birthday or deathiversary. There are many unique ways to privately create a ritual that helps you mourn the loss.

Chapter 25

Mother Didn't Leave Me Enough for a New Kitchen Sink

*A*fter we left Tacoma, Dan, Karla and I drove out to West Port to visit with Dan's mother and stepfather.

Lee was very ill. His doctors told him his time was short, but he didn't want to spend the time he had left in the bedroom. He wanted to be out in the living room, spending time with us while we were there. Lee was unable to hold any food down, but I knew he loved ice cream. I offered to mix up a little bit of vanilla ice cream with a splash of root beer. He decided to give it a try. Surprisingly, it went down and stayed down. He asked for another. It was just a juice glassful, but it was something.

As we got ready to head to California, we knew we were saying our last goodbyes. It was a very difficult thing to do. We hugged, we kissed, we cried. He insisted on standing up to say goodbye for the last time. It was his way of honoring us. Lee was an amazing stepfather. In fact, Betty's kids called him Dad. He was their Dad. Their biological father was their Father. But Lee raised them and loved them as his own. The grandkids were his, through and through. They make no bones about that fact, to this day.

When I returned home from vacation, Mellie said that Lisa had been calling. She was eager to talk to me; so, I called her, as soon as I walked through the door. Lisa told me that a guy from MetLife wanted to talk to me. She said, "Call him and then call me back and tell me how much you get." My training kicked in. I needed her approval. I did what I was told. I did what was expected of me.

It was Sunday, so I left a message stating that he could reach me at home on Monday morning.

The day we got home from vacation Betty called. She said that if Dan wanted to see his Dad before he died, he'd better come back as soon as possible. He'd have to fly; there was no time to drive. So, Monday morning, I dropped Dan off at the airport for a 6 am flight.

When I got home from the airport, the phone was ringing. It was the guy from MetLife. As soon as I hung up talking to him, I called Lisa. I told her how much *my* inheritance was. I said, "Figure out the value of everything you got. If it's less than what I got, I'll make sure you get enough to make it even." She called me back the next day and said, "Let's call it even. That will just make it easier on me." Of course, I knew what all she had ended up with. I don't know what I would have done if she'd asked for some of my inheritance, knowing hers was at least as much as mine.

All the while, I was walking on concrete, and all my furniture was in the den or the garage because my home was waiting to be repaired from the flood. My stress level was through the roof.

That evening, Dan called from his Mother's. He said that he had gotten there just in time to say goodbye. He informed me he would be staying through the service. His Dad's ashes were to be scattered at sea.

I told him about my inheritance, and that I was expecting to receive confirmation of a Total Control Account policy in about a week. He told me to put Mellie on the same flight the following morning that he, himself, had taken that morning. She hadn't gotten to say goodbye, so he wanted her to be able to attend the service. Thank goodness for the inheritance. It could not have come at a better time.

The next morning, I took Mellie to the airport and headed home. As soon as I walked in the door, I realized that our seventeen-year-old Dachshund was in crisis. I was a frantic mess. I called my sister and asked her to come to me. I told her that I desperately needed her. I told her what was happening and that I needed to get my dog to the veterinarian and have him put to sleep. I believe it was the first time I'd asked for help since my mother refused to help me during my miscarriage, but I was in such a frantic state, I knew I couldn't drive myself and my sick little dog. Lisa came and took us to the veterinarian. I am ashamed to say, I handed them my little Dachsey and left — one of the biggest regrets of my life. I could not bear to watch him die. I was in an emotional crisis.

When I got home, I had to call my husband and tell him that his best little buddy was gone. We agreed that he wouldn't tell Mellie about our little Dachsey until they were heading back home.

After much consideration, my sister and I, the two people who knew our Mother best, decided that she would like to have her ashes scattered at Papa's Place down in Hugo. I called the current owner of the property, her cousin, who was living in Idaho and asked how he felt about us scattering Mother's ashes on his property. He told me, "I think that is perfect. She loved it there, and we all have such great memories of growing up down there. Yes, please do, scatter her ashes at Papa's."

Lisa and I waited until the weather cooled to plan a trip to Hugo, just the two of us, which is how our mother would have wanted it. I packed an ice chest with some cheese and crackers, fruit, and two wine coolers. I probably should have packed beer instead, in honor of Mother, but neither of us cared for beer.

I drove to my sister's house, picked her up, and was told what route I should take to Hugo. I had planned to take the Interstate, a straight shot to Hugo, but Lisa insisted it would save gas to take the back roads. I tried telling her that I was more comfortable taking the interstate, but she pushed back. Lisa fell into our mother's position of authority like the classic narcissist. As my training kicked in, I did what I was told.

Enough About You, Let's Talk About Me[20]

> Dr. Carter states, "Narcissists have little faith in others' ideas (or, put another way, in anyone else's ideas besides their own), so when someone has a different idea, they instinctively try to find what is wrong. It would never occur to them that they might learn something from someone else. They simply don't trust others. Everything they say and do communicates a very low regard for others' decision-making skills."

We took the back roads. Lisa, who was navigating, got us lost. We drove so far off-course we were in Texas before we realized we were lost. After much backtracking, we found our way to Hugo. We went to Papa's, set out a couple of lawn chairs, and placed the ice chest between us. We had our snack and toasted mother with the wine coolers, and then we tried to approximate where we remembered the barn being. Mother often talked about watching Papa milk the cows, always squirting milk at the cat waiting nearby. So, we scattered her ashes as close as possible to where we thought that might have taken place.

I laughingly told Lisa I would be taking the Interstate back. I had anticipated one tank of gas for the whole trip but hadn't planned for the detour. When I realized how low we were on fuel, we were on a Turnpike, with one gas station midway. We coasted in on fumes, and Lisa sat in the front passenger seat like the Queen of Sheba. She let me gas-up the car, clean the windows, and pay for the gas, all without offering any help whatsoever.

When I got home, I typed up a "faux-funeral brochure." Similar to one that would have been handed out at a funeral with information about the deceased. I described what Mother specifically asked that we *not* do, and then described what we *did* do. I mailed one to each of her extended family. Lisa and I felt we had honored our mother's wishes to the best of our ability.

A few years later, her cousin, the owner of Papa's Place, passed away. The property was left to his son. The whole family was informed of his plan to scatter his father's ashes at Papa's Place and invited anyone interested to come down. Dan and I went, of course. When it came time, my cousin asked me where exactly I had scattered Mother's ashes. His Dad wanted his ashes scattered in the same place. That confirmed, for me, that I had done right by my mother.

Unloved Daughters and Their Siblings[21]

While the patterns of sibling relationships may look similar in broad strokes, there are major differences when a mother is unloving.

First of all, the differential treatment is usually conscious and deliberate and even acknowledged, although it will usually be accompanied by a rationalization for the behavior, ***the unloved child will be labeled as stupid, stubborn or lazy in comparison with***

her "gifted" sibling and will be made to feel "less than" on the daily.

Second, many unloving mothers actively orchestrate their children's behavior by pitting them against each other or by co-opting the siblings so that the daughter becomes the odd girl out (a term called triangulation, a term coined by Murray Bowen[22]). Sometimes, ***the behavior is aimed at keeping the family's attention on the mother or making sure that the mother's vision of what's happening becomes the family truth.***

Third, ***an unloving mother will usually do what she can to make sure that sibling relationships are neither close nor intimate unless she is in control of them***.

Thus, the lack of maternal love is often not the only loss sustained; sibling relationships, a sense of belonging to a family, and connectedness are among the others, all of which affect the daughter's sense of self in myriad ways.

Daughters who were the odd girl out in their families of origin often report that they have difficulty forging close friendships with women and have trouble trusting their own judgments in relationships generally. They also report that they're highly sensitive to rejection and criticism.

Shortly thereafter, I received a packet from Lisa with some paperwork she had gotten from a lawyer, asking me to sign and forward it to his office. Essentially, it was saying that I had no rights to her inheritance. I was surprised that she would hire a lawyer to protect her inheritance from me, but I would never ask why she felt the need to go to that extreme. However, the only reason I can think of would be that she ended up with far more than Mother's MetLife policy had paid to me. Did she seriously think she had to protect her inheritance from me?

A few days later, Lisa and I were talking on the phone. I told her I had mailed the paperwork to her lawyer, hoping she might enlighten me as to why it was necessary. She did not.

In May of 1999, Lisa and I were talking on the phone. I told her we had hired some old guy to paint the outside of our house. I was laughing because, although he was doing a great job, and he was finishing up, it had taken him over a week to complete the job. That's when she said that her husband and son had replaced the siding and were currently replacing the framing around the windows on their house. I told her I thought that probably looked nice, and that I wanted to see it. We made plans for the following week, the day before my birthday. I would pick her up at her house, and we would go to lunch.

The morning we had planned to meet, Lisa called. She said she had business in town. "How about we just meet at the bank and go to lunch from there." I agreed.

We met at the Credit Union and went next door for Chinese. When we finished eating, she began to tell me that her lawyer had told her she didn't have to pay taxes on her inheritance. But then she had received a letter from the federal government saying she was late paying her taxes and would have to pay the penalty. Lisa said she told the lawyer to sell the stocks Mother left her from AT&T to pay the taxes, but that his secretary didn't make sure that was done right away. Lisa said his secretary waited until after the weekend to sell the stocks, and that in the meantime, the value had gone down so much that she lost $1,600. on the sale of the stocks.

That's when she said, "As it turns out, I didn't get enough from what Mother left me to buy a new kitchen sink." I will never forget those words, not as long as I live. Of course, I had been taught not to let anything show on my face. But my mind was saying, "She's lying. She just told me about the new siding. She's trying to pull something." I told her I would check to see how much was still in the MetLife account. I said she could have whatever was left, just to see her reaction. She instantly perked up and said, "Okay!"

I fumed all the way home. When I walked in the door, Dan and Mellie were sitting on the couch. I told them what had happened. Dan said, "Well, it's your money, you do what you want, but let me ask you this. Will you have anything to do with her after this?"

I said, "Never!"

"Then why give her anything?" he asked me.

I called Lisa and said, "Turns out, there's nothing left in the account." She hung up on me. I was never so disappointed in anyone in my life, until a few days later, when I received a letter from her, spewing venom, and dated on my birthday. She said that Mother had intended to have Lisa's name put on that policy; she just hadn't had a chance to get it changed.

I thought, *in eight years, she never had a chance.*

While I chose not to respond to her letter, I couldn't help but think she had hired an incompetent lawyer to keep me from getting my hands on her inheritance, and now wanted mine.

Isn't it ironic?

Alanis Morissette

Chapter 26

Grief Is as Individual as a Fingerprint

*M*ellie was taking classes at the Vocational-Technical center through the high school to become a Certified Nurses Aid. By graduation, she was a C.N.A. The neighbors next to us were both Respiratory Therapists. They told her that she could go to school to become a Respiratory Therapist and then continue her education while still working. We took Mellie to another Vo-Tech to sign her up for R.T. classes. The academic counselor was hesitant to let her sign-up for the classes. The counselor said that most of the R.T. students had been in the medical field for years when they transferred to the R.T. field. We assured the woman we had every confidence in Mellie's ability to keep up with the curriculum. We were willing to gamble our money to put her in the class.

Mellie jumped in with both feet. She started a study group, which met after hours. She made sure everyone got their assignments in, calling some of these people at home. Mellie even made plans with her classmates to go on a river float trip over a holiday. She got excellent grades and took a position at a local hospital upon finishing her first year in R.T. school.

She continued her R.T. classes the following year and took additional classes at a city college to get her Associates degree.

Mellie moved into a house with her best friend from high school. Kim had bought a little farmhouse near her parents, about three miles from us. Kim didn't like staying there alone, so she asked Mellie to move in with her. I saw more of Mellie after she moved out than when she lived at home. She would stop by after classes every day to have lunch with me.

On Friday, September 15, 2000, Mellie stopped in for lunch. I was running out the door to go pick up Karly for a doctor's appointment. Mellie was standing at the kitchen counter, making herself a sandwich the last time I saw her. I said, "I love you!" She said it back, and out the door I went.

That night, Dan was out all-night riding with the Oklahoma City Police Department Mounted Patrol. He got in bed at about five o'clock on the sixteenth. At about six o'clock, Karly came knocking at our bedroom door. She was crying and saying, "Mellie has been in an accident." I jumped up and opened the door. Karly had the phone in her hand.

Mellie and Kim had been to a party the night before. They got home just fine, but then decided to drive into the city for breakfast. When Kim pulled into the parking lot of the restaurant, she said Mellie was asleep in the passenger seat, so she decided just to go home.

As they were driving down Tenth Street, two miles from home, Kim fell asleep as well. The truck went off the road and hit a stand of trees.

Kim had to kick out the windshield to get out of the truck. She then ran half a mile back to the nearest house to call for help.

It was Kim's father calling us that morning. When Karly answered, he thought it was me and told her everything he knew. He went over it again when I got on the phone. He said that a helicopter had come and Medi-Flighted Mellie to the same hospital where she worked. I told him we were heading to the hospital right away.

When the three of us arrived at the emergency room, I ran to the desk and said I was looking for my daughter and gave them her name. It registered in my brain that there was medical staff crying all around me. I didn't make the connection that these were Mellie's co-workers. A doctor came through the swinging doors and said that she had been flown to a different hospital, not that one. We later found out that word had gotten to them about our Mellie, and that was why everyone was in tears.

We got in the car and headed to the other hospital. We were in a nightmare. You know the one. Where you're running as hard and as fast as you can, but you just can't get there. It felt like hours before we finally got to the right place and started getting answers. At this point, I still didn't know what to expect. I assumed some surgery would be involved, and she would be fine.

Dan told me later when Medi-Flight is called; it rarely turns out that way. We were told that she was being worked on; they would keep us updated. I was asked to do some paperwork, get her insurance information to billing, etc.

We were surrounded by men and women in uniform. One member of our police family lived across the street from Mellie's boyfriend. They were friends, and he knew Tom was dating a police officer's daughter. Tom had worked the night before and would be leaving work soon, so his neighbor called him and told him to wait for him at work. Tom was brought to the hospital to wait with us.

Dan was not himself, he was certainly worried about our baby girl, but he was also extremely tired. I had never known him to not be in control of any given situation, but in this instance, he had shut down. I went to get the paperwork taken care of, and all the insurance information filed. It was surreal, having to answer their routine insurance questions, as though my daughter weren't dying in the next room. I had to make a conscious effort to stay in the moment and answer their questions.

The doctor, a good friend of Dan's, came out and told us that our daughter had been revived numerous times. Twice in the helicopter, and several times since arriving at the hospital. While waiting for the results of some tests, he said they hadn't given up on her. However, at this point, the tests showed that she was brain-dead. He needed us to tell him what we wanted him to do. I told him to stop abusing her body and let her go. Then I looked at Dan and asked, "Right?" He and Karly agreed.

Dan's friend, Jeff, a police officer, had gone in to see Mellie. He told us that we did not want to see her in that condition. As a police officer, Dan had been in similar situations where he told family members that he would advise them not to see their loved ones torn and broken bodies, as it's not something you need in your head. You will never forget that sight. We trusted our friend to advise us in this situation. We waited until her heart stopped for the last time, and we left the hospital.

Jeff drove us home in our car, while his wife followed us in theirs. When we pulled up at our house, there were police cars everywhere, just waiting for us to arrive. Kim was parked in front of our house with her parents. She got out and came to us, crying and begging us to forgive her. We held her, assuring her as best we could, and asked her parents to take her home. We couldn't deal with her right then. We had to deal with our emotions, as well as all these people.

I ran in the house and put on a pot of coffee. I began picking up any clutter I saw. I washed any dishes in the sink. That was my go-to reaction. I had to make sure everyone was taken care of.

I have been described as a nurturer. I don't see myself that way. I see myself as someone who is obsessed with the need to please; to take care of others before myself. That's not healthy. That is what I was doing when my daughter died. I began taking care of others instead of myself.

Then I had to make the phone calls. I had to call friends and family to let them know. In between those calls, I got calls from other people finding out about our loss. I went into the bedroom to make the calls. I didn't want to be with all the people coming in and out of our home. I wasn't comfortable with the looks, the questions, the sympathy, any of it. I didn't know how to act. I wasn't taught to accept a compliment, let alone condolences.

Mindfulness & Grief, Heather Stang, M.A.[23]

> "While we can make a list of common reactions that include thoughts, feelings, and cognitions, we know that no two people will have exactly the same story of love and loss. That is why prescriptive models of grief don't work."
>
> She continues to say, "Adapting to your loss includes remembering the person who died, reconstructing your relationship, and finding a way to exist in the world without that person."

I called my father, who called and told my sister. Lisa called me and basically asked how it happened and who was driving. That was it. She didn't ask how I was doing. She has never once, in the nineteen years since we lost our daughter, asked how I was coping with the loss.

Dan and I had to make funeral arrangements. Mellie was being cremated, and we decided to have a service.

My mother's cousin, a minister in Texas, agreed to perform the service at a local church that many of my cousins attended. My cousin, Dale, a favorite of Mellie, agreed to write and read the eulogy. He had spent an evening with us, as well as Mellie's friend and roommate, Kim. We told him funny stories about Mellie because she had such a great personality, and we wanted that to come through.

Another of my cousins agreed to perform two songs for us. He was wonderful.

A few weeks before Mellie died, Dan and I were sitting in our living room talking about what we wanted done with our bodies after we died. At that time, Dan said he wanted his ashes scattered on our favorite ski trails. I said I really didn't have a preference. If I died after him, I would want my ashes scattered where his ashes had been scattered.

Mellie came in, so naturally, we asked her, "If you were to die tomorrow, what do you want done with your body?"

She didn't hesitate, "I want my ashes scattered at sea with Grandpa."

Dan's stepfather, Lee, had died in 1998. He was a veteran of World War II, Korea and Vietnam. As such, the Coast Guard took his family out in the ocean where they scattered his ashes and provided the family with the exact coordinates. That's where Mellie wanted her ashes scattered.

Dan and I both agreed the accident wasn't Kim's fault any more than it was Mellie's fault. In fact, he and I went to court with Kim and her parents. We stood in front of the judge and told him we did not feel that Kim should be charged with manslaughter, as it was purely an accident, and that either of them could have been driving that night. The judge took into consideration our statements and gave her probation with Community Service. The charges finally came down to Negligent Homicide. Because she was underage at the time, she was also charged with Driving Under the Influence. Any amount of alcohol in an underage driver's blood, even the slightest bit, is considered DUI. Kim was two months shy of turning twenty-one. Blood tests of both girls showed they had probably been sipping a beer all night.

Kim attended several Impaired Driving Classes as a guest speaker during her time on probation. She had a poster-sized picture of our beautiful Mellie, and one of her wrecked truck to put on display as she told the story of how her best friend had died. All because they had been out all night and decided to drive to a restaurant for breakfast. She had to confess to having been drinking while underage, as well. She was not allowed to make excuses, only to take responsibility and try to convince the people in the room not to make the same mistakes.

Kim told us that the first time she had to get up in front of a crowd and tell her story, it was the hardest thing she'd ever had to do. She said that it got easier because afterward young people always came up to her and told her that her story had made an impression on them. More so than when someone in their fifties tried to relate to them. I hope Kim's story saved some lives.

In October, we flew into Seattle, rented a car, and headed out to the ocean. Dan had been in contact with his siblings. He chartered a boat to take about twenty of us out to the exact location Lee's ashes had been scattered. Anyone who didn't plan to make the drive back to Seattle had a room rented at the Westport Inn and Suites. The day we planned to go out, we all caravanned to Westport Charter for the boat. Unfortunately, when we got there, they said that the winds were too high. They wouldn't be able to take us out. Last-minute change of plans, we all drove to the Jetty.

The Jetty was a favorite place of all the grandkids. So many memories were created at The Jetty. Hundreds of pictures taken there. I could do a whole scrapbook of all the grandkids growing up at The

Jetty. Dan and I decided it would be perfect. Dan's mother, Betty, said that some of Lee's favorite memories with the grandkids were at The Jetty. She loved the idea, too.

When we got to the Jetty, the sky was overcast, and the wind was blowing like crazy. It was cold and dreary. Generally, the weather sucked. Dan and his brother, Glen, climbed up and over the giant boulders. As they looked for a safe place from which to scatter the ashes, the clouds broke. The sun came out. The wind died down. Suddenly, it was a beautiful day at the ocean.

Dan leaned out and scattered the ashes. We all had climbed up as far as we felt safe. Originally, we were all going to scatter long-stemmed red roses from the boat. Instead, they were tossed out to sea from the Jetty. Then several of the kids noticed there were two seals not too far off the Jetty, watching us. We all cried and laughed and hugged each other. It was perfect.

One of Grandpa Lee's favorite jokes with Mellie was, "Hey, did I ever tell you about the deer I saw by our house." It was a story he'd told about one hundred times, so when he asked her if he'd told her, she always answered the same way.

"Yes, Grandpa, you told me." She said it with that long-suffering tone that every teenager has. It was *their* joke.

As we drove away from The Jetty, Grandma Betty said, "I can picture them together, holding hands and walking down the beach. Together forever."

Karly said, "And he's asking her, 'Hey, did I ever tell you about the deer I saw by our house?'" We all laughed, and it was a good way to leave our Baby Girl.

After we lost our daughter, I felt like I was floundering. I still had a fifteen-year-old to think about, and we certainly wanted her life to be as happy as possible. We had always been such a happy family. We didn't want that to change for Karly. She needed to grieve, but none of us wanted to get stuck in that place.

That first day, one of Karly's friends came to the house to pick her up and take her to a house where all her friends had gathered to support her. She certainly didn't want to stay home with all the strangers coming in and out. I wished I could go with her.

Karly and I went to grief counseling, separately. Dan stayed up late, sometimes all night, talking to his friend, Jeff, on the phone. Jeff and his wife are devout Christians, and that may have helped Dan. I don't know how their conversations went. Dan said those conversations got him through the toughest times.

I went to one of the Big Book Stores in the city. I went to the Grief section and took down one of every book on losing a child. I stacked them on a table and got a cup of coffee. If I had to, I would be there all day.

I picked up the first book and turned it over to read the back. If it said anything about depending on God or religion to get me through, I set it aside. I needed to know what to expect in a future that would no longer include my daughter. How was that going to look? I found one book, one that sounded like what I was looking for. I took it home and put it on a shelf.

A few weeks later, our friends from Canada came down for their annual visit. Their friend had lost her son just a few years earlier, and when our friends told her about our loss, she gave them a book to bring to me, with a note inside. She said it was a book that helped her "tremendously." It was the exact same book I had put on the shelf a few weeks earlier.

Of the hundreds of books out there on grieving the death of your child, it was that book. Bewildering, to say the least. *When the Bough Breaks: Forever After the Death of a Son or Daughter,* by

Judith R. Bernstein. Dr. Bernstein's book really helped me. It is filled with stories from parents, describing what they went through over the next several years. It gave me some insight into what I might expect, which was what I needed.

When my children were young, I was not kind to them. I didn't have the patience I should have had. I expected too much of them at such a young age. I cursed at them. I was the toxic influence in their lives. That is the biggest regret I have — they did nothing to deserve to be spoken to so harshly. I can't even remember anything they did that caused me to blow my top. But I do remember, specifically, the last time.

At about this same time, my mother had told my children that she and PawPaw were having sex in front of the TV while they watched porn. I was torn about what I should do. I hadn't yet grown the backbone necessary to cut my mother out of our lives. Then one day Mellie came home from a friend's house, and I lashed out at her. There was a flyswatter sitting next to me. I grabbed the flyswatter and swatted her upper leg with it yelling at her for going off without asking permission.

Mellie cried and grabbed her little leg telling me, "I did ask. You said I could go. You were watching your Soap." Oh my God, what kind of monster had I become. I was so completely absorbed in my Soap Opera I had just wanted her to go away. I held her and apologized over and over. I told her there was no excuse for me to treat her that way, and things were going to change.

I decided then and there to be a better mother to my children. And a better wife to my husband. I went to my counselor and told her, not only about what I had done, but what had occurred with my mother a few days earlier. That's when she told me that I needed to cut my mother out of my life. And that I needed to pay attention to the choices I made based on my mother's influence. *Question my choices.* She also explained about addiction. She said I had an addictive personality that included not only smoking but also my addiction to "my soap opera."

I stopped watching that soap. In fact, I stopped allowing TV shows to monopolize my time. I quit smoking, which was one of the best decisions I've ever made. I still love watching my favorite shows, but they are not the priority in my life.

I wasn't a perfect mother, but my children and I had a wonderful and close relationship after that. I made amends with them and should be able to forgive myself, but it's hard. The guilt is suffocating.

After Mellie died, Dan and I told ourselves that we were lucky because we were both in a good place in our relationship with her. We had nothing to regret. And that's true, about our relationship at the time. But I will always regret the years that I was impatient and unkind to my children. I wish I could do them over.

As I write this, I realize I'm still learning. I see that blaming and complaining is useless, and that making excuses is passing the blame. I realize that I have created all the good and all the bad in my life. I made some bad choices, and now it's time to forgive myself, right the wrong, and move on.

My mother has been dead for over twenty years. It's time to stop using her as an excuse for my bad decisions.

Christmas '97. Mellie in the back with Karly, JoJo and Dan.

Chapter 27

05-05-05

I realized I needed more counseling to get through my loss. I sat down with Dan and cried for the first time in front of him. Not just silent tears, but I explained that I hadn't grieved because I wasn't comfortable with my emotions. He just held me and let me pour out my feelings to him.

I told Karly I was going to get some grief counseling and asked if she'd like to talk to someone. She agreed, stating she could benefit from counseling, as well. I made our appointments at the same time, with two different counselors in the same location. That worked out well. The counseling was helpful for me and seemed to be helping Karly.

After we lost Mellie, the three of us decided we needed to move. It was so hard living in the house where she had grown up. Everything reminded us of her, not that moving would make us forget her. It had become Mellie's habit to stop by every day after her morning classes to check in with me and have a little lunch. After she died, every time I heard a car door, my heart would leap into my throat, wanting so desperately for it to be her.

Where we were living, we had a Yukon mailing address, but our girls went to Mustang schools. When we decided to move, we made sure we stayed in the same school district. Dan and I found a house we all loved in Mustang. Just seven miles from our current location at the time.

Dan had helped Mellie research and find her first new car, a car she bought with her own money. They had left the house right after lunch one day in March of 2000. They didn't come back until after dark. Mellie proudly drove up in a brand new, Black 2000 Ford Mustang, 5-speed with black leather interior. She was glowing. She said the salesman kept trying to get her to agree to some terms her Dad made clear was not going to happen. Dan was the Fleet Manager for the Oklahoma City Police Department. He knew what was required when buying a car, and what was extraneous bull shit car dealers tried to sell you. Mellie said once the finance officer realized her Dad was not going to let her commit to paying for any extra crap, they wrote up a clean contract, and she bought the car.

When Mellie died, six months later, Dan was determined to keep her car. It meant the world to him; he had been there for her, and they had gone together to be sure she got the best deal possible.

We paid off the Mustang from the insurance money we got after the accident. I started driving it, just to feel closer to Mellie. When Karly got her learner's permit in October, I began teaching her how to drive the Mustang. I had been taking Karly out on back roads, teaching her to drive my car, for close to a year by this time. The next step was teaching her to drive a standard transmission. By the time she got her driver's license, she had no problem driving the Mustang. Karly drove the Mustang to school for the next two years.

Once Karly had her permit, she and I got in the habit of me picking her up after school so she could drive us home. One day, about a month after Mellie died, Karly came out to the car angry and on the verge of tears. She told me that one of her teachers had said to her it was time she got over the death of her sister.

I said, "Let's go. I want to speak to the principal." I charged into the office like a mother rhinoceros. I told them I wanted to speak with the principal "right now." They could tell I was serious and got us in to speak with her right-away. I told the principal I was disgusted that one of her teachers could be so callous and uncharitable. As it turned out, Karly did not want to go back to his class, and we got no argument out of the principal for Karly to change classes.

The following year, Karly started her junior year. She got her prerequisites done in the morning at the high school, then drove to the Vocational-Technology school for afternoon classes. Karly took Commercial and Graphic Arts in her junior and senior years at the Vo-Tech. The school offered a program to high school students; if you attended for two years, you could attend the next two years, right out of high school, for free.

Her senior year, Karly made a trip to Portland, Oregon with a group of high school students for a tour of the Arts Institute campus. She met other students from all over the country with similar interests and fell in love with the campus. She came home from Portland jazzed about the possibility of attending their school.

Karly was accepted to the Portland Art Institute, and we were so proud of her. We had a conference call with one of the school's admissions counselors. Everything was looking good until Karly decided she didn't want to go so far from home.

It was a difficult time for Karly. She was still in counseling for depression after Mellie died. There was a lot going on, and she wasn't ready to leave Mom and Dad. We supported her decision and offered to help any way we could.

Karly chose not to pursue anything in the arts. Instead, she decided, after graduating high school, she would take advantage of the opportunity to get two years of free education at the Vo-Tech.

Of all things, she took Telecommunications Cabling and Electronic Repair. A complete 180 degrees from the arts.

The first year of her new classes focused on the Cabling. Karly learned to assemble and install Ethernet cabling, connect and configure switches, hubs, and routers and support network communications. It didn't sound like anything I'd be interested in, but she had a great head for that type of work. In fact, Karly excelled in that two-year course. At the end of 2004, Karly was a licensed Voice and Data Cabling Technician.

Karly was sent to the Skills USA State Competition in May of 2005 where she won First Place in Cabling. What an achievement. In June, Karly went to Nationals, which took place in Kansas City, Missouri and, as the only female in the competition, won Second Place, nationally! That was a huge accomplishment and was a great addition to her resume.

In the summer of 2004, the Vo-Tech decided to upgrade the cabling throughout the school. The instructor chose a group of his best students to perform the job. Obviously being the most qualified, with her Skills USA wins, Karly was made Lead Technician and Supervisor on the job. It was hot, dirty work, but she gained so much grit and confidence, it was amazing to see how she blossomed.

When Karly went back for the second year, they were focusing on the Electronics Repair portion of that class. The instructor had died suddenly just as the class was getting started, so the school hired a new instructor to teach Electronics, but they asked Karly, who was nineteen at the time, to teach the Cabling portion, while she was taking the Electronics class. They paid her a small salary while she was going to school; however, the value of having that on her resume was priceless.

At the end of the school year, in May of 2005, Vo-Tech had their graduation ceremony. Karly was a stand-out, not only for her grades but for her contributions to the school. She received her awards from the Skills USA competitions at the graduation ceremony, where Karly chose to give her National Skills USA medal to the instructor's widow, giving much credit for her awards to his instruction. Karly's husband was beaming with pride, sitting with Dan and me in the audience.

Near the end of Karly's senior year, she began officially dating Bryan. They had been seeing each other for a while, but our rule for dating while she was in high school was, the boy had to be within a year of her age, and preferably, attending school. Either still in high school or college. Bryan was four years older and had been attending college while Karly was in high school.

As soon as Bryan got his bachelor's degree in education, in addition to his Associates Degree in illustration, he began teaching third grade at an inner-city school. He thrived, becoming a favorite of the students and his co-workers.

Bryan and Karly continued dating for the next year, while Karly continued taking classes at Vo-Tech. By Christmas of 2004, Bryan had asked Karly to marry him. They began planning their wedding for the fifth of May 2005.

Dan and I were surprised. Our "baby" was getting married? Karly would be twenty by the time they got married. Dan and I were only nineteen when we married, so we couldn't hold their ages against them. And to be honest, the two of them were very well suited. Even more so now, fifteen years later.

Karly and Bryan wanted an outdoor wedding, originally wanting to have it in a creek at the Martin Park Nature Center, in their bare feet. It would have been unique, just like them, but with one of their grandmother's in a wheelchair, and two more not at all stable on their feet, it would have been impossible to get them down to the creek.

Bryan and Karly found a location with an outdoor venue on flat ground. Because they had decided on 05-05-05, a Thursday, the venue was willing to work with them. A small ceremony, with parents and grandparents only, was scheduled for that Thursday, followed by a terrific luncheon hosted by the groom's parents at Cattlemen's Steak House in Oklahoma City, and a honeymoon in Las Vegas.

Ten days later, on a Saturday, Dan and I hosted the reception at the same location, where the wedding ceremony had been held. Karly and Bryan had invited one hundred guests, but the caterer said to count on about 75% of the invited guests. The reception was being catered by the venue, with a beautiful wedding cake and groom's cake being made by a local baker. The venue had offered to make the cake, but since we had already ordered the cakes, we declined.

As we neared the wedding reception, the guest list was reaching about 98% of the invited guests. I called the venue and asked if they could get their caterer to make that additional cake for us after all; flavor and style of their choice. As it turned out, they provided us with the most amazing chocolate cake any of us had ever tasted.

Originally, Karly had planned to wear a nice sundress. One day while she and I were out looking at venues, I casually asked, "Just for the fun of it, do you want to try on some wedding dresses?" Karly and I agreed, trying on wedding dresses could be fun. What she didn't count on was falling in love with one. She was stunning in a halter/sheath gown.

Bryan's mother took him shopping for a new suit. At the wedding, Bryan stood under the arbor in the gardens of the venue, clean-shaven in his new suit and looked about as happy as any groom I have ever seen. He had the biggest smile on his face as Dan walked Karly, in her beautiful gown, from the building out to where Bryan waited to marry his perfect mate. The young couple had the most important people in their lives around them as they repeated their vows to honor and cherish each other. Their parents, grandparents, and Dan's sister, who had driven his stepmother down for the ceremony were in attendance. Karly and Bryan each had their best friend standing up for them. A small, intimate ceremony that suited them both very well.

Shortly after their wedding, Karly graduated from Vo-Tech, this time receiving her Electronics Assembly/General Electronics Technician certificate. Dan and I, along with her new husband, Bryan, were all in the audience as she walked across the stage.

New Year's Eve, 2005, Mellie's friend, Kim, got married. Kim and Karly had become good friends after Mellie passed away. Kim asked Karly to be a bridesmaid in her wedding. Kim had two older sisters who were also in the wedding. It was a lovely ceremony.

Kim had told us on many occasions that she felt people in town were talking about her. Kim's father owned a business in town and was a well-known member of the community. Kim said, "When I go into shops in town, I swear I feel people start whispering about me." I told her I thought she probably imagined it. If anything, the people in our community felt bad for her because of the accident, but I told her, "I doubt anyone is speaking negatively about you."

Dan and I took our seats at Kim's wedding, sitting with Karly's husband, Bryan. We prepared for the ceremony to begin. The music started, and Kim's Matron of Honor, her sister, started down the aisle. That was when I heard the woman behind me, speaking just loud enough for the people sitting around her to know she was the authority on who was in the wedding party, say to her date, "That is Kim's oldest sister." Then the middle sister came down the aisle, and I heard, "That's Kim's middle sister." And then, Karly came down the aisle. The woman behind me said, "That's the sister of the girl Kim killed." I just about turned around in my seat to see what kind of person could be so callous. However, I didn't want to do or say anything to ruin Kim's special day. Nor did I want Kim to know that she was right. Not only were people talking about her, they were doing so in the worst possible way. And this was a friend or family member speaking.

After the ceremony, the photographer came in and began taking pictures of the bridal party and the families. A lot of the guests stayed seated to watch. At one point, Kim asked Dan and me to join her, her groom, and Karly. Before taking the picture, the photographer asked me what the relationship was. I told her Karly was our daughter, and Kim was like another daughter to us. It was at this point I saw the woman who had been sitting behind me get up and leave with her date. I looked for her at the reception. She never showed up.

In April of 2007, Karly and Bryan had their first son and named him Jace. Jace was a handful. I suppose what I'm saying is, he was exhausting. When Jace stayed with Bryan's parents, there were two, sometimes three adults to share the responsibility. Judy retired to be available to stay home and babysit fulltime. Judy also had her mother living with them fulltime. Bryan's father, Jim, cut back on his hours at work to spend more time with his grandson. They lived nearby, so dropping Jace off with them on his way to work was easy for Bryan. Karly and Bryan enjoyed knowing their son was being cared for by people who had his best interest at heart.

However, when Jim and Judy were unavailable, I drove into Oklahoma City to meet Karly at her office where I would pick-up Jace and bring him to my house. That child had the energy of triplets. Dan was still working fulltime, so I had Jace all to myself, which would have been great if Jace liked to sit quietly and cuddle. Okay, okay. I hear myself. That's unreasonable.

If there was a mudpuddle handy, Jace was in it. If it made noise, Jace banged on it. Jace is the joy of all four of his grandparents. That boy is smart as a whip and went ninety miles an hour all day long. Dan and I thought it was just because he was a boy. We'd only had girls, so we had nothing to compare. Later, Jace's Mom and Dad learned Jace has ADHD. With some medication and coaching, Jace managed to settle down enough in school to live up to his potential. Now that Jace is older, he's learned to control himself better at home. He is currently on a low dose medication to help him focus at school, but eventually, he'll be weaned off the medication altogether. Bryan and Karly didn't think they'd have any more children. Jace filled every bit of their hearts so completely.

Luke was born in March of 2013. Once Jace was going to school fulltime, Karly and Bryan decided they wanted another child. Thank goodness they did. What a blessing. Luke was this chill little dude from the moment he was born. Luke was perfectly happy quietly sitting around watching his brother climb the walls.

When Luke was three years old, Dan retired from the Police Department. The first year he was home he wanted to spend as much time with the boys as possible. Dan had worked two and three jobs to support us for so long; he missed out on a lot of time with our girls. He said he wanted to take this opportunity to spend time with Karly's boys. Dan would have a fight on his hands though.

Bryan's mother, Judy, had been keeping Luke fulltime. She didn't want to give up any of her time with that precious little boy, and who could blame her? Judy was convinced to let us have him a couple of days a week.

I miss Mellie every day, but I am so grateful for the time we had with her. I still have Karly, and now I have a son, as well as two grandsons to lavish my love upon. I have a good life now — a joy-filled life. I wouldn't change my life now, but I must admit, if I could, I would change several things from my past — no point wishing for that which cannot be changed.

Postscript

I chose to not think about any trauma in my life. I just thought, what was the point. I didn't want to get stuck in that place, so rather than think about it, I convinced myself one of two things; either it didn't happen at all, or it wasn't so bad. But, of course, the trauma festers within you and affects you whether you intend for it to, or not. For me, therapy was what helped me most. In 2017, there were an estimated 46.6 million adults aged 18 or older in the United States with any mental illness. This number represented 18.9% of all U.S. adults. These numbers represent anyone who has sought help from a psychologist or counselor for any reason. In the 1970s, Americans didn't seek help; they suffered in silence.

As of May 2019, 87% of Americans agree that having mental health issues is nothing to be ashamed of. Clearly, the stigma of seeking help has lessened; however, there are still people afraid it will have a negative effect on their job or family.

Since beginning the research phase of my book, a great number of memories have resurfaced. At first, I thought writing my book would be cathartic. After some time, I realized I wasn't sleeping well. In fact, I was hardly sleeping at all. Every time I fell asleep, I was having nightmares. Eventually, I had to return to a counselor. The stress of reliving the trauma from my time in the Air Force, and the strain of the years spent covering up for my mother, I was falling apart. I began to notice intrusive thoughts and compulsive behaviors.

I'm doing so much better today. I'm learning to control my

defensiveness. My counselor and I figured out that when someone criticizes me, even constructive criticism, I'm hearing my mother telling me that I'm not good enough. Rather than puff up and take offense, I take a breath and remind myself, this is not my mother, and they are not telling me I'm bad or inconsequential; they are simply making a comment about something I have done or said. *We are having a conversation. It is not necessary for me to defend myself.* That was huge for me.

I hope my book is a benefit to others and in some way, helps them gain strength and understanding to overcome their own traumas.

To the veterans who have suffered sexual assault, stand up for yourselves. Once I began to talk about the trauma I experienced in the military, I began to hear from other women about their experiences.

Things need to change. We may have to make a huge stink to get any changes made, but it is such a worthy cause. It's 2019, and women are still being raped and assaulted by their fellow soldiers. It must stop. Talk about it. Tell your story. Make people aware. You are not alone. I promise.

Author Biography

JoJo Maize is a veteran of the United States Air Force and sexual assault survivor, before and during her time in the Air Force. An Oklahoma State University Alumna, JoJo currently lives in Yukon, Oklahoma, with her husband of 40+ years. She retired early from the State of Oklahoma, Purchasing Division, and now happily shares babysitting responsibilities of her two grandsons. She has tried, unsuccessfully, to sell real estate during an economic bust in the Oklahoma City market. However, she has successfully had real estate articles published in local newspapers. JoJo is currently a member of a writing group in El Reno, Oklahoma, *Creative Quills.* She enjoys traveling the highways and byways of the United States with her best friend (her husband). Today JoJo is researching her next book, a creative fiction based on some of the stories she has learned of her ancestors while doing genealogy. She anticipates it will be a fun project, bringing joy and laughter to the author, as well as the reader.

End Notes

Chapter 1

1. Mayo Clinic Staff, November 18, 2017, Narcissistic Personality Disorder, Accessed 23 February 2019 through https://www.mayoclinic.org/diseases-conditions/narcissistic-personality-disorder/symptoms-causes/syc-20366662

Chapter 3

2. Frank G. DeLuca, Orvar Swenson, John H. Fisher, and Adele H. Loutfi. First published 1 April 1962 *The "Lazy" Bladder Syndrome in Children* Accessed 13 March 2019 through https://adc.bmj.com/content/archdischild/37/192/117.full.pdf

3. Carter, Les Ph.D., (2018) *When Pleasing You Is Killing Me.* (First Edition) Dallas, Texas: Les Carter

Chapter 5

4. Narcissistic Supply, Wikipedia. Accessed 3 March 2019 through https://en.wikipedia.org/wiki/Narcissistic_supply

Chapter 7

5. Carter, Les Ph.D., "Covert Narcissism: Control With a Sly Twist" *Surviving Narcissism, YouTube,* 11 October 2018, https://www.youtube.com/watch?v=nWjHr44zuis

Chapter 8

6. Sam Edwards, (2019) 5 Ways to Spot a Sense of Entitlement. Accessed 2 Aug 2019 through www.AConsciousRethink.com/4561/5-ways-sense-entitlement-reveals/

Chapter 9

7. Wikipedia contributors, "Narcissistic personality disorder," accessed 21 June 2019 through *Wikipedia, The Free Encyclopedia,* https://en.wikipedia.org/w/index.php?title=Narcissistic_personality_disorder&oldid=902172826

Chapter 10

8. Stephanie Kriesburg, Psy.D., (s.d.) *Women with Narcissistic Parents: Stuck in Worry. (Emotional Inheritance for Women with Narcissistic Parents)* Accessed 27 March 2019 through https://adaa.org/learn-from-us/from-the-experts/blog-posts/consumer/women-narcissistic-parents

Chapter 11

9. "Child Grooming," accessed 3 August 2019 through https://en.wikipedia.org/wiki/Child_grooming

Chapter 13

10. SoulGPS, 23 August 2018 *How Narcissists Use Sex to Exploit & Control You* Accessed 14 June 2019 through https://medium.com/@SoulGPS/how-narcissists-use-sex-to-exploit-control-you-9b26be74069f

11. Wikipedia contributors, "Narcissistic rage and narcissistic injury," accessed 21 June 2019 through *Wikipedia, The Free Encyclopedia,* https://en.wikipedia.org/w/index.php?title=Narcissistic_rage_and_narcissistic_injury&oldid=902356735

Chapter 16

12. Wikipedia contributors, "Pied Piper of Hamelin," accessed 19 March 2019 through *Wikipedia, The Free Encyclopedia,* https://en.wikipedia.org/w/index.php?title=Pied_Piper_of_Hamelin&oldid=902851258

Chapter 19

13. Les Carter, Ph. D (2018) *When Pleasing You Is Killing Me: Setting Boundaries with The Controllers in Your Life* (First Edition) *Page* 42 United States: Les Carter

14. Wikipedia contributors, "Agnosticism," accessed 20 March 2019 through *Wikipedia, The Free Encyclopedia,* https://en.wikipedia.org/w/index.php?title=Agnosticism&oldid=902687804

Chapter 20

15. Carter, Les. "When a Narcissistic Parent Coaches a Kid to Reject You" *Surviving Narcissism, YouTube.* Dr. Les Carter, Ph.D. 4 March 2019 https://www.youtube.com/watch?v=mFLVpelZ8Aw&t=707s

16. Les Carter, Ph. D (2018) When *Pleasing You Is Killing Me: Setting Boundaries with The Controllers in Your Life* (First Edition) Page 103 United States: Les Carter

Chapter 21

17. N. s.d. s.l. *Generalized Anxiety Disorder* Accessed 25 February 2019 through https://www.anxiety.org/generalized-anxiety-disorder-gad#resources

Chapter 22

18. Collier R. A short history of pain management. *CMAJ.* 2018;190(1):E26–E27. doi:10.1503/cmaj.109-5523 Accessed 20 April 2019

Chapter 24

19. Beyond the Dash, *How to Memorialize a Loved One Who Asked for No Funeral* 28 September 2018 N. s.l. Adperfect https://beyondthedash.com/about/

Chapter 25

20. Les Carter, Ph. D (2005) Enough *About You, Let's Talk About Me: How to Recognize and Manage the Narcissists in Your Life* (First Edition) Page 49 United States: Jossey-Bass

21. Peg Streep, (2015) *Unloved Daughters and Their Siblings: Five Common Patterns,* accessed 26 May 2019 through https://www.psychologytoday.com/us/blog/tech-support/201506/unloved-daughters-and-their-siblings-five-common-patterns

22. Murray Bowen, "Triangulation (Psychology)" accessed 7 Aug 2019 through Wikipedia, The Free Encyclopedia, https://en.wikipedia.org/wiki/Triangulation_(psychology)#The_Perverse_Triangle

Chapter 26

23. Heather Stang, (2018) *Mindfulness & Grief: With Guided Meditations to Calm the Mind and Restore the Spirit (*First Edition) Page 120 United States: CICO Books

Made in the USA
Monee, IL
22 May 2021

68354262R00177